REVOLUTION

Volume 17

NATIONALISM AND COMMUNISM

NATIONALISM AND COMMUNISM

Essays, 1946–1963

HUGH SETON-WATSON

LONDON AND NEW YORK

First published in 1964 by Methuen & Co Ltd

This edition first published in 2022
by Routledge
4 Park Square, Milton Park, Abingdon, Oxon OX14 4RN

and by Routledge
605 Third Avenue, New York, NY 10158

Routledge is an imprint of the Taylor & Francis Group, an informa business

© 1964 Hugh Seton-Watson

All rights reserved. No part of this book may be reprinted or reproduced or utilised in any form or by any electronic, mechanical, or other means, now known or hereafter invented, including photocopying and recording, or in any information storage or retrieval system, without permission in writing from the publishers.

Trademark notice: Product or corporate names may be trademarks or registered trademarks, and are used only for identification and explanation without intent to infringe.

British Library Cataloguing in Publication Data
A catalogue record for this book is available from the British Library

ISBN: 978-1-032-12623-4 (Set)
ISBN: 978-1-003-26095-0 (Set) (ebk)
ISBN: 978-1-032-18038-0 (Volume 17) (hbk)
ISBN: 978-1-032-18041-0 (Volume 17) (pbk)
ISBN: 978-1-003-25258-0 (Volume 17) (ebk)

DOI: 10.4324/9781003252580

Publisher's Note
The publisher has gone to great lengths to ensure the quality of this reprint but points out that some imperfections in the original copies may be apparent.

Disclaimer
The publisher has made every effort to trace copyright holders and would welcome correspondence from those they have been unable to trace.

Nationalism and Communism

ESSAYS, 1946-1963

by Hugh Seton-Watson

METHUEN AND CO LTD
11 NEW FETTER LANE LONDON EC4

First published 1964
© *1964 by Hugh Seton-Watson*
Printed in Great Britain
by the Camelot Press Ltd
London and Southampton

TO DOUGLAS YOUNG
AS A TOKEN OF THIRTY YEARS OF FRIENDSHIP
AND MANY HOURS OF TALK
ON THESE AND KINDRED THEMES

Contents

Preface   *page* ix

PART ONE   TWENTIETH-CENTURY HISTORY

Nationalism and Multi-national Empires   3
Twentieth-century Revolutions   36
Industrialization and Revolution   51
Russian Revolutionaries   68
Hitler's Revolution   77

PART TWO   EASTERN EUROPE AFTER THE WAR

The Danube States in 1946   85
Czechoslovakia in 1947   119
Greece in 1948   128

PART THREE   COMMUNISM IN EASTERN EUROPE

The Hungarian Tragedy   143
The East European Communist Parties, 1944–58   163
Five Years after the Hungarian Revolution   173

PART FOUR   INTERNATIONAL PROBLEMS

Soviet Foreign Policy on the Eve of the Summit   189
The 'National Bourgeoisie' in Soviet Strategy   203
The Great Schism   222
Commonwealth, Common Market, Common Sense   240

Preface

The essays and articles collected in this book are united by the general theme of national and social revolution, which is so obvious a feature of twentieth-century history. Nationalism and Communism are mass movements, in the sense that they express mass discontent and that they mobilize the masses of town and country for action. These essays discuss only certain features of revolutionary movements. Little is here said about the economic sufferings or aspirations of peasants or workers. I have written something about these things elsewhere,[1] though of course I cannot claim to have covered more than a small part of the ground, and indeed even the enormous literature which has appeared in the last half-century in many different languages on the social problems of peasants and workers is still inadequate for so vast a theme. But I think that I am at least entitled to claim that I do not lack interest in social problems, or underrate the role of the masses in revolutionary movements.

These essays are, however, concerned mainly with revolutionary leadership. If no revolutionary movement can prosper without mass support, it is equally true that none can even begin without leadership. The formation of revolutionary *élites*, the social conditions and the personal motives which impel men to revolutionary leadership, are still insufficiently understood. Western writers tend to consider this problem in terms of 'the rise of a middle class'. This, it seems to me, is a mistake, largely due to a natural tendency to regard the formation of a bourgeoisie in Western Europe, between the end of the Middle Ages and the end of the eighteenth century, as the normal pattern in the historical development of societies. The truth is rather that the formation of a bourgeoisie is an exceptional and uncharacteristic phenomenon, confined to a part of the European continent and its successor societies in North America and the Pacific. The social group which has played the leading part in political movements in 'underdeveloped societies', from

[1] Especially in my *Eastern Europe between the Wars* (1945), *The Decline of Imperial Russia* (1952) and *Neither War nor Peace* (1960).

post-Petrine Russia to mid-twentieth-century tropical Africa, has not been a 'middle class' but an 'intelligentsia'. The difference is more than semantic. The argument is worked out in some of the essays in the first part of this book.

The date and place in which each essay appeared is stated in a footnote at the beginning of each. There are only minor verbal changes in the texts. Some titles have been changed. In certain cases explanatory footnotes have been added. The essay on 'Nationalism and Multi-national Empires' appears here for the first time. It is based in part on lectures given in Paris, Stockholm and Ankara. Two short essays on 'Russian Revolutionaries' and 'Hitler's Revolution' are reviews of two outstanding books – *Il popolismo russo* by Professor Franco Venturi of Turin and *Die Auflösung der Weimarer Republik* by Professor Karl Bracher of Bonn.

The area in which I have personally had most opportunity to see national and social revolution at work is Eastern Europe, with which the second and third parts of this book are concerned. The second consists of articles written during journeys to Eastern Europe in the period of Communist seizure, or – in the case of Greece – attempt at seizure, of power. The third part consists of essays on the development of the Communist régimes in these countries during the last fifteen years, as seen from a distance.

In the fourth part the subject is essentially the impact of the revolutionary forces of nationalism and Communism on international politics – on the relations between the Soviet Union and the West and between the Soviet Union and China, and on the situation of Britain in world politics in 1963.

In conclusion I should like to express my thanks to the editors of the periodicals, mentioned in the text, from which most of these articles have been reprinted, and to the colleagues and students who during two decades have provided so much stimulus to thought.

One: Twentieth-century History

Nationalism and Multi-national Empires

There have been many great empires in human history, and the subjects of many of these have included people of different religion, language and social customs. But the expression 'multi-national empire' can only be used of the period since the birth of the modern concept of secular nationalism. Nationalism, as we understand it, hardly existed before the French Revolution.

NATIONALISM AND LEGITIMACY

In the traditional empires of the past, subjects were expected loyally to obey and serve their ruler, whose position was believed to be sanctioned by divine law. The monarch was the ruler appointed by God, and responsible only to God. He in turn accepted the devotion of his subjects, and had the duty to protect them. This did not, however, imply equality among his subjects. Not only were there social privileges and hierarchies, rich and poor, but whole categories of persons might be regarded as second-class subjects. This was notably the case in Christian and Moslem empires. Here the division was one of religion. In the Mogul Empire in India, the Hindu majority were second-class citizens, enjoying fewer rights than Moslems. So were the Jews in medieval Christian states in Western Europe, the Christians in the Balkan provinces of the Ottoman Empire and the Moslem Tatars in the Russian Empire of the seventeenth and eighteenth centuries. This does not necessarily mean that they were persecuted for their religious beliefs, though this did happen from time to time in all these cases. It was also possible for individuals to change their religion. If they were converted to the dominant religion, they enjoyed its rights.

The principle of nationalism emerged gradually in Western Europe, and was theoretically formulated in revolutionary France. Nationalism is essentially secular and essentially democratic. It gradually replaces (though it does not necessarily completely eliminate) loyalty to the religious community and loyalty to the ruler by loyalty to the nation. It is of course true that, under most earlier forms of government, both monarchical and republican, devotion to the fatherland (*patria, patrie*) was recognized, and encouraged, but even if this included love of a city or a piece of land, a heritage of literature and art, or loyalty to a way of life, the essential focus of patriotism was still the ruler and the faith.[1] It is true also that the word 'nation', in its Latin form and French and Italian derivatives, can be found in medieval Europe. The University of Prague, founded in 1348, had German, Czech and Polish *nationes*, and in Dante's Italy the expressions *nazione fiorentina* or *nazione milanese* were used. But the idea that the 'nation' is the focus of loyalty for the citizens of a State was not yet born. The conception of loyalty to the nation, as it arose in eighteenth-century France, rejected the divine sanction of government, and implied that the collective personality of the nation is more important than the individual person of the monarch. Most nationalists in the nineteenth century continued to practise their religions – Christian or Moslem or other. Many, perhaps even most, nationalists were not opponents of the institution of monarchy. Fundamentally, however, the idea of nationality contains within itself that of the sovereignty of the people. Thus, the rulers of 1815 (Metternich, Alexander I of Russia and others) were right to feel that nationalism was a subversive idea, a threat to the power both of churches and of dynasties.

Nationalism, as a political movement, dates from the Revolution of 1789. Thenceforth, it was increasingly claimed that the interests of whole nations (interpreted of course by those who claimed to represent their will) should have first priority in political life, both domestic and international. Nationalism, in fact, provides a new principle of *legitimacy* for government, an alternative to the traditional legitimacy of monarch and religion.

However, the problem then arose, how was one to define the nation. Nationalisms have become an effective force only where there has been national consciousness among at least an important section of the people concerned. The growth of national consciousness always precedes the birth of nationalism. Historically this growth has had different origins in different countries.

[1] It is impossible to find a historical generalization which will fit all particular cases. I realize that these words apply only very partially to the Greek city states, and that even the Roman Republic differs in important respects. But they do, I think, apply to the great majority of pre-modern forms of government.

THE GROWTH OF NATIONAL CONSCIOUSNESS

In the oldest nations, national consciousness was *the product of the State and the monarchy*. England and France are the obvious examples. The English monarchy arose from the union of a number of Saxon kingdoms, and was later strengthened by the Norman conquest. The French monarchy resulted from the extension of the power of the Capetian kings from their original small territorial base in the Ile de France. In both cases the monarch had to struggle against powerful regional forces as well as independent-minded social *élites*. In both cases the subjects of the monarch included people of several languages. In England there were Cornishmen, Saxons and Frenchmen, not to mention the Welsh, who remain nationally different to this day. The Franco-Saxon synthesis created the English language itself. In France there were Bretons, Normans, Provençaux, Burgundians, Flemings, Germans, Basques, and Catalans in addition to the Frenchmen who were themselves a product of a Gallo-Roman synthesis. A third case is Scotland. Saxons, Celts and Norwegians each had a share in the creation of the Scottish nation, and traces of these different origins can still be found. In Spain the monarchy created the nation from people of Roman, Visigothic, Arab, Basque and still older origins. To this day Catalans, Castilians, Andalusians, and Basques remain different, yet Spanish nationality has been one of the great facts of human history, and is still a reality. The growth of the Russian nation has points of similarity with that of the French and Spanish. After the Tatar conquest of the thirteenth century, the region around Moscow played the same role, as a nucleus of the Russian State, as the Ile de France had played for the French. The expansion of Muscovy, like that of Castile, had also a religious character: it was a crusade against the Moslems (Arabs in Spain, Tatars in the Volga valley and southern steppes).

National consciousness can also be created by foreign conquest. The obvious examples are the nations of America. The Spanish, Portuguese, English, and French immigrants brought their own traditions with them, but developed a national consciousness separate from that of their homelands. The Brazilian and the Hispano-American nations were also created by intermarriage with indigenous peoples (in the Brazilian case to some extent also with imported negro slaves), whereas the English and French exterminated most of the indigenous people, and the English refused intermarriage with their negro slaves. Whether the North American French are a nation is a matter of argument in the Province of Quebec. To a Scot it seems clear that they are, even if, like the Scots, they do not possess a State of their own. In Africa European governments created states by arbitrarily drawing lines on the map in agreement with other European governments. In this way such huge states as Nigeria, Congo, and Sudan came into existence. Within these artificial frameworks a sense of nationality certainly grew among a limited number of educated Africans: how wide and deep the belief in the existence of a Nigerian, Congolese, and Sudanese nation has spread, still remains to be seen.

National consciousness can also be preserved by the memory of a State. Poland is the obvious case. Throughout 150 years of partition, the Polish educated classes (nobility, priests, and secular intelectuals) kept alive the tradition of Polish patriotism. The same is true of Hungary from 1526 to 1867: the period of foreign rule was longer, but the foreign rulers made less determined efforts to destroy the patriotism than in the case of the Poles. In other cases one may say that memories which have virtually died out have been artificially revived: the Czechs and Bulgarians fall into this group. India is a special case. Here the sense of religious and cultural unity was continuous under many different foreign rulers, but the belief in an Indian statehood was artificially developed in the nineteenth century, and based on romantic and questionable interpretations of the history of the sub-continent.

National consciousness has been *derived from religion* in the case of peoples ruled by foreigners whose religion is different from their own. Obvious examples are the Catholic Irish; the Moslem Bosnians; and the Turkic, Iranian and Arab peoples ruled by Britain, France and Russia. The subject peoples of the Ottoman Empire in the Balkans always regarded themselves as distinct from their rulers: they were Christians, and the rulers were Moslems. For a long time 'Christian' was more or less identified with 'Greek', since the great Christian State of the Balkans, the Byzantine Empire, had been a Greek State, and the Orthodox hierarchy was in Greek hands. The medieval Serbian State had been independent of Constantinople until the Turkish conquest, and after the conquest many Serbs found refuge under Austrian rule. Thus the Serbs were never so subject to Greek influence as the other Balkan Orthodox.

Nationalism and Multi-national Empires

It was not until the mid-nineteenth century that the Roumanians and Bulgarians acquired a national consciousness, in relation to the Greeks, comparable to the religious consciousness which they had always had in relation to the Turks.

The Moslems of Bosnia are an interesting case. Their language was always Serbo-Croat, not Turkish, and they were the descendants of the inhabitants of the medieval Bosnian State. But once converted to Islam, they identified themselves with their rulers, and were accepted by them. They were never Turks, but they were *Osmanli*. When they came under Austrian rule in 1878, they insisted on being distinguished from the (Catholic) Croats and (Orthodox) Serbs who shared their homeland and spoke the same Serbo-Croat language as themselves. In the Yugoslav State which succeeded Austria in 1918, they remained a separate community, and became known as the Moslem 'nationality' (*nacionalnost*): Islam became recognized as a *national* category.

In the Moslem countries ruled by European Great Powers, the sense of separateness was of course based on religion. The peoples were Moslem, their rulers Christian. As politically conscious *élites* developed, they put forward demands on behalf of the Moslem people. Their main concerns were to adapt Islam to the modern world and to obtain greater autonomy in all fields (political, cultural, and economic) in relation to the imperial Government. Thus we have the democratizing, modernizing movements in Egypt and among the Volga Tatars. It was only after some decades that the concept of a Tatar nation and an Egyptian nation arose, and much later still that the Egyptians spoke of themselves as Arabs. In Algeria right up to the present the conflict has been conceived, by the great majority of those involved, as one between *français* and *musulmans* – that is, between a *national* and a *religious* category. This is still true today, even though an increasing number on the Moslem side regard themselves as Arab nationalists, and though all Algerian Moslems are so regarded by all Arab nationalists outside Algeria.

The last category on which national consciousness has been based, and in modern times by far the most important, is *language*. In the old nations of Europe, national consciousness grew from other roots, despite diversity of language, but the national language was forged in the process, and became the expression of a nationality which was already there. Thus, the English, French, Spanish, and Russian languages have become the expression of nationality and patriotism (including American, Canadian, Australian, New Zealand, and Scottish as well as English; Belgian and Swiss and Canadian as well as French). In more modern national movements, which began on the basis of a sense of distinction from the rulers, based on religion, further differentiation has taken place on the basis of language. This process has clearly been connected with cultural and social secularization, with the declining influence of religion on society. There have even been some cases of nationalities artificially created on the basis of languages, not only by nationalist intellectuals or politicians but even by imperial governments seeking to disrupt nationalist movements directed against themselves.

In the Ottoman Empire, the Roumanians and Bulgarians became aware, during the nineteenth century, that they were different from the Greeks, because they spoke different languages. The struggle against Greek supremacy was conducted in the economic field and within the ecclesiastical hierarchy. As the Ottoman State itself began to disintegrate, the rivalry between Bulgarians, Greeks, and Serbs took the form of assassinations and gang warfare between *komitadji* bands, recruited from the subjects of the Ottoman Empire and subsidized by the governments in Belgrade, Athens, and Sofia. Linguistic distinction was the main basis of nationalism, but it was buttressed by claims based on romantic interpretations of history (*revendications historiques* or *revendications hystériques*). The frontiers of the State of the Serbian emperor Dushan (1332–56) or the Bulgaro-Macedonian Tsar Samuel (d. 1015) were claimed as sacred for all time. The Roumanians provide a special case of some interest. They based their nationality not so much on conquering heroes of the past (Michael the Brave, who united Transylvania with Wallachia in 1599, is an exception) as on the foreign conqueror of their country, the Roman Emperor Trajan, after whom until recent times every Roumanian provincial town named at least one hotel. Roumanians, it was claimed, were Latins not only by language but by *race*, being descended from Trajan's legions. Even if every Roman legionary in Dacia had performed prodigies of reproduction, it is difficult to see how the miscellaneous riff-raff of Spaniards, Berbers, Englishmen, Syrians, or Thracians could have produced a pure Latin progeny from the conquered Dacians of Roumania, even if all the Slav and Magyar and other invasions of subsequent centuries were treated as *non avenus*. However, the Roumanian nationalists, having satisfied themselves that they were Latin, and therefore culturally

Nationalism and Multi-national Empires   9

superior to Slavs or Turks, claimed for themselves all territory in which Roumanian-speaking peasants could be found. This linguistic nationalism was combined with a more modest interest in the genuine historical past of the Roumanian principalities of Moldavia and Wallachia. Thus, in the Roumanian case too, state tradition had a part (though secondary to the linguistic factor) in the formation of national consciousness.

In Central Europe, the Slovak nation arose on a linguistic basis in the nineteenth century. It is of course true that, before the Hungarian conquest in the ninth century, there was a state (of which very little is known) called the Moravian Empire, whose inhabitants were the ancestors of the modern Slovaks. But it is an anachronism to trace back the modern nationalism of the Slovaks to this time. A *Slovak nation* did not exist before the nineteenth century. Then, from the various Slav dialects spoken by the peasants of the mountain valleys of northern Hungary, there was created a standardized Slovak literary language. Newspapers, poems, and prose works published in this language became the basis of a Slovak national consciousness, from which there emerged by the end of the nineteenth century a Slovak nationalist movement. The religion of the majority of Slovaks was the same as that of the majority of Hungarians – Roman Catholic – though the Protestant minority played a role, out of proportion to its numbers, in the process of linguistic standardization and literary-political awakening. The Slovak nationalists fought first against the Hungarians (till 1918), and then against the Czechs for their independence.

Another nation roused to national consciousness in modern times as a result of the standardization of a literary language is the Ukrainian nation. The people of the Ukraine were descendants of the population of the first Russian state of Kiev. During centuries of Polish rule they acquired social and cultural characteristics distinct from those of the people of central Russia, who passed during the same centuries under the rule of Tatar khans and then of the Princes of Moscow. When the Ukrainians were incorporated in the Muscovite State in two stages, in the mid-seventeenth century and at the end of the eighteenth century, they had a very different mentality from the Muscovites, and the dialects they spoke were distinct from the Great Russian language. In the nineteenth century a great poet, Taras Shevchenko, and several lesser writers created a standardized Ukrainian literary language. A small but growing educated *élite* created, on the basis of linguistic, social, and cultural distinction, a Ukrainian national consciousness which spread to the peasant masses. In the mid-twentieth century the Ukrainians are a nation.

Among the Moslems of the Ottoman Empire language did not become a political factor until the twentieth century. 'Turk' was a word denoting crude peasants in Anatolia: an educated gentleman in Istanbul was not a Turk but an Osmanli. Only when the last European provinces were almost lost, and the loss of the Arab provinces was well within sight, did political leaders in Istanbul begin to think and speak of themselves as Turks. In the Republic founded by Kemal Atatürk the linguistic category became decisive: the people of the Republic were those whose language was Turkish, and the State was given the name *Türkiye*. But the Turkish language had become the basis of nationalism some decades before this outside the Ottoman Empire, in the Tatar provinces of the Russian Empire. The democratic and modernizing movement of the Volga Tatars acquired a linguistic basis. The attempt was made to create a single literary language, acceptable to the Crimean, Volga, and Azeri Turks. This was not successful, but the idea of a solidarity of peoples of Turkic language (the differences between which were comparable to those between Romance or Slav languages) made considerable progress. Panturkism was a serious force among the educated Moslems of the Russian Empire, and spread even to Turkestan. In the Civil War of 1918–20 both Russian Whites and Reds repressed Turkic nationalism. In the Soviet Union lip-service has been paid to national self-determination, but in practice the linguistic factor has been manipulated to split up the peoples. Dialects have been artificially magnified into 'languages', with appropriate infusions of Russian words, and adapted to the Russian Cyrillic alphabet. In the Soviet view, Uzbek, Turkmen, Kirgiz, Kazakh, and Kara-Kalpak are separate 'nations', and Azeri Turks are quite distinct from Anatolian Turks. Here language has been used as an instrument not to disrupt but to perpetuate imperial rule.

Arab nationalism is another special case. The essential common factor among Arabs is classical Arabic, the language of the Koran. This was once a common factor uniting all Moslems, but the growth of secular education all over Asia and Africa has diminished the importance of Arabic for Turks, Persians, Malays, Indian, and tropical African peoples of Moslem faith. In the Arab lands a common secular language has developed, the language of the Arabic press from Agadir to Baghdad. Yet the languages spoken by Moroccans, Egyptians, and Syrians differ hardly less than those spoken by Frenchmen, Italians, and Spaniards or by Azeris, Turkmens, and Uzbeks. Fortunately for the Arabs, the British and French rulers made no such attempt to manufacture languages as did the Soviet Russian rulers in the Caucasian region and Central Asia. The common element provided by the modern Arabic language, in which the influence of the secular school is strengthened by the religious associations of the sacred language, valid even for those who no longer practise the Moslem religion, has undoubtedly made Arab nationalism a political reality, even if the ancient divisions of geography and history and the more modern divisions of economics and of state structures still prevent Arab unity.

The relative importance, in the development of the national consciousness of each nation, of these different factors – monarchy, state machine, historical memory, religion, and language – largely determined the relative importance of different social classes in the leadership of each nationalist movement. Monarchs and aristocracies played a leading part in England and France. In cases where historical memory was preserved unbroken under foreign rule, such as Poland, Hungary, and perhaps India, surviving social *élites* – landowners, Catholic priests and Brahmins – were decisive. In countries colonized from Europe, national consciousness was formed by social *élites* of immigrant origin – Anglo-, Hispano-, or Lusitano-American landowners or senior officers or businessmen, of whom some were descended from the metropolitan aristocracy but many were of much humbler origins. In countries where national consciousness has been derived from some combination of the religious and linguistic factors – and these form the great majority of cases in the last hundred years – the dominant social group has been the intellectual *élite*. One must here stress the vital distinction between the traditional *élite*, which in nearly all such cases has been the priesthood, and the modern *élite*, which is derived from a secular system of education introduced from Western Europe or from North America. Both the traditional and the modern *élite* have been concerned with the religious factor, but whereas the traditionalists have usually been content with negative and sterile opposition to the foreign rulers, the modern *élites* have sought to modernize religious institutions and even religious thought, in order to strengthen the people's capacity to resist the foreigner, and this has usually increased the speed of secularization, even when the original reformers have been firm believers, with no desire to weaken the influence of the faith.

Language was, however, the principal instrument of the modern *élite* in the East European empires and the Middle East. In these countries the development of linguistic nationalism steadily strengthened the importance of the modern *élite* – or intelligentsia – within the nationalist movements. In the overseas colonies of the West European Powers, on the other hand, language was not in most cases an important factor. The leaders of Indian, or West African, nationalism, precisely because the population of their countries was multi-lingual, could not make language the foundation of national feeling: on the contrary English and French, no less than the vernacular languages, were used to propagate their nationalist doctrine. There was seldom hostility towards the language or culture of the former Imperial Power as such, and in many of the new states the European language was retained for the conduct of Government business, at least at the higher levels of administration, after independence.

It is a general characteristic of all those nationalist movements of the last hundred years which have arisen within an 'underdeveloped' social and economic framework,[1] that they have been led by a modern secular *élite* or intelligentsia. It is necessary here to say something of this social group, and to give some historical examples of its leadership.

THE INTELLIGENTSIA

Intelligentsia is a Russian word, and it is in nineteenth-century Russia that the phenomenon first appeared. The predicament of the Russian intelligentsia, and the tensions and frustrations which inclined so large a part of it to revolutionary sympathies, and an important minority to revolutionary action, have often been discussed. But

[1] Almost all modern nationalist movements have in fact arisen within such a framework. It is difficult to think of any which have arisen in advanced industrialized and urbanized societies. Perhaps one could so regard the progress of Australia and New Zealand to complete independence from Britain. But in neither of these cases was there any militant nationalist movement. In Western Europe the unsuccessful Flemish and Catalan nationalist movements are perhaps better examples. In none of these cases was the leadership in the hands of the intelligentsia. Rather, the leaders came from a bourgeoisie which included businessmen, shopkeepers, farmers and members of intellectual professions.

the intelligentsia is not a specifically Russian phenomenon. It is something which is to be found in all societies which have been forced at a late stage into the processes of modernization. That is to say, it is to be found in some stage of the recent history of all nations except those of Western Europe, North America, and the Anglo-Saxon democracies of the Pacific. The intelligentsia is a modern secular intellectual *élite* which, unlike those of the Western nations, has not grown up organically with its society – as happened in the West between the sixteenth and nineteenth centuries – but has been deliberately created by rulers who have set themselves the political task of bringing their countries at forced speed into the modern world. Inevitably this small new modern *élite* finds itself isolated from the great mass of its compatriots. Where the political system is autocratic or oligarchical, as in Imperial Russia or the Ottoman Empire, the contrast between the political ideas which the intelligentsia has learnt as part of its modern education, and the brutal political reality, still further increases the frustration caused by the social and cultural isolation. Where the rulers belong to a foreign religion or language, this is a further aggravating factor. The Russian intelligentsia in the Russian Empire was primarily concerned with social justice and political liberty, while the non-Russian intelligentsia (Poles, Tatars, or many others), although certainly not indifferent to these principles, were primarily concerned with the rights of their nations. All alike suffered from the repressive police of the Tsars. In the British Empire the intelligentsias of the old and new nations of Asia and Africa have usually enjoyed more liberty than those of Russia, Turkey, or other empires. But this advantage has been largely outweighed in their minds by the colour bar and other forms of arrogance displayed by members of the imperial nation towards 'the natives'.

The intelligentsia is not easily defined. At the beginning of the process of modernization – for example, in the first decades of the nineteenth century in Russia – it amounts only to a few hundred persons, mostly children of upper-class families, and its effective spokesmen are a few brilliant writers, such as Belinski or Herzen. As the country's economy becomes more complex, and the demand for modern skills leads to the rise of modern professions (law, teaching, engineering, or medicine), the members of the intelligentsia become more numerous. But intelligentsia is not identical with intellectuals, or with the free professions. Essentially, the intelligentsia consists of members of the modern intellectual *élite*, in a still underdeveloped society, who are above all interested in general political and social ideas. Membership of the intelligentsia does not depend on the level of intellectual attainment, though there is of course a minimum intellectual level below which no one could be considered to belong. A brilliant scientist, who is devoted to his science and fully occupied with it, is certainly an intellectual, but is not a member of the intelligentsia. On the other hand a man of modest scholarly attainment may be a member of the intelligentsia if his attainment is still far above the general level of his society, and if he is above all concerned with general political and social ideas. An example is the late M. Patrice Lumumba. Among the Africans of the Congo, who had been almost completely excluded from a higher education (though encouraged and helped to develop technical skills) Lumumba was intellectually outstanding, and political ideas and politics were the most important thing in life for him.

The intelligentsia is obviously recruited chiefly from the intellectual professions, but its members are also to be found among business-men, bureaucrats and army officers. The phenomenon of a 'military intelligentsia' is of special interest. The original motive which has driven rulers to embark on forced modernization has usually been military need. Peter the Great, Mohammed Ali, and Mahmud II were determined to catch up with the military strength of the West. Young army officers were among the first persons whom they sent for training to the West. In these countries the profession of arms had always held great social prestige, and so had attracted able and ambitious people. It is thus not surprising that officers should have been among the first to have been affected by revolutionary ideas. In Russia the first revolutionaries were the Decembrists of 1825. After they had been suppressed, great efforts were made to keep political ideas out of the army in Russia, and this effort was mainly successful. In the Ottoman Empire, and in its Arabic-speaking successor states, the interest of young army officers in politics, and the overlapping between civil and military intelligentsias, has continued to the present time. Nasser is the outstanding example, but many of the military conspirators in Iraq and Syria belong to this category, and even the great Kemal Atatürk had something of the military intelligentsia about him.

Whether recruited from landed nobility, free professions, the army, or even from merchant families, the intelligentsia form the distinct social group, which has had a distinct political role to play. The issue is only confused if one speaks, as has become fashionable for example in recent years in regard to Latin America, of a 'middle class'. The point about societies in process of forced modernization is that they do not possess *a* middle class, or a bourgeoisie, but several middle classes, distinct in outlook and origin from each other, and not united, as the West European bourgeoisie became united between the end of the Middle Ages and the Industrial Revolution, by a common ethos. The politically significant and operative group is the intelligentsia, and it is this group which has provided the leadership of social and national revolutionary movements.

THE INTELLIGENTSIA IN NATIONALIST MOVEMENTS

In the Habsburg Monarchy in the nineteenth century the Czech and Hungarian nationalist movements do not fit this pattern. The Czechs were the only nation of the Monarchy, apart from the Germans, who had a more or less homogeneous bourgeoisie of the Western type, uniting all the middle classes with a common bourgeois ethos. It was this bourgeoisie which led the Czech national movement. The familiar Marxist term 'bourgeois nationalism' is exactly applicable to the Czech movement. The Hungarian nationalist movement, however, up to 1867 was led by the nobility. Its leaders included persons of noble origin who were employed in an intellectual profession: Louis Kossuth himself is an example. But essentially the strength of the movement lay in the landowning class rather than the intellectual *élite* as such. Among the Croats and the Galician Poles, both intelligentsia and landed nobility had a part to play. The Croats of Dalmatia also possessed a bourgeoisie in the Western sense, formed by centuries of overseas trade under Venetian rule. Among the remaining national movements within the Monarchy – the Slovenes, Slovaks, Roumanians, and Serbs – the role of the intelligentsia was overwhelming. The leaders were lawyers, journalists, school-teachers, priests, and pastors. It should also be noted that, as methods of government in the Monarchy were much more liberal than in Russia, and as the differences between the ruling Germans and Hungarians and the subject nationalities were much less sharp than between European colonial rulers and Asian or African subjects, the distinction between intelligentsia and intellectuals, discussed above, has less validity. Rather, perhaps, one should say that the leaders of these nationalist movements came from the intellectual professions. The expression 'bourgeois nationalism' does not, however, seem applicable: it is too vague.

In the Ottoman Empire, the role of the intelligentsia was more important in the later than the earlier movements. The leaders of the Serbian risings of 1804 and 1815 were local notables, prosperous farmers with little formal education. At this time there hardly existed a Serbian intelligentsia in Ottoman Serbia, unless the Orthodox priesthood be so considered, but among the Serbs of the Monarchy, across the rivers Sava and Danube, the number of persons with a modern education was considerable. The leaders of the Greek struggle for independence included merchants, aristocrats, intellectuals, and local notables of the same type as in Serbia. In the preparation of the movement, which was much longer and more systematic than in the Serbian case, the Greek intelligentsia played a predominant role. In Roumania the intelligentsia played a decisive part in the revival of national consciousness, connected with the development and purification of the Roumanian language. But Roumanian independence was achieved not by a national struggle against the Turks but by the intervention of the European Powers. In so far as Roumanians played a part in these events, the most important social group was the landowning aristocracy. Bulgarian independence too was achieved by external action, by the Russian army. But in Bulgaria there was also a national rising, heroic but pitifully ineffective. This rising was prepared and led by conspirators who provide a classic example of a revolutionary intelligentsia. They were indeed in contact with the Russian revolutionary intelligentsia of the 1870's.[1] The last revolutionary nationalist movements among the Christians of the Ottoman Empire took place in Macedonia at the end of the century. These were led by elements of the intelligentsia, largely village school teachers or priests or children of priests. The Macedonian movements can, however, hardly be regarded as 'pure' nationalist movements, since they were largely controlled by the Governments of the neighbouring states of Bulgaria, Serbia, and Greece, each of which was pursuing territorial aims hostile not only to the Ottoman Empire but also to the other states. Nationalist movements, based on language, arose much later among the Moslem peoples of the

[1] The mental climate of the Bulgarian revolutionary emigration in Russia is vividly described in Turgenev's *On the Eve*.

Ottoman Empire. The Albanians were led by tribal chiefs or landowning *beys*. The pioneers of the Arab nationalist movement, both in Egypt and Syria, came from the intelligentsia, and the same was true of the Turkish nationalist movement which first became influential after the Young Turkish Revolution of 1908 and triumphed after the victory of Kemal Atatürk.

In the Russian Empire the intelligentsia provided the bulk of the leadership of most of the nationalist movements. Exceptions were the Baltic Germans and the Finns, both of which were culturally and socially similar to the nations of Western Europe. In Russian Poland the intelligentsia was the most active element. Its importance was increased by the fact that after the rebellions of 1830 and 1863 many Polish landowners lost their properties, and Poles of noble birth, being excluded from public service as they were not considered reliable by the Russians, and scorning business as an unworthy occupation for noblemen, had no other opportunity open to them but the intellectual professions. It was this Polish intelligentsia, largely though not wholly of noble origin, which provided the political leadership of the Russian Poles. Even the socialist movement which developed from the 1890's had among its leaders such noblemen as Joseph Pilsudski.[1] The Ukrainian nationalist movement was completely dominated by its intelligentsia. The same was true of the socialist movement in Georgia, which had a mildly nationalist character. There was no strictly nationalist movement of any importance in Georgia. The Armenian nationalist movement was led by its intelligentsia, which included many priests or children of priests. In the two Protestant Baltic nations, the Estonians and Latvians, the leading nationalists came largely from teachers and pastors, though in the case of Latvia the industrial workers of Riga began at a rather early stage to make themselves felt politically, not as nationalists but as socialists. The Moslem democratic movement in the Russian Empire had its strongest

[1] This, like most of the general observations in this essay, is inevitably an oversimplification of a complex situation. There were Poles employed in Russian Government service, but in provinces outside Poland. There were other Poles who accepted Russian culture, and became Russians, ceasing therefore to count as Poles. There were even some Poles in business by the first decade of the twentieth century, though Polish industry and trade were predominantly in the hands of Jews or persons of German or other foreign extraction. The Polish socialist movement certainly had Polish industrial workers among its leaders, especially in the years after 1905, but intelligentsia (including Jewish intelligentsia) were still numerous among them.

support among the Tatars of the Volga valley, with the city of Kazan as its centre. Here the most active social group was the intelligentsia, whose nucleus consisted of school-teachers from the modernist schools which were set up at the end of the nineteenth century, in opposition to the traditional Islamic schools based on study of the Koran. Rich Tatar merchants contributed generously to the support of these schools. So did individual Moslems from other parts of Russia, of whom the most important was the Crimean Ismail Bey Gaspirali, who set himself the task of popularizing a uniform language based on Ottoman Turkish. His particular aim was not achieved, but his efforts did have the effect of interesting the Tatars and other Moslem peoples of Russia in their languages, most of which belonged to the Turkic group. Moslem nationalism, based on the religion of Islam, was replaced by Tatar nationalism or Pan-Turkic nationalism, based on language. All this was essentially a creation of the intelligentsia. The fact that Tatar merchants gave financial help provides a certain plausibility for calling the movement one of 'bourgeois nationalism'. But the truth is that there was no real Tatar bourgeoisie, and that not the merchants but the intelligentsia led the movement.

In the British and French empires too the intelligentsia provided nationalist leadership. The modern intellectual *élite* in India was at first recruited from outstanding families, Brahmins and Moslem landowners and the like, but as its numbers increased it included persons of humbler origin. A recent study of the formation of the middle classes in India shows clearly the preponderant role of the intellectual professions.[1] In both British and French Africa nationalist leaders have come from the intelligentsia. It seems that the French African leaders have on the whole been intellectually more distinguished than the British. It is interesting to note that two of the outstanding British African leaders obtained a large part of their education in the United States.

The role of the intelligentsia does not cease with the attainment of national independence. The experience of the Balkan states is here of interest. The revolutionary intelligentsia which had played a heroic part in the struggle for Bulgarian freedom in 1876 provided many of the rulers of the new state. This generation became rich and self-satisfied, and began to rule with methods not so different

[1] B. B. Misra, *The Indian Middle Classes: their growth in modern times*, Oxford University Press for Royal Institute of International Affairs, 1961.

from those of the Turkish pashas whom they had replaced. The next generation revolted against the *embourgeoisement* of their elders, and turned to the ideas of social revolution. The social injustices and political repression, the gulf between the upper layer and the masses and the contrast between modern democratic principles and the reality of their country – the same factors which had driven the Russian intelligentsia to revolutionary ideas and action – operated for many decades in the liberated Balkan states. At the same time, however, the Balkan intellectual youth were held back from subversive action against their governments by the nationalist issue. Every one of the new Balkan states had an *irredenta*, had claims for territory against the Habsburg or Russian Empire or against the remnant of the Ottoman Empire. In the face of the national enemy, even the revolutionaries – or at least a very large part of them – could be persuaded in a crisis to rally round the Government. This state of affairs even continued after the First World War. In these years the social and political problems still remained unsolved. The gap between rulers and masses had still not been closed, political freedom still not achieved. The intellectual youth thus continued to be radical or revolutionary, to denounce the régimes in power. Yet every one of the East European states either had an *irredenta* or was concerned to maintain its swollen frontiers against its neighbours' claims. Hungarians and Bulgarians demanded territory inhabited by their kinsmen; Croats, Slovaks, and Ukrainians demanded self-government or independence; and Czechs, Poles, Roumanians, and Serbs clung on to what they had seized. Appeals to nationalism, whether offensive or defensive, could usually rally support.

These same problems exist today in the new states. The heroes of the independence struggle are now respectable politicians or bureaucrats in power, and the young generation of intelligentsia are restive. This can be seen in India, Nigeria, and Senegal, to take three cases only, and will certainly be seen in other countries. And in the new states as in the old Balkans, the best way to disarm the younger generation is to appeal to nationalism. In Africa as in the old Balkans, territorial disputes are numerous, and will no doubt increase with time.

OFFICIAL NATIONALISM AS THE NEW LEGITIMACY

We have noted that the growth of nationalism in nineteenth-century Europe undermined the traditional basis of legitimacy.

Looking back today we can say that the imperial governments were faced with the decision whether to stick to the old principles of legitimacy, or to try to create a secular ideology of state to replace the diminishing loyalty to a divinely sanctioned monarch. The Habsburg Emperors, in the 'Austrian' part of their dominions,[1] and the Ottoman Sultans in Europe and Asia, made no such attempt. Loyalty to the dynasty remained until the end the only claim, and the only non-material bond holding the diverse subjects together. It must be admitted that this bond remained effective until a remarkably late date. Many Ottoman Christians remained loyal to the Sultan until late in the nineteenth century, and *Kaisertreue* was a real factor even among many Czechs, South Slavs, and Roumanians until 1918. The British Empire, too, made no attempt to create an ideology of state. The British Monarchy was the bond, though in contrast to the Houses of Habsburg and Osman the King or Queen of England exercised no real power. The Monarchy stood for a mixture of concepts, never precisely defined, which included the supremacy of Parliament, the Rule of Law and a British way of life which was but dimly intelligible to the Asian or African subjects of the Empire, yet in its great days impressed them. The French Empire went somewhat further towards creating an ideology. Its *mission civilisatrice* included a more clearly understood concept of a French culture, and even a French nationality, which were to be accessible to all. There was an intention of creating Asian and African Frenchmen, regardless of birth or colour, even if the intention was only made effective in a few cases. No comparable intention existed at all in the British case.

The traditional principles of legitimacy did not, however, save the Habsburg, Ottoman, British, or French empires. When the opportunity came to achieve independence, the nationalist leaders seized it and their compatriots followed them. The Ottoman Sultans were defeated in a series of wars, and on more than one occasion were compelled by the European Powers to surrender territory even when they had not been defeated. The Habsburgs lost their empire through defeat in one world war. The British and French lost large parts of their empires by defeats in another world war, but were

[1] By this is meant those Habsburg territories not belonging, after 1867, to the Kingdom of Hungary. The only official designation of these miscellaneous territories was 'the lands represented in the Reichsrat'. 'Austria' is an unhistorical name for these territories, but as a common-sense abbreviation its use can be defended.

able to reassert their power since they ended the war as victors. However, this was but a temporary recovery. In the next years the French were defeated in Indo-China, and forced into an intolerable stalemate in Algeria, from which the only escape was surrender. In Morocco, Tunis, and tropical Africa they voluntarily abdicated. In Britain the abdication of the imperial *élite* was even more thorough than in France. In Cyprus, Malaya, and Kenya some blood was shed by both rulers and subjects; in India the massacres (by the hundred thousand) were strictly confined to the people of the country; in West Africa the transfer of power was peaceful.

The manner of the ending of the British Empire was more elegant than that of the other three. This was helped by fostering the myth of the Commonwealth. This name, which had well described the relationship existing between the genuinely like-minded peoples of Britain, Canada, Australia, and New Zealand and the once comparatively like-minded white South Africans, was extended to cover the relationship of these peoples to half a milliard Asians and Africans who, except for a small number of high civil servants and intellectuals, had virtually nothing in common with them at all. The myth of the larger Commonwealth played a useful part in making the transition less painful for the people of Britain. Even so, it is chastening to Western pride to reflect that most of the lands of the British and French empires were under their rule for less than 100 years; that British rule in India and Habsburg rule outside the Vienna–Prague–Budapest triangle each lasted about 200; but that the Ottoman Sultans ruled most of their European subjects for more than four centuries.

The two multi-national states of the nineteenth century which did attempt to create an ideology of state were the Russian Empire and the Kingdom of Hungary. The nationalism of the dominant nation, Russians and Hungarians, was to fill this need. It was to be made compulsory for all, and all were to be absorbed within one nation.

In Hungary this aim was proclaimed by the nationalist leader Louis Kossuth already in the 1840's, when he was in opposition to the paternalist absolutism of Metternich, and Hungary enjoyed very little autonomy under the Habsburg Crown. In 1848 Kossuth attempted to put it into practice, incurring the hostility of Croats, Serbs, Roumanians, and Slovaks, who were driven to support the Habsburgs in the suppression of Hungarian liberty. Later in life, in exile, Kossuth recognized his mistake and urged reconciliation and co-operation between the Hungarians and the other nations who lived in their midst. But when after 1867 the next generation of Kossuth's compatriots attained power, under the new constitutional agreement which gave the Hungarians almost complete sovereignty within the historical boundaries of Hungary, they showed that they had not learned the lessons of 1848. Hungarian language and culture were to be imposed on the smaller nations. The administration, courts, and schools were to be devoted to this purpose.

In Russia, official nationalism made its appearance in the 1830's, with special reference to the Poles, who by their rebellion of 1830 had shown themselves disloyal to the Tsar. But Nicholas I thought in dynastic rather than in nationalist terms. He had no wish to Russify his subjects of non-Russian language and culture, provided that they obeyed him loyally. He prevented the attempts made by some ardent Russian patriots to impose Russian culture on the Baltic provinces. It was not until the 1890's that official nationalism developed into systematic Russification, and was extended even to nations which had an unblemished record of loyalty to the Tsar – the Finns,[1] Baltic Germans, Volga Tatars, and Armenians. Every effort was now made to impose on them the Russian language, culture, and nationality. Russian provincial governors, priests, school-masters, and police worked to this end.

It is only fair to point out that there were honourable, even humanitarian aims behind these policies. Russian and Hungarian nationalists believed that their culture was superior, and that they were doing the smaller nations a favour by absorbing them into it. The Hungarian leaders were liberals, who had inherited the belief of most European liberals, derived from the time of the French Revolution and the Vendée insurrections, that centralism is progressive and all forms of regionalism are reactionary. Non-Magyars who accepted assimilation were treated as equals, and had the same opportunities of advancement as persons of Magyar origin. The same was broadly true of the Russian Empire. Poles or Tatars or Balts or

[1] Finland was not part of Russia, but was joined to it only by a personal union. From 1809 onwards the Emperor of Russia was also Grand Duke of Finland. The institutions, law, official language, and social organization of the two countries were intended to be kept quite distinct. It was not until the 1890's, as a result of the pressure of Russian nationalism within the Russian bureaucracy and a part of Russian public opinion – which found a sympathetic response in the minds of the last two Tsars, Alexander III and Nicholas II – that the attempt was made to absorb Finland into the Russian Empire and to Russify its cultural life.

Ukrainians who became Russians, accepting the Russian language as their own, and preferably also accepting conversion to the Orthodox Church, enjoyed the same opportunities (or absence of opportunities) of personal freedom or social advancement as subjects of Russian birth. But both the Russian and the Hungarian Government were determined (the Hungarians by more humane methods than the Russians) to destroy the nationalist movements within their states, and both governments failed. Certainly both Hungarian and Russian civilization exerted some attraction on the smaller nations. Budapest and St Petersburg were centres of a splendid culture. The same was of course true of Vienna, and even of Constantinople in the period of the decline of Ottoman power. Yet the educated *élite* of the small nations in its majority rejected Russification or Magyarization, and chose nationalism, and the bulk of the nation in each case followed its own *élite* in preference to its foreign rulers. The disaffection of the nationalities was an important contributory cause of the collapse of Austria-Hungary and Russia in 1917–18, and when the collapse came the nationalities rushed to break away and set up independent states of their own.

OFFICIAL NATIONALISM IN SUCCESSOR STATES

The break-up of the Kingdom of Hungary, and the loss of the western territories of the Russian Empire,[1] might have been expected to serve as a warning against the attempt to make the nationalism of one nation the basis of legitimacy of a multi-national state. Unfortunately the very same nations which had revolted against this principle, endeavoured to make it the foundation of the new states which they founded. In the Polish Republic and in the enlarged kingdom of Roumania, Poles and Roumanians formed about two-thirds of the population. In Czechoslovakia the Czechs, and in Yugoslavia the Serbs, each formed less than half – a smaller proportion, in fact, than the Russians in the old Russian Empire or the Hungarians in the old Kingdom of Hungary. All four were multi-national states, and all four insisted on pretending to be states of one nation, in which persons of other national origin could only be

[1] Finland, Poland, Estonia, Latvia, and Lithuania, became independent of Russia, and the south-western border province of Bessarabia was united with Roumania. These territorial changes were reversed in 1939 and 1940 by agreement between the Soviet Union and Nazi Germany. After the Second World War the only one of these countries which still retained real independence (though at the cost of some territorial loss) was Finland.

tolerated guests for a time, and the longer-term aim was the assimilation of all into the nationality of the dominant nation. The fact that the Czech political leaders claimed to speak for a "Czechoslovak nation", and the Serbian political leaders for a "Yugoslav nation", does not modify this, for the majority of Croats and Macedonians in Yugoslavia, and of Slovaks in Czechoslovakia, were discontented from an early stage, and after a decade or so were hostile or indifferent to the existence of the State. All four of these states failed to satisfy their component nationalities, and all four were in a state of almost constant hostility with all their neighbours – not only with the losers of 1918, Hungary and Bulgaria, whose compatriots were unwillingly incorporated in the victor states, but also with their fellow-victors, who advanced claims against each other. The mutual hostility, and the rival petty imperialisms, of these small states, enabled Hitler to play them off against each other and impose his rule on all alike, and when he was overthrown they fell into the clutches of his totalitarian heir, the Soviet Government.

The situation of the new states of Asia and Africa in many ways resembles that of the East European states after 1918. Can Nigerian nationalism prove an effective ideology of state, to unite Hausa, Ibo, Yoruba, and other peoples into one nation, or will it prove as fictitious as pre-communist 'Czechoslovak' or 'Yugoslav' nationalism? The new states have an advantage over their East European predecessors in that linguistic distinctions have not yet crystallized to the same extent into national consciousness. On the other hand they have a disadvantage in that the dominant groups do not possess so strong a sense of national identity as did the various dominant nations in Eastern Europe. In fact, both centripetal and centrifugal forces are weaker. However, it is clear that most of the problems of multi-national states, nationalism and small-power imperialism, familiar from the history of the Balkans, will present themselves, or are already presenting themselves. African politicians would do well to suppress the contemptuous undertone of their use of the word 'Balkanization'. They will need compassionate understanding of the plight of others, and a humility in the face of their tasks in which Balkan politicians forty years ago were sadly lacking.

COMMUNISM AS THE NEW LEGITIMACY

But official nationalism of one dominant nation is not the only secular ideology of state which has been used to replace traditional monarchy and religion as the basis of legitimacy. The multi-national Soviet empire is based on Marxism-Leninism. Marxism-Leninism, its followers claim, is a science of human history and human society, with laws as certain as the laws of chemistry. All human communities are bound to pass through certain stages of social development, culminating in socialist revolution followed by growth into communism. Marxism-Leninism is not only a science which explains these stages: it is also the invincible weapon of the class which has the Messianic historical role of bringing this process to its achievement – the proletariat. Marxism-Leninism is the 'theory of the proletariat'. It is the theory which explains what are the true interests of the workers, and how they must be defended. Marxism-Leninism does not come naturally to the simple working man: he has to be instructed, organized, and led. These tasks can be performed only by the trained Marxist-Leninists, organized in the Communist Party. The party leaders understand the worker's interests as mere flesh-and-blood men and women at the factory bench cannot. The party by its very existence embodies the immanent interests of the working class of the whole world. Whether the workers know it or not, their interests are what the leaders of the Communist Party at any moment say they are. All Communist parties are modelled on the Communist Party of the Soviet Union, itself created by the great Lenin. In November 1917 this party undoubtedly had the support of a larger number of workers in the city of Petrograd than did any other party. In the insurrection of that month, the party seized power, and after years of civil war extended its rule to the greater part of the former Russian Empire. In the opinion of its supporters to this day, these were not mere military victories. They were a turning-point in the history of the whole human race. They introduced the Era of Socialism in the world. The claims made on behalf of Marx to have discovered the laws of human history, and the claims made on behalf of Lenin to have created the party embodying this wisdom and embodying the immanent interests of the workers of the whole world, are considered to have proved the legitimacy of the Communist Party, which is no less absolute, no less identified with a specific group of men succeeding each other from generation to generation, and no less binding on all its subjects, than was the legitimacy claimed for divinely sanctioned monarchs. This legitimacy is binding not only on those Russians who never accepted Marxism-Leninism, but also on non-Russians who form 40 per cent. of the population of the Soviet Union, including peoples, such as those of the Caucasus and Central Asia, among whom an indigenous industrial working class did not exist at all in 1917 and among whom such a class is still today only a comparatively small minority.

In Central Asia there is no doubt that enormous material progress has been made during forty years of Soviet régime. The natural wealth of the region has been systematically exploited and new industries have been created. Central Asians can use their own languages in public business, and most local jobs are held by local people. There is a modern system of schools, in which the language of instruction is the local language, and of higher education, in which both the local language and Russian are used, in varying admixtures. As a result of these changes, the social structure of the Central Asian peoples has been transformed. Central Asians are now to be found not only in agriculture but also in all the professions and in all ranges of industrial skill from the manager to the low-grade manual worker.

These great changes have been planned and executed on orders from above. The Central Asian peoples have never had the slightest influence on policy: they were not asked whether they wished to remain in the Soviet Union, what kind of an economy they wanted, or for what purposes they wished the resources of their country to be used. It is arguable that if there had been independent Central Asian states, the resources would have been less efficiently used, and the standard of living of the peoples would be lower today than it is. There is no doubt that the standard of living is higher in Soviet Central Asia today than in Persia, Afghanistan, or Pakistan. The Soviet leaders can claim to have improved the lot of their subjects. But the essence of the argument is the same as that which can be used by Sir Roy Welensky. It may be that the Soviet achievement is greater than that of the British or French colonial rulers. It should, however, be remembered that the cultural level of the Central Asians at the time of the Russian conquest was incomparably higher than that of tropical Africans at the time of European conquest. It should also be remembered that the ratio of the metropolitan people to the colonial peoples was very much more favourable to the Russians than to the West Europeans (4 Russians to 1 Central Asian, as opposed to 1 Briton to 8 Indians). Asians and African nationalists claim, not only on behalf of themselves but also on behalf of African peoples who are not yet independent, that self-government is more important than good government. Dr Nkrumah has declared that the keys of the political kingdom must be given first. But these keys have always been denied to Central Asians. It may be argued that socialism is a better form of government than capitalist democracy, that Stalin and Khrushchev have done their job of colonial development better than Welensky: the fact remains that it has been the same sort of job.

COMMUNISM AND RUSSIFICATION

The Central Asians have remained colonial subjects, with no right of self-determination, and they have been ruled by the same Communist Party as the Russians and the European subject peoples of the Soviet Union. But has this rule been exercised in the name of the Russian people or of some other force? The answer must be that power has been wielded by a totalitarian state based not on nationalist but on Communist principles, but that there are also definite elements of Russification, which suggest some continuity with Imperial Russia and some similarity to other non-Communist empires. The use of the Russian language exceeds the inevitable needs of central administration. The Central Asian 'languages', artificially manufactured from dialects in order to divide from each other the Turkic peoples which 100 years ago belonged essentially to one culture, are filled with Russian words, on a scale exceeding the inevitable needs of technical vocabulary. Key posts in the management of industry, political administration and party hierarchy remain in Russian hands. (For example, first secretaries of republican and provincial committees of the party are usually Asians but second secretaries are usually Russians; Ministers in Republican governments are Asians but heads of departments in ministries are often Russians.) In Kazakhstan a mass influx of Russian settlers in Khrushchev's 'Virgin Lands' is reducing the Kazakhs to a diminishing minority in their own homeland. Ever since 1917 the local Russian populations have been chauvinistic and intolerant towards their Asian neighbours, even though the Moscow authorities have exhorted them to behave in a fraternal manner. The Tashkent railway workers and small officials ever since 1917 have played a part very similar to that of the European workers in Northern Rhodesia, the 'poor whites' in the American South or the *pieds noirs* in Algeria. In Central Asian cities residential segregation exists in practice. Russians and Asians meet at their place of work, but they seldom meet socially or intermarry. Official Soviet historical literature has also done its best to deprive the Central Asian peoples of their past, well knowing how dangerous nationalist interpretations of history can be. The Russian conquest of the Caucasus and Central Asia is represented as an objectively progressive phenomenon, since it brought these peoples into touch with the superior culture of the great Russian people, and expedited the development of their society from feudalism to capitalism, and thence to socialism. This, of course, is simply a Marxist-Leninist version of the doctrines of Kipling, or of President McKinley, who declared his intention to 'take the Filipinos and lift them up and Christianize them'. In recent years some of the worst distortions of the Stalin period have been dropped, but Soviet historians still write not of the conquest of Central Asia, but of their fusion (*sliyanie*) or union (*prisoyedinenie*) with Russia.

It is sometimes argued, outside the Soviet bloc and by non-Communists, that in the Soviet Union a new national consciousness has been created, that a 'Soviet nation' has been formed, which includes persons of Russian or Ukrainian or Georgian or Yakut origin but is distinct from the Russian or other nations. A comparison is made with the melting-pot of the United States, in which the immigrants were absorbed into a new nation. In my opinion this is a wrong comparison. The American nation was a new nation, created from many ethnic stocks in a new land, though based on a foundation of English language and law. The immigrant groups had left their old homelands, and plunged into a society which was not theirs, but which was continuously evolving, and they made their contribution to this evolution. At any given time, however, the immigrant groups were a minority in relation to the mass of those who had grown up in, or had been absorbed into, the Anglo-Saxon cultural and social tradition. In the Soviet Union large compact national groups live in their own traditional homelands, with which they are bound by powerful cultural and sentimental bonds. The domination of the Russians over them is a foreign domination, which certainly has its good features but remains foreign. The American nation is a fact, but the 'Soviet nation' is a fiction, similar despite obvious differences to the fictitious 'Yugoslav' and 'Czechoslovak' nations between the world wars.[1]

[1] Whether the 'Czechoslovak' and 'Yugoslav' nations are a fiction today is more difficult to say. My own belief is that, owing to the memory of the fratricidal

There are of course no organized nationalist movements directed against Soviet rule, no Uzbek equivalents of the Indian National Congress or the Egyptian Wafd. But this proves only that the Soviet security police are efficient, and that no political opinions may be expressed that differ from those of the Communist Party. Yet the experience of other empires is significant. The British in India and the French in Indo-China created, by introducing modern European education on a rather modest scale, modern intellectual *élites*. The Hungarian governments of 1867–1918 provided education for a considerable minority among their non-Hungarian subjects. All these people owed to the foreign government the opportunity to acquire modern knowledge and skills, to become men or women of the nineteenth or twentieth century. But this did not make them supporters of alien rule. Nehru and Ho Chi-minh were products of English and French education, but they used their abilities and education to lead their peoples in the struggle for national independence. The same is true of the Slovak, Transylvanian, and Serbian intellectuals who were subjects of Hungary before 1918. The Soviet régime has created a proportionately large intellectual *élite* among the peoples of the Caucasus and Central Asia. It would be astonishing if these men did not have in their hearts the determination one day to secure national independence. If it exists, it will one day be translated into action.

It is worth stressing the historical tragedy of the Turkish peoples of Russia. It is a curious historical irony that the main route of expansion of the Turkish State in its prime was into the Christian Balkans, while the first territorial expansion of the Muscovite State was among the Turks of the Volga basin. If ethnic and religious, rather than strategic and geographic, factors had been decisive in the fifteenth and sixteenth centuries, the Russian Empire would have stretched into the Slav lands and the Ottoman Empire would

---

slaughter of Serbs, Croats, and Moslems in the Second World War, and owing to the growth of a new generation whose homeland is not Serbia or Croatia but Yugoslavia, the Yugoslav nation is already a reality for a very large part of its members, and within a decade or two will be a reality for all. In Czechoslovakia, on the other hand, the persecution of Catholic Christianity by Czech Communists and other abuses of the Communist régime, may have the effect of widening the gulf between Czechs and Slovaks. There are, however, undoubtedly forces making for unity. It should also be noted that the peoples of Czechoslovakia and Yugoslavia are far closer to each other than are the different peoples of the Soviet Union, or the different linguistic and tribal groups of India, Nigeria, and many other new states.

have reached to Kazan. The truth is that the Volga, the 'Russian river' (*russkaya reka*) of which the ballad tells, was until the mid-nineteenth century ethnically a Turkish river. But though during the nineteenth century the Balkan Christian peoples became freed from Ottoman rule, thanks to the support of the European Powers and especially of Russia, the Turks of the Volga and Urals were even more firmly subjected to Russian rule. During the last decades of Tsardom national consciousness and nationalism rapidly grew among these people, and the collapse of the Imperial régime gave them a sudden hope of liberty. But they were once more suppressed, this time in the name of a 'proletarian revolution' which was not theirs; and incorporated in the 'Soviet brotherhood and friendship of peoples' for which they had never asked. It is a pity that a 'world opinion' so solicitous for the rights of Angolans or Kikuyu should so totally ignore the Soviet Turks.

It can of course be argued that, of the Balkan Christians, at least the Roumanians and the Bulgarians have fared little better, for they too have ended up as the subjects of a totalitarian Soviet empire. The case of the Greeks is different, but in its way it too is an example of the tragic irony of history. In the Ottoman Empire the Greeks were the traders and the intellectuals of the whole empire. They were successful and influential in the whole Eastern Mediterranean and Middle East and all round the coasts of the Black Sea, including the south of Russia. But the creation of an independent Greek state, and the expansion of its territory during the last 140 years, has coincided with the liquidation of Greek influence in the wider world. We need only recall the list of cities from which Greeks have been forced out, whether by sudden violence or by gradual suffocation – Bucarest, Odessa, Smyrna, Constantinople, and now today, slowly but relentlessly under the leadership of that exponent of progressive Arab nationalism President Nasser – Alexandria itself.

NATIONALISM TODAY AND TOMORROW

The terrible experiences of the 1930's and the Second World War largely discredited nationalism in Europe. It had degenerated into a doctrine of power, and had reached its culmination in the life and actions of Adolf Hitler. The nation became an idol, a modern Moloch for whom the furnaces of Auschwitz were filled. Membership of the master nation conferred the right to exterminate inferior nations, whose members were not human beings but vermin to be wiped off the face of the earth. The best-known example is, of course, the Nazi view of the German race and of the Jews. But it was not the only example. The East European nations produced minor Hitlers of similar outlook, who did their best to put these inhuman doctrines into practice. Such were the leaders of the Roumanian Iron Guard and the Hungarian Arrow Cross. Perhaps the most diabolic figure of all was the Croatian Fascist, Ante Pavelić, who was personally responsible for the slaughter of several hundred thousand Serbs and Jews. Nationalism by 1944 had come a long way since the French Revolution. Europeans could see it as a Janus: one face showed the venerable features of Garibaldi, the other the grinning mask of the death-camp commandant.

In Western Europe since the Second World War men have moved away from nationalism. Frenchmen and Germans, both reduced by defeat and occupation to destitution and despair, began to see, as they recovered, that their old enmity had lost all sense. The belief in Franco-German reconciliation, confined at first to a few in each nation, spread to ever larger groups, especially among the young. The growth of this belief, tragically underrated in Britain, was perhaps the main force behind the movement for European unity, to which economic factors also contributed, and which was assisted both by American encouragement and by Soviet hostility. The movement affected the other nations of Western Europe, but for obvious political reasons it could find but little public expression in Spain and Portugal, and none at all in the countries under Communist rule.

The movement towards European unity in the West is a strong and noble force. But it would be unwise to assume that the old Adam of narrow nationalism is quite dead. Side by side with the generous ideals and the enlightened self-interest, there is also evidence of the pursuit of national greatness at the expense of others. Most obvious are of course the Carolingian ambitions of Charles de Gaulle, to whom the new Western Europe seems to mean a new variation on the theme of the Frankish or French empires made familiar by Charlemagne and Napoleon. In Germany the old nationalism seems to be no more than a minority view, and the hard core of this minority, the Germans expelled from Prussia, Silesia, and Bohemia, is growing weaker as the older people lose their influence on the young. Nevertheless there is some irredentist nationalism left, and it might revive at a time of crisis. On the other hand the desire for the reunification of Germany, which means essentially the restoration of liberty to eighteen million Germans under Communist rule in the Soviet zone, is a natural human emotion, and can hardly be reckoned as nationalism. Almost all Germans, however European in outlook, feel this desire, and it is entirely reasonable that they should.

In Eastern Europe the issue of nationalism presents itself somewhat differently. Certainly in 1944 disillusionment with nationalism was widespread, probably even more so than in the West, for it had brought even greater suffering. But when it became clear that another imperial rule had been imposed on them, in some ways as harsh as Hitler's and certainly far harsher than those of Habsburg or Romanov, the peoples of Eastern Europe, including the intellectuals who previously had most strongly reacted against the abuses of nationalism, began once more to value above all their patriotism and national traditions. Independence became for them the greatest good. This was most strikingly shown by the peaceful revolt of Poland in October 1956 and by the Hungarian Revolution. Since 1957 the Soviet leaders have held the East European Communists on a looser rein, and life has become more tolerable in consequence, both for Communists and for the rest. They have taken as much liberty as it is safe to take. That they have not tried to take more, does not mean that they would not like more. The Poles, for example, accept Gomulka's policy of loyal co-operation with Soviet Russia. This does not mean that the vast majority of Poles, and probably Gomulka too, would not like to break away from Russia altogether.

Nationalism against Russia is not permitted, but nationalism against Germany is encouraged, at least in Poland and Czechoslovakia. Acting on Goebbels' principle that the big lie, endlessly repeated, is effective propaganda, the Prague and Warsaw spokesmen assert that the Federal Republic is ruled by Nazis and militarists, and treat Adenauer as Hitler's direct heir. How much effect they have on their audience, it is impossible to judge. That there is a large volume of distrust for all Germans among Poles and Czechs can hardly be doubted. However, though varying degrees of nationalism, in the old sense, against Russia or Germany or both, are certainly present in Eastern Europe, and though the old nationalist passions between neighbours (for example, between Hungarians and

Roumanians about Transylvania) may still be alive beneath the surface, there is also evidence that the idea of European unity enjoys sympathy, and that the progress already made in this direction in the West exerts great attraction.

In Asia and Africa nationalism is comparatively new, and seems immensely popular, while in Latin America it has increased in recent years. The only Asian country in which it appears to have declined is Japan. Disillusionment caused by defeat, and an increased understanding of the exceptional dependence of Japan on international trade and peace, have created a strong mood of internationalism. Even so, nationalist passions are capable of revival, both in a traditionalist and in a Communist form. In India the nationalist enthusiasm of the people has been to some extent counterbalanced by the internationalist outlook of Jawarhalal Nehru and his circle, who though Indian patriots are also citizens of the world. As for China, it is doubtful whether nationalism is an appropriate word to describe the outlook of leaders or people. Rather, it would seem that patriotic pride in restored greatness, traditional Chinese imperial ambitions and Marxist-Leninist ideology have been fused into a totalitarian doctrine which differs radically from nationalism.

It is tempting to argue that the intensity of nationalism to be found today outside Europe and North America varies in inverse proportion to the population of a country and to the number of years that it has enjoyed independence. There is some validity in this correlation, but it is also misleading. It is true that nationalism is especially violent in those countries which are still colonies of Western Powers. Whether beneath the totalitarian surface nationalism is still strong among the non-Russian peoples of the Soviet Union is hard to say, but the historical experience of other empires suggests that it is likely to be. But nationalism in independent countries is not simply related to the length of their independence. Nationalism can be provoked not only by direct foreign rule but also by a humiliating degree of foreign tutelage. 'Neo-colonialism' has become a well-known slogan among Asians, Africans, and Latin Americans. There are many cases where the slogan corresponds to reality. Persia has been independent – with several fairly extensive interruptions – for over 2,000 years. But since the early nineteenth century Persia has suffered much from the intervention of European governments or business interests. In the 1960's many

Persians believe, rightly or wrongly, that their independence is limited, to an intolerable extent, by American political and economic influence. In Latin America there is no doubt that American interference – more often by business firms than by the United States Government – has been far-reaching, and has often taken offensive forms. In the 1960's it is smaller, but it has not disappeared. From the mid-1950's there developed, especially among the young generation of the intelligentsia, a pathological hatred of the United States, which was made the scapegoat for every social or political abuse in the sub-continent. This campaign of hatred coincided with Communist aims, but was certainly not created by the Communists. Perhaps its most striking expression was the bestial reception given by Peruvian and Venezuelan students to Mr and Mrs Nixon in 1958. In the independent African states, suspicion of 'neo-colonialism' has become almost paranoiac at times. The Communist Powers have done their best to exploit it, to create the conviction that the presence of any Western business interests is proof that a country is not independent, that 'the imperialists' still rule it by new and more subtle means. However, this propaganda has sometimes turned against the Communist Powers too. Technicians from the 'socialist camp' are not immune to African xenophobia or search for scapegoats.

Many of the new states are multi-lingual and multi-tribal. The development of linguistic nationalism is a dangerous possibility for them. Two great states are especially vulnerable, India and Nigeria. At least in India there is a common religious and cultural tradition of great antiquity. Indians have felt themselves to be Indians for centuries. Even so the appeal of regional patriotism and linguistic separatism should not be underrated. But 'Nigeria' is an invention of the Europeans. The creation of a Nigerian national feeling is an artificial process. Can this new secular ideology of state compete with Ibo or Yoruba or Hausa loyalties? Nigerian nationalism has the advantage over Russian and Hungarian official nationalism, that it is not identified with any existing national or linguistic group. It has the disadvantage that it cannot command the innate devotion even of a minority.

Another feature of the East European scene of the nineteenth and early twentieth centuries has already appeared in Africa. Irredentism and small-state imperialism are already flourishing. Morocco demands Mauritania. The Kenya nationalists insist that the Somalis who live in the province of Kenya bordering Somalia may not join their kinsmen: the territorial integrity of a state arbitrarily created by Europeans is sacrosanct. Both Indonesia and the Philippines look covetously at British Borneo. Ghana and Togoland quarrel about the rights of the Ewe people, divided between these two states by colonial boundaries of the past.

Europeans and Americans are inclined to interpret history as showing that nationalism is a temporary phase in the development of human societies, which must give way to larger associations, and ultimately to world government. It may be so, but it is not certain. Looking at the East European situation of 1963, one is inclined to say that national independence was but a brief transitional period between the fall of the empires of Habsburgs, Romanovs and Ottomans and the establishment of the empire of the Bolsheviks. One then wonders whether the independence of Asians and Africans will not prove to be an equally brief transitional period between the fall of the British, French, and Dutch empires and the establishment of new empires – Chinese, Russian, Egyptian, or some other. Such speculation is based on the assumption that the Soviet rule over Eastern Europe has come to stay for a long time. Yet within a few decades it may have disappeared without trace. The future of nationalism is unpredictable.

Twentieth-century Revolutions

The first half of the twentieth century is richer than any previous period of human history in the activities of revolutionary movements. Some have failed, others are still engaged in the struggle. A few have achieved revolutions of historic importance. But there is one important feature of the twentieth-century revolutionary movements which distinguishes them from those of the nineteenth century. The earlier movements arose in culturally and economically advanced countries, while those of the present century have for the most part affected backward regions and peoples.

These movements are much discussed at present by journalists and politicians, but have received little attention from historians. In current discussions the main emphasis is usually placed on the mass aspect of the movements and on economic factors. It is assumed that their strength comes mainly from the unrest of subject nations, industrial proletariats and impoverished peasants. The victories which they have won are usually attributed to mass support. The conclusion is that revolutions can best be averted if the wealthier nations invest large sums in the development of backward economies. Better food crops, new jobs in industry, and more extensive trade will reduce the mass poverty and deprive the revolutionaries of their opportunity.

It would be absurd to deny that revolutionary movements thrive on mass poverty and mass discontent, or that improvement in the standard of living of the masses makes for political stability. But two further factors deserve consideration. The first is the origin and the nature of revolutionary leadership. The second is the political framework within which revolutionary movements develop. Both these factors have, of course, been minutely studied by historians of the revolutions of the eighteenth and nineteenth centuries in Western Europe and North America. They have, however, been somewhat neglected in connexion with the twentieth-century movements in Eastern Europe, Asia, and Africa. Such attempts as have been made are too often the work of uncritical admirers or passionate

---

This article was first published in the *Political Quarterly*, July 1951.

Twentieth-century Revolutions

adversaries. Yet even a brief examination of these two factors may make possible some significant conclusions about the twentieth-century revolutionary movements of backward peoples.

West European and American political commentators and economists are too inclined to consider world problems from the point of view of the economics and political traditions of Western Europe and North America. But the 'western society' on which their ideas are based is not the typical society of the world. It exists only in Scandinavia, north-west Europe, North America, and the British Dominions of the Pacific. If northern Italy and Germany are added, the whole area has a population of less than 400 million out of a world population of more than 2,000 million.

The society of this 'north-western corner' of the world, which has grown up since the end of the Middle Ages, has certain specific features. The class structure is balanced. The level of skill and the standard of living of workers and farmers are on the whole high. There is a numerous and influential middle class, in which the three subdivisions of business, free professions and administration play their parts. Education is widespread and long established. The tradition of representative institutions, both national and local, is deeply rooted. Though there are great differences in wealth, all citizens belong to the same century. Class structure, education and constitutional forms vary considerably within different regions and countries of the north-west corner, but all share these general characteristics, in contrast to the lands outside the corner.

If the typical classes of the north-west corner are skilled workers, educated farmers, and business men, the typical classes of the outside world are unskilled labourers, uneducated peasants, and bureaucrats. In Southern and Eastern Europe, Asia, Africa, and Latin America the great majority of the population are primitive and poverty-stricken peasants. In the last decades the rapid industrialization of certain regions has reduced the number of peasants and increased the number of unskilled workers in mines or factories, little if at all less primitive or poor. One reason for the poverty of the peasants has been the survival of great landed estates and of various semi-feudal legal forms. This was the case in Russia before 1917 and in Hungary until 1945. It is still the case in southern Italy, Spain, Egypt, and large parts of Asia, Africa, and Latin America. But experience has shown that the distribution of landlords' estates among the peasants – which was done in parts of Eastern Europe after 1918, in other parts after 1945, and in Japan, Korea, and China after the Second World War – is not the end of the peasants' poverty. A more basic cause of poverty is rural overpopulation. The numbers of people in the villages have grown more rapidly than the output of the soil has been increased or than new jobs in industry have been created. Overpopulation means underemployment for the peasants, and a reserve of half-employed peasants keeps down the level of wages for all but the skilled minority among the urban workers.

For those sons of workers who are able by ability or good fortune to rise in the social scale the best opportunities have usually lain in the State service. But the growing influx of recruits from below inflates the bureaucracy intolerably. As the numbers of bureaucrats grow faster than the national wealth, their material conditions deteriorate. An enormous underpaid civil service breeds corruption: only by bribery can the poor official feed his family. To corruption must be added a tradition of arrogance and brutality. The official is accustomed to despise and bully the human cattle whom it is his duty to push, pull, or drive whither his masters bid. This has certainly long been the practice in Spain, Hungary, Poland, the Balkans, and Russia. It is still more so in Turkey, Persia, China, or Japan. In colonial countries the situation has been somewhat different. Western administrators have tried, with varying success, to bring to their colonies the more civilized methods of administration prevalent in their own countries, and have also resisted the pressure to inflate the numbers of officials. But the lower ranks of their administration have been filled with local people who have imperfectly acquired the higher standards, while the limitation of numbers has contributed above all to the frustration of the subject nations. As soon as they attain independence the colonial peoples rapidly expand their civil services. The world must be shown that they are not 'unfit to govern', and jobs must be found for the boys. Corruption increases faster than ever, and the new bureaucrats feel even more strongly than the old how distinct and superior a caste they are.

In this type of society, which until recently was typical of most of the world outside the north-west corner, the masses were too inert and the bureaucrats too powerful. If there was to be radical change, leadership must be found. The source of such leadership has been the small educated class – the 'intelligentsia'.

The intelligentsia is a product of Western influence. Already in the eighteenth century Western ideas and ways of life were known to the aristocracies of Poland, Hungary, and Russia. During the nineteenth century schools and universities developed in these countries, slowly it is true, but with important effects. The professional class was formed from two directions, from the children of the landed gentry for whom there was no place on the family estate, and from the children of small officials, merchants, and village shopkeepers who had just enough money, ability or 'connexions' to mount the educational ladder. Even the reactionary but incompetent Ministers of Education of mid-nineteenth-century Russia were unable either to reserve higher education to members of the nobility or to purge it of progressive ideas. In the Balkan countries liberated from Turkish rule no social hierarchy barred the way to education. The Balkan governments were keen to extend education: the obstacle was the meagre wealth of the states. Though the intention was education for all, the more prosperous families were in fact privileged. The children of the army officers, officials, innkeepers, pig-merchants, and village usurers from whom the ruling class of the new states was formed, had better chances than the children of peasant smallholders, miners, railwaymen, and factory workers. In Asia the process started later. In the Middle East the Islamic system of education was open to comparatively poor children, but it was more or less unrelated to the needs of the nineteenth and twentieth centuries. The same was true of the Confucian system in China. The introduction of Western ideas and influences was largely the work of such institutions as the French schools in the Levant, the American Robert College at Constantinople, the American University of Beirut, the European and American missions in China. Japan alone among Asiatic countries systematically copied European education and diffused it among her subjects. In Latin America considerable efforts had been made in education ever since the Spanish and Portuguese conquests.

The best education available at the most modern schools and universities in Eastern Europe, Asia, and Latin America has been little inferior to that available at the same time in the Western world. Some institutions in Africa have recently approached or attained the same standard. The best scientists, writers, doctors, or engineers produced by this education have been as good at their jobs as their Western counterparts. They have entered the twentieth century, while their peoples, suffering from social injustice and political oppression, have remained in the eighteenth, or fifteenth, or tenth century.

Many, probably most, members of the East European and Asian intelligentsias accepted this fact. Some believed that by becoming twentieth-century people, and doing twentieth-century jobs, they were working for their own nations' good, and would help to raise their nations to their level. Others were so engrossed in their special skill that the wider issues did not occur to them. Others simply enjoyed the life of a French lawyer or an American engineer, rather than that of a Hungarian worker, a Lebanese peasant or a Chinese coolie. Their lives were more agreeable than those of their compatriots: let the latter fend for themselves.

But the minority, and in some countries a very numerous minority, rebelled. They were horrified by the contrast between themselves and their peoples, between the fifteenth and twentieth centuries. The social injustices were intolerable, and the political factors which perpetuated them – the dominance of a privileged class or a privileged nation – must be swept away. There were young Slovaks who were not content, by learning the Magyar language and so reaching a Magyar university, to merge themselves in the Hungarian ruling class, but insisted on fighting for the national and social liberation of the submerged Slovak nation. There were Russian or Chinese intellectuals, of both distinguished and humble birth, who could not ignore the landhunger in the villages, the maltreatment of peasants by landlords or police, the dead weight of a bureaucracy suspicious of every generous initiative.

To these idealist motives must be added personal motives for revolt. Semi-feudal legal survivals or foreign rule were not only socially or nationally unjust: they were also obstacles to the ambitions of the local intellectuals. Poles, Ukrainians, Balts, and Caucasians in the Russian Empire; South Slavs, Slovaks, and Roumanians in Hungary; the Asiatic and African subjects of European colonial empires found their way to power and wealth barred by members of the dominant nations. In Hungary, Roumania, and Poland between the world wars many of the best posts in business and the free professions were held by Jews. University graduates who found no jobs attributed their difficulties to sinister Jewish conspiracy. Idealism and interest alike led them to anti-semitic Fascism. Chinese in Siam and Malaya, Indians in East Africa, Greeks in the Middle East, and Europeans throughout Asia, form a host of 'Jewish problems', seem to the young intellectuals of each country to have robbed them of their birthright, and drive them to revolutionary nationalism. Balkan university students denounced their professors as 'reactionary' because they failed in their examinations. Egyptian or Indian students have beaten or murdered invigilators who objected to their bringing cribs into the examination hall. To join an extremist party – Fascist, nationalist, or Communist – was emotionally satisfying and required less sustained mental effort than plain hard work. For most of the revolutionary intellectuals of the backward countries the broader and the personal motives existed side by side. The personal motive is perhaps more powerful in colonial countries, where the presence of the foreign power is a constant irritant, and where the level of education is lower than in Eastern Europe, Japan, or even the Middle East. The half-educated are perhaps more frustrated, and more inclined to revolutionary shortcuts, than the fully educated.

It was through the intelligentsia, created by the development of Western types of education, that the modern political ideas of Western Europe reached the countries of Eastern Europe, Asia and Africa. It should be noted that the ideas reached the backward countries ready-made, before the economic, social, and political conditions to which they were related had arisen. Examples are Russia in the 1870's, Bulgaria in the 1890's and China in the 1920's. Even nationalism was preached by the intelligentsia when national consciousness hardly existed among the masses. Examples from Europe are the Slovaks and the Ukrainians. In Asia and Africa this has been still more the case.

The relationship between the ideas of the intelligentsia and the social condition and consciousness of the masses has varied according to the stage of general economic and cultural development. This is well illustrated by the case of Russia. In the Russia of the 1870's, when the intelligentsia was separated by a chasm from the masses, the intelligentsia's best hope of victory for their ideas was to organize a secret conspiracy of professional revolutionaries. In the Russia of 1913, in which a middle class and skilled working class were becoming important factors, the peasants were becoming educated, and even the intellectuals were beginning to find a legal outlet for their energies and abilities, political action by mass parties, as in Western Europe, was becoming possible. This was what the Menshevik faction of Russian socialism advocated, and every year after

1905 seemed to strengthen their case. Lenin, who clung to the older conspiratorial type of party, seemed a reactionary utopian. But in the Russia of 1917, when the Russian State collapsed and the europeanizing work of fifty years was undone, Lenin was the realist and the Mensheviks the utopians.

Between the world wars Hungary, Poland, and Japan to some extent resembled the Russia of 1913. Large-scale industry was fairly well developed. Skilled workers, technicians, and businessmen were numerous. Political power, however, did not belong to these classes, not even to a very large extent to the businessmen. It was held to some extent by landowning families, and to an increasing extent by a bureaucracy whose higher officials were descendants of landowners, who had succeeded in impressing even on its lower ranks – recruited from the poorer classes – the traditional outlook of the landowning class – gentry, *szlachta* or *samurai*. The peasants were still economically backward, had too little land, and were in many cases victims of exploitation.

The Balkan countries between the world wars had some points of resemblance to the Russia of the 70's. Industry was still backward, skilled workers were few, and the middle class was weak. When dictatorships were installed in the 1920's the police were no less powerful, and probably more cruel, than the police of Tsar Alexander II. On the other hand, the Balkan nations had no landowning aristocracy or semi-feudal survivals; their education was making great progress and they had far more experience of self-government than the Russians.

In Asia and Africa development was, of course, slower. The most modern provinces of Egypt, India, and China bear some resemblance to the Russia of 1913, but in the backward provinces conditions remained as primitive as in the Europe of the Middle Ages. In large parts of Africa things are very much more primitive still. In these countries the local man who has received a twentieth-century education is cut off from his people by a deeper gulf even than were the Russian intellectuals of the mid-nineteenth century.

The impact of ready-made West European political ideas on these various types of backward societies had effects at least as far-reaching as the impact of West European trade and technique. The political ideas were reflected in political movements, in which inevitably the leadership came from the intelligentsia. In Russia, China, the Ottoman Empire, and the Balkan states the radical intellectuals were forced by the repressive policy of dictatorial governments to resort to more or less revolutionary and conspiratorial methods. In Austria-Hungary, Japan, and the British and French empires they enjoyed greater freedom of action, though this fell short of 'Western democracy' as understood in Britain and France. In general, the radicalism of the intellectuals and their importance in the revolutionary movements varied in inverse proportion to the economic and cultural development of their peoples. As the masses became more prosperous, more skilled and more educated, broadly based mass movements became more possible, the leadership of intellectuals became less essential, and it became more reasonable to hope for improvement by comparatively peaceful means. It is the combination of backward masses, extremist intellectuals and despotic bureaucrats which creates the most conspiratorial movements.

These movements may be, in European terminology, 'extreme Left' or 'extreme Right'.

The earliest example of the 'Left' type were the Russian Populists of the 1870's. They held unrealistic views about the revolutionary potentialities of the Russian peasants, and about the possibility of transforming the traditional organs of village self-government into organs of a socialist society. But as conspirators they were efficient, at any rate judged by the technical standards of the time. They created a small but well disciplined organization, which assassinated several high officials and finally killed the Tsar himself. Their technique was later copied and improved by Lenin, whose Bolshevik party was from the first intended to be an organization of 'professional revolutionaries'. The Bolshevik technique of conspiracy has in turn served as the model for the Communist parties in all countries. Some of these have been forced by police persecution to operate 'underground' during most of their existence. But even those which have enjoyed the political liberties of a democratic state were obliged by the Twenty-One Conditions of the Second Comintern Congress of 1920, to maintain, parallel with their 'legal' organization, an 'illegal' apparatus. The efficiency of Communist conspirators has varied greatly in the last thirty years. Among the more efficient were the illegal parties of Bulgaria and Yugoslavia between the world wars. In both countries the intellectual youth was strongly attracted to Communism. Students and graduates of Belgrade and Sofia universities succeeded in popularizing Communism and the Soviet Union and built up cadres which were to prove valuable during the resistance movements in the Second World War. Another country in which Communism made a most powerful appeal to the young intellectuals was, of course, China.

An interesting example of a 'right' type of revolutionary movement in a backward country is the Roumanian Iron Guard. Led by university students and graduates, it was able during the slump of the early 1930's to exploit the misery of the peasants and the idealism of the intelligentsia. It promised vague social reforms, including a further distribution of land. Oppression was identified with the Jews, liberation and justice with the German Nazis. Like the Russian Populists, the Iron Guardists 'went to the people', studying their living conditions more honestly and more thoroughly than the elder generation of liberal politicians had done, and at the same time propagating their ideas. Like the Communists, they infiltrated themselves into official organizations and into oppositional parties. Like the Communists, they were savagely repressed by the police. Parallels with the Roumanian Iron Guardists can be found among the nationalist movements of Asia and Africa. One example are the conspiratorial groups of young officers in Japan, who had more or less fascist ideas, wished to regenerate their country, were anti-parliamentarian and anti-Western traditionalists. Another is the Moslem Brotherhood in Egypt, a combination of modern nationalism and Islamic conservatism. Like the Roumanian Iron Guardists and the Japanese secret societies, the Moslem Brothers make use of assassination as a political weapon.

Communism is today the most important of the revolutionary movements among the backward peoples, but it is not and will not necessarily be the only one. Communism, as developed by Stalin and Mao Tse-tung, is only the most important example of a wider phenomenon, the revolt of the backward peoples, led by a section of their intelligentsia, against the West.

The obstacle to the seizure of power by the revolutionary movements has been the bureaucratic State machine. Communist theory has paid much attention to this problem. But in fact no Communist movement in this century has, solely by its own efforts, captured or destroyed the State machine. In three cases only Communists have seized power – in Russia, Yugoslavia, and China. But in all three cases the State machine was smashed not by the revolutionaries but by a foreign invading Power.

In the chaos of the collapse of Tsardom the Bolsheviks were more clear-headed, better disciplined and less scrupulous than their rivals. They were also more efficient demagogues. By promising the people at once the things they most needed, and which in fact they knew that they would not be able to give them, they won considerable popular support. Lenin, who for more than a decade had devoted himself to the study of power, built a new army and a new police machine. He made good use of the quarrels between his Russian rivals and between his foreign enemies. He was also able to some extent to exploit Russian patriotism against Poles and Japanese. His skill in all these matters gave him the victory, but he would not have had a chance to begin if Ludendorff had not crushed the armies of the Tsar. Nor would all his skill have availed him had not Russia possessed the advantages of geographical remoteness. The British, French, and American publics were not convinced that it mattered to them what happened in distant Russia. Their governments, dependent on their votes at election time, soon abandoned their very small attempts at intervention. In Hungary, where the collapse of the old régime gave the Communists a similar opportunity, they were crushed. This was no doubt partly due to the fact that Bela Kun was not so good a leader as Lenin. But it was still more due to the geographical accessibility of Hungary to the armies of the victorious allies and of their smaller protégés.

In Yugoslavia the old police régime which had kept down the Communists was destroyed by the German and satellite invaders. In China the same thing was done by the conquering Japanese. In both countries the Communists assumed the leadership of national resistance. The Chinese Communists had already acquired valuable experience of guerilla warfare in their struggle against Chiang Kai-shek. The Yugoslav Communists had no guerrilla experience in their own country, but they possessed cadres of brave and disciplined underground organizers, and some of their leaders had learned the art of warfare as volunteers in the Spanish Civil War. In both countries the Communist-led resistance forces liberated considerable areas, in which they set up a civil administration and conscripted the population into their armies. Thus by the time the Germans and Japanese were defeated by the Allied Great Powers, both the Chinese and Yugoslav Communists possessed disciplined military and civil bureaucracies, ready to take over power in the rest of their country. The factor of geographical remoteness also operated in their favour. If either the Germans or the Japanese had sent overpowering forces into the fastnesses of the Yugoslav and Chinese Communists, they could no doubt have crushed them. But the commitments on the main war fronts and the difficulty of the Communist-held terrain made it not worth their while to do so. After the defeat of the invaders, the two countries were outside the area of the Western armies, which might have been expected to be unsympathetic to the Communists. Belgrade and Manchuria were 'liberated' by the Soviet armies. The supply of American arms to the forces of Chiang Kai-shek was even less effective than the supply of arms from France and Britain to the Russian Whites in 1919–20.

In other areas also Communist-led resistance forces gained experience of military leadership and civil administration, but were not able to seize power. The European example is Greece, where a large 'liberated area' was held in 1943–4 and again in 1947–9. In Asia there were similar areas in Malaya, Burma, and Indo-China. These areas were not, however, geographically remote enough. British forces defeated the Greek Communists in 1944, and American aid enabled the Greek National Army to defeat them again in 1949. In Burma the Communists and nationalists came to blows, and the Government of Burma, granted independence by Britain, gradually gained control of most of the country. In Malaya Communist guerrillas are still a very serious nuisance, but there is no prospect of their obtaining power over the country unless they are supported by an invading army. In Indo-China the outlook is uncertain, but hitherto the Viet-Min rebels have not been able to conquer the most populous and wealthy provinces.

There have, of course, been numerous occasions when Communist régimes have been installed by the military intervention of Soviet Russian forces. This was done in Georgia in 1921, in Outer Mongolia in 1922 and in the Baltic states in 1940. An unsuccessful attempt was made in Finland in 1939. The 'democratic government' set up in Terijoki under the Comintern veteran Otto Willi Kuusinen merely made itself and its patrons ridiculous. It was abandoned when peace was made with Finland, and it was not revived after the defeat of Finland in the war of 1941–4. Another failure took place in 1946 in Persian Azerbaidjan, where a puppet administration was created under the 'Democrat' Pishevari, who had played the same role more than twenty years earlier. The Soviet Government yielded because the Powers which it then still nominally regarded as its allies were strongly opposed. But Pishevari, who with true Bolshevik self-criticism had publicly analysed the mistakes he had committed in 1920, repeated the performance in almost identical terms in 1946. These failures, however, seem small in comparison with the successes achieved in Eastern Europe after 1944. In Poland and Roumania the Russians put in their puppets by open display of force. In Bulgaria and Hungary they forced the removal from public life of political leaders whose courage and popularity were an obstacle to Communist victory. In Czechoslovakia the presence of Russian forces in 1945 made possible the seizure by the Communists of the key posts which enabled them to seize power three years later. In 1948 the signal for action was given by Moscow, and the presence of Russian troops round four-fifths of Czechoslovakia's frontiers was a decisive factor. Gottwald's 'February revolution' was made by the police. It can be compared with Mussolini's march on Rome by sleeping-car in 1922, and still more closely with Hitler's elevation to the German Chancellorship and subsequent elimination of his opponents in 1933. The roles of the ailing President Hindenburg and the ailing President Beneš are strongly similar.

The establishment of Communist régimes in Eastern Europe has historic importance, for it has brought 100 million people under Moscow's control. If the Chinese Communists were to establish similar régimes in Korea and parts of South-East Asia that too would be an important victory. But neither can tell us anything of the technique of revolution, for these régimes were not created by revolution. The imposition of puppet governments by imperialist Powers is nothing new in history, even if some of the details of its execution by Moscow's agents are original.

Certain tentative conclusions may perhaps be drawn from this survey.

The first is that few revolutionary movements of the twentieth century have attained power solely by their own efforts. Two exceptions are the triumph of Kemal Atatürk in Turkey and of the Kuomintang in China in 1927. At least in the second case there can be doubt as to how complete was the triumph and how revolutionary the movement. The three most impressive revolutionary triumphs of the century (Russia, 1917–20, Yugoslavia, 1941–4, and China, 1945–9) were won only because a foreign enemy had smashed the State machine which the revolutionaries had previously been too weak to destroy or to capture. The triumphs of Asian nationalism (India, Burma, Indonesia) were won by the willing or reluctant surrender of the colonial Powers. Other Communist successes were won by Soviet or Chinese conquest. Fascism was set up in Italy and Germany, and Communism in Czechoslovakia, by consent of the civil and military authorities. The various violent changes of power that have from time to time taken place in the Balkans, Latin America, and the Middle East have been *coups d'état*, not revolutions. If Communist and other revolutionary movements have won through Russian conquest, through defeat of their enemies in war, or through the surrender of the legal rulers, then their victims in the free world must make sure that they are not defeated in war and that they do not yield positions of power. This is a question of military strength, national unity and the enlightenment of the free peoples. It is the first priority, and seems at last to be recognized as such by the governments concerned. Even so, much remains to be done in revealing to the free nations the true nature and the urgency of the danger.

The second conclusion is that the leadership of revolutionary movements comes principally from the intelligentsia. No good is done by denouncing intellectuals or screaming about *la trahison des clercs*. The Western nations must win the friendship of the young intellectuals of the backward nations. Immense harm is done by personal affronts. Nothing has done so much to make possible the monstrously distorted picture of the United States which is believed in good faith by thousands of Asiatic and African educated men and women, as the knowledge of the inferior status of American Negroes. Every London landlady who refuses to let a room to a 'coloured' student is worth a platoon of troops to Stalin. Dr Malan and his apartheid are worth a division or two. But the avoidance of insults and injustices is not enough. More attention should be given to the education of the backward peoples. Education should be so devised as to produce experts devoted to the practical service of their peoples, not semi-literate demagogues. This immensely difficult task faces not only the education officers of the colonial Powers but also the leaders of the independent Asiatic states. The experience of each can be useful to the other. Both in colonies and in independent states there are many devoted educational workers. Their efforts in the cause of all humanity do not receive sufficient recognition or sufficient material aid. Their own governments' resources are slender and their other tasks are many and urgent. The United

Nations, which should be a force of progress in this field, is little but a forum for irresponsible demagogy. The representatives of the oppressive pashas of Egypt, or the corrupt rulers of the Philippines, have little right to blame the British administrators of Tanganyika for failing to create a social and cultural utopia. But their declamations are treated more seriously than they deserve even by enlightened citizens of countries friendly to Britain. If the free nations mean anything by their statements that they are united in defence against Muscovite totalitarianism, they should help, not harm each other in this most vital task of education. If revolutions can be prevented by strength, the spread of revolutionary movements can be prevented by sound education. There is no task more urgent than to prevent the frustration and mental distortion of the educated youth of Southern Europe, Asia, and Africa.

The third conclusion is that economic action against revolutionaries is not in itself enough, and should be used with care. It is a delusion to suppose that the mere expenditure of some millions of dollars will make it possible to present to the 1,000 million people of non-Communist Asia, Africa, and Latin-America a magic, ready-made 'social justice'. The poverty of these regions is deeply rooted, and pressure of population is making it worse. It will be very long before the standard of living of the whole of these regions can be appreciably raised. This the governments of Western Europe and America no doubt know. But public opinion does not know it. Well-meaning talk of 'solving' the economic problems of Asia and Africa by some sort of new Marshall Aid creates illusions among the Western peoples, and rouses hopes that cannot be satisfied among the peoples of Asia and Africa. This does not mean that economic aid is not essential. Without it, Asia and Africa would certainly be lost. But economic aid cannot create universal prosperity. It can only reduce misery, remove the most glaring contrasts in wealth and the most horrifying injustices, and create at least in certain naturally favoured regions the means of rapid further development. Clearly industrialization is desirable where the conditions favour it. But it should be treated as a practical measure, not as a matter of dogma. There is no need to emulate the Stalinist mystique of vast heavy industries built by armies of conscripted labourers. It is also utopian to imagine that a large part of the funds allotted to the economic development of backward countries will not be wasted. Corruption of officials is the result of excessive numbers and insufficient pay. Until officials can be secured tolerable living conditions, and until the flow of educated young people can be directed to other employment than the bureaucracy, corruption will continue. Improvement depends on the creation of large numbers of engineers, doctors, scientific workers and industrial technicians. Here economic development and the improvement of education are inseparable.[1]

Great financial sacrifices will have to be made by all the Western nations for the development of the backward countries. The aim should be to reduce both poverty and corruption; the means should be to create the right industries, the right technicians, and the right education. None of these tasks can be achieved unless the military power of the free world deters aggression. Nothing can be done in any direction unless the Western governments not only make their plans but explain them to their own peoples and to that section of the backward peoples which is accessible to information – that is, to the educated section. None of these tasks will be completely achieved even in the most favourable conditions. But partial success is enough to save the free world. Neither the Communist nor any other revolutionary movements are invincible. The history of their seizure of power shows that their claims to scientific infallibility and predestined victory lack any serious foundation.

[1] In the twelve years that have passed since this was published, the Western colonial empires have been largely dismantled, and the problems of economic aid to 'undeveloped' societies have received far more attention in the press and publications of the Western world. There have been many changes of régime: among the victims have been the 'oppressive pashas of Egypt' mentioned above. However, the problems mentioned above are as far from solution as ever, and neither the ignorance nor the demagogy have notably diminished.

Industrialization and Revolution

INDUSTRIAL REVOLUTIONS AND SOCIAL CLASSES

The twentieth century is an age of revolutionary movements, but these have had their triumphs not in the Western lands which were the homes of the great classical revolutions but in the 'underdeveloped' countries of Eastern Europe and Asia. The twentieth century is also an age of political dogmas, based on ideas which were once live but have become fossilized and no longer explain the phenomena to which they are said to relate. Fossilization does not, however, deprive them of power over men's minds. The most important body of such dogma is of course Marxism, with or without its Leninist and Stalinist accretions. But all too often the slogans of less dogmatic schools of thought – 'private enterprise', 'conservatism', 'democratic socialism', and even 'democracy' itself – are used rather as magic incantations than as significant terms.

Those who wish to understand the revolutions of the twentieth century – which affect us all in a much more complicated and pervasive way than those who are either frightened or bored by talk of the 'communist challenge' will admit – must get away from dogmas and slogans and look at the social and political processes of the recent past and the present. And these derive directly or indirectly from the Industrial Revolution. West Europeans and North Americans, who understandably regard this as a thing of the fairly remote past, should not forget that for Russia, Japan, or Eastern Europe it is the recent past or the present, and for large parts of Asia, Latin America, and Africa the future. Too little has been done to compare the effects of the Industrial Revolution, in terms of the formation of social classes and political power, in the many different regions and stages of its development.

The Industrial Revolution in north-west Europe and North America was planned by no one, it was the work of individuals seeking their own profit. It derived from private capitalism, which was of course much older than modern factory industry and which

---

This article was first published in the *Manchester Guardian* in January, 1954, as four articles under the general title 'Some Myths of Marxism'.

for various well-known reasons advanced earlier in Protestant countries. But since the mid-nineteenth century a different type of industrialization has made its appearance. It is the work not of individuals but of governments, its aim is not private profit but imperial greatness. Even in such Western countries as France protection gave powerful support to private industry. But in Imperial Russia and Imperial Japan, though ownership and profits were mostly left to individual capitalists, Government control and initiative were on such a scale as to make industrialization an instrument of State policy. Tendencies similar though not so pronounced can be found in the industrialization of some East European countries between the world wars. The most complete example of industrialization by decree is of course the Soviet Union under the Five-Year Plans. Its example has been followed by the 'People's Democracies' of Europe and Asia.

The nature of the distinction between types of industrialization has been obscured by controversy about words and slogans. To Stalinists, to a lesser extent to all Marxists, and also to the doctrinaires of private enterprise the essential distinction is between a society in which all industry is State owned and all other industrial societies: the first is 'Socialist', the others are 'capitalist'. Surely the truer line of distinction is between societies in which the direction of industrialization and the control of industry are principally, though not necessarily entirely, in private hands and those in which they are principally, though not necessarily entirely, in the hands of the State.

The Industrial Revolution, whether conducted by private enterprise or by State initiative, creates new social classes. The replacement at the base of the social pyramid of peasants by factory workers is too familiar to require comment. But the changes at the top of the pyramid are more obscure. Here we find not the single 'bourgeoisie' of Marxist demagogy but several distinct social groups which often differ as much from each other as from the peasantry or working class. Their social and political roles vary in different regions with different political and cultural conditions. The most important of these groups may be called, for lack of more precise terms, the business class, bureaucracy, and intelligentsia.

Businessmen are private individuals who organize industry for their own interest. Controlling their factories, they also control, at least in the early stages of industrialization, the lives of the workmen employed in them. As long as no external checks limit their power the control tends to turn into exploitation. In the classical countries of early capitalism certain moral, aesthetic, and political values were associated with the rise of the business class. One was a dreary puritanism in private life combined with a conviction of moral superiority to persons of humbler social status. Another was militant aesthetic philistinism, a liking for pompous forms in art and architecture and poetry, coupled with fierce hatred of orginality in the arts or letters. A third was nationalism, sometimes generous and liberal while the business class was struggling for recognition within its own society but increasingly selfish and illiberal as it gained an established position. The illiberal phase produced the whole ideology of imperialism which found expression in Europe at the turn of the nineteenth and twentieth centuries.

Bureaucracy is, of course, much older than the Industrial Revolution. But the more complicated social and economic conditions of industrial society increased the tasks of governments and the number of bureaucrats. In countries where industrialization came late and resulted less from private than from State initiative, the bureaucracy became its chief instrument. The general ethos of the bureaucracy in countries of State-initiated industrialization was very different from that of the business class in countries of classical capitalism. But as rising classes conscious of their growing power they had in common a propensity to aggressive nationalism and imperialism. This at least was common ground between men so dissimilar as Rudyard Kipling, Chancellor Bülow, the Russian police chief von Pleve, and President McKinley.

The intelligentsia is a social group that persistently evades definition. Essentially it consists of those who possess the many special skills required in an industrial society. In the countries of classical capitalism the development of these skills was, like the Industrial Revolution itself, a spontaneous process. On the whole the demand for intellectuals kept pace with their supply, and in an expanding economy there was usually scope for their talents. In the countries of State-initiated industrialization the intelligentsia was a more artificial growth, the creation of more or less enlightened despots. In all these countries, with the notable exception of Japan, relatively far more was done for the higher than for the lower levels of education, The intelligentsia, the product of local or foreign universities, thus belong to the culture of the twentieth century, while the peoples from which it sprang lived much as they had lived

1,000 years before. This contrast only increased the importance of the intelligentsia as a social and political force. It was through it that modern ideas, technical, literary, or political, reached these lands. The contrast also inflicted on many a deep sense of emotional frustration, which caused them to sympathize with revolutionary ideas of some sort or another. In the countries of classical capitalism, with their much slower and more spontaneous economic and social growth, the intelligentsia as a separate social and political force can hardly be said to have existed. Eighteenth-century France perhaps had something similar, but the parallel is rather superficial.

It is no coincidence that the word 'intelligentsia' is Russian. Lenin was aware of the political implications of frustration and revolutionary feeling among the intelligentsia, but even he did not fully appreciate the significance of the intelligentsia as a distinct social group. Neither the Stalinist nor the Western branches of Marxist doctrine have given it its rightful place in revolutionary theory. But the revolutionary intelligentsia is no specifically Russian phenomenon: it has made its appearance, in the last fifty years, in one 'underdeveloped' country after another. Nor do the revolutionary feelings of members of the intelligentsia caused by both ideal and personal motives, both by indignation at the gulf between their own life and that of their peoples and by resentment at various political obstacles which prevent them from pursuing their ambitions, necessarily drive them to Communism or to the Left. Revolutionary fascism and revolutionary nationalism may be equally attractive: the examples of the Roumanian Iron Guard or the Moslem Brotherhood of Egypt are instructive. What is certain is that none of the revolutionary movements of 'underdeveloped' countries in the twentieth century could even have begun without leadership from the intelligentsia.

INDUSTRIALIZATION AND POLITICS

The countries of classical capitalism have been, with a few partial exceptions, countries of liberal government, though not necessarily of the British type of parliamentary democracy. The countries of State-initiated industrialization have been, with even fewer exceptions, countries of political despotism. The countries of classical capitalism were marked, even at the outset of their industrial revolutions, by a relatively high level of education and the prevalence of the rule of law. Industrialization strengthened these features.

Industrialization and Revolution

When contrasted with political conditions in Eastern Europe or Asia, all the political régimes of Western Europe in 1914, however great the differences between them then appeared, now seem in retrospect to have approximated to a single type.

The evil results of industrialization – exploitation of the workers, aggressive nationalism, imperialism, and philistinism in the arts – were painfully felt, but in the course of time they were mitigated, and in some cases removed, by the growth of political liberties. This was possible because political and economic power were not in the same hands. The capitalists certainly had great political influence, but they did not run the Government, whether of Gladstone or of Bismarck. This is a point which few Marxists and no Leninists have understood. Freedom of speech and press enabled the grievances of the workers to be freely discussed, and created a social conscience among educated people which was one of the driving forces for reform. The other driving force was the power of the workers, who being free first to form trade unions and then to vote for Parliament were able first to influence and then to dominate government. Writers and artists who pursued ideas or forms unpopular with the philistine majority had to endure poverty and insults, but nobody prevented them by force from exercising their skill. Often rebellious individuals or groups among the wealthy or the influential gave them protection or material support.

A public conscience was also created about imperialism. The pressure of Liberal and Socialist opinion in Britain, and to a lesser extent in France, has been a major factor in constitutional changes in the British and French empires. At the same time the growing freedom of speech and organization permitted the educated *élites* of the colonial peoples to form societies and parties which grew into great mass movements and forced imperial governments to make concessions. Colonial history in the twentieth century has its episodes of repression and bloodshed, like the Amritsar shooting of 1919 or the Algerian massacre of 1945. But the use of repression is limited both by public opinion in metropolitan countries and by the scruples of colonial officials brought up in a liberal tradition. For all the rhetoric of colonial nationalists and Communist propagandists, it remains true that no liberal capitalist government has used extermination as a weapon against its workers or its colonial subjects.[1]

[1] Despite the long struggle of Mau Mau in Kenya, the campaign of terrorism and repression in Cyprus, and the bitter war in Algeria, which came after these

Once the Industrial Revolution had run its course in the countries of classical capitalism, a certain social balance was achieved. In Britain the peasantry has almost disappeared. In other Western countries a large part of the nation remains agricultural, but it is strongly affected by urban social and cultural values. The gap between town and country is not closed, but it is growing very narrow. In the industrial working class the proportion of skilled men is large. The level of education is generally high, the standard of living of all but the wealthiest has risen, and there is no desperate proletariat. The British workers of the Chartist period, uprooted from the society of the village but without a place in the new society of the city, suffered both material exploitation and emotional bewilderment. They were a potential revolutionary factor. The British workers since 1900 have often been poor and angry, but they have had a place in society and means to fight for better conditions. They have used the means, and cared little for revolution. This does not mean that all social problems have been 'solved' in a Western 'free world' of perfect felicity. New problems have arisen, no less frightening than the old. The rule of Hitler has shown some of the horrors that can overtake a highly civilized nation and a highly developed society. But it cannot be said that any Western society today is dominated by a revolutionary class struggle. The French and Italian Communist parties are led by men who use the slogans of the classical class struggle of Marx's day, and whose aim is revolutionary power. But the great majority of the French, and even the Italian, workers who vote Communist seek not revolution but better conditions within a society that is changing not by cataclysm but by law.

In any case the experience of the last thirty years suggests that when the State fabric in a Western society is shaken, what emerges is not a revolutionary class struggle but armed bids for power by totalitarian parties whose *raison d'être* is not the defence of any social class but absolute power as an end in itself. This happened in Italy in 1919-22 and in Germany in 1930-3, and would happen if for any reason parliamentary government should break down at present

---

articles were written, I still think the argument is essentially sound. Even in Algeria, though there were cruelties on both sides, the French did not carry out mass reprisals, of the Nazi or Stalinist type, against the Algerian Moslems. And pressure of democratic opinion in France was undoubtedly a factor in the ultimate solution, even if it needed the iron will and political heroism of Charles de Gaulle to complete the process.

in France or Italy. The French and Italian Communist parties enjoy workers' support, but they are not workers' parties. They are totalitarian power cliques led by professional power-maniacs. Should their bid for power become an immediate threat – which today it is certainly not – and should the democratic forces be unable to resist them, it is almost certain that anti-Communist totalitarian forces would emerge to fight them. Whichever of these two might win, democracy would be destroyed.

In countries of State-initiated industrialization quite different social and political forces can be observed. Here the great majority of the people were peasants, and these were poor and unskilled. Where great landowners possessed large slices of the arable land – as in Russia before 1917, Hungary before 1945, or Persia today – the rural class struggle was a bitter reality. But even where, as in the inter-war Balkan states, all holdings were fairly small, poverty was a scourge. Overpopulation, which was not absolute but was a result of the disproportion between the numbers of peasants and the means of livelihood in existing economic conditions, meant widespread underemployment and undernourishment. The peasants of Eastern Europe and Russia were unable to improve their lot, as the peasants of Western Europe had done in the first half of the nineteenth century. This was partly because, at the time their countries began their industrial revolutions, they were culturally far behind the French peasants of 1800. It was also because, having decided for political and strategic reasons to embark on industrialization, the Governments of Russia and other Eastern countries devoted their energies and resources to industry and ignored the peasants except as a source of revenue. Industrialization hurriedly pursued for reasons of State policy laid a heavier burden on the peasants than industrialization resulting from unplanned private capitalism.

State-initiated industrialization in these countries produced, like private capitalist industrialization fifty to a hundred years earlier in Western Europe, an industrial working class. Its situation resembled that of the desperate proletariat, materially exploited and emotionally disoriented, of Western Europe under early capitalism: it was quite different from that of the West European working class in the twentieth century. Like the British workers in the days of the Chartists, but unlike the British workers of 1900, the Russian workers of 1900 were, and the Indian workers of 1953 are, a potential revolutionary force. The ruling class of countries in an early stage of

State-initiated industrialization has been a bureaucracy. Businessmen and great landowners have played a secondary but at times important part in it. Revolutionary leadership has invariably come from the intelligentsia, the reasons for whose disaffection have already been briefly mentioned.

The social régime in most of these countries has borne some resemblance to that of Western Europe under early capitalism. But the political régime has been entirely different, and this difference is fundamental to an understanding of the twentieth-century revolutions. It was political liberty and representative institutions that enabled the régime of early capitalism to evolve into the Western democracy of today. It is the absence of these that has made it almost impossible for a régime of State-initiated industrialization to advance beyond the stage of exploitation and repression. The absence of political liberty was an obstacle to the cultural progress without which peasants and workers could hardly even learn to defend their interests. The more closely the State-initiated industrial revolutions combined political with economic power, by subjecting both Government and industry to the same bureaucracy, the more defenceless were the worker and the peasant, the more revolutionary was the intellectual.

Theoretically, advance from these intolerable conditions may be either towards constitutional and liberal government or towards some form of revolutionary dictatorship. The first method has been tried, with few encouraging results. In the 1920's it had success in Poland, the Balkans, and Japan which proved ephemeral. Constitutional progress in Russia from 1906 to 1914 was ended by war and defeat, but even before this it had met with formidable obstacles. Two great Asian countries today give some hope. In Japan the social structure is more compatible with democracy than that of any Asian country, but political traditions are anything but hopeful. In India the value of liberty is more widely recognized than elsewhere in Asia, but social and economic problems present fearful perils. Of the second direction, revolutionary dictatorship, there are many examples.

REVOLUTIONARY DICTATORSHIP

No great revolutionary movement in an 'underdeveloped' society has seized power entirely by its own efforts. Where they have succeeded the revolutionaries have owed their victory in large part to blows struck against their enemy by third parties, that is, to the collapse of the régimes under the impact of war. But whether, when chaos gave them their chance, the revolutionaries triumphed depended on whether they were well led, as the Russian Bolsheviks in 1917-20, the Chinese Communists in the 1930's and 1940's, and the Yugoslav Communists in 1941-5: or were crushed by overwhelming external force, as the Hungarian Communists in 1919 or the Greek Communists in 1944: or were placed in power by foreign bayonets, as in the Danube Valley in 1944-8.

It is possible to trace three stages in the growth of revolutionary movements in 'underdeveloped' societies. In the first there are only groups of revolutionary intellectuals, with no mass support at all. The second stage comes when they make contact with the masses in the place where they are both physically and mentally most accessible, in the towns. This first mass support is historically important, but it is far too small to give any real chance of seizing power. The third stage comes when they make contact with the great masses, which in such countries means the peasants. This is both physically and mentally possible only when the State machine has been badly shaken and traditional loyalties such as patriotism and religious belief are losing their hold on peasant minds. And in the twentieth century this condition has usually been produced only by war.

Revolutionary movements in 'underdeveloped' societies in the twentieth century have been either predominantly nationalist or predominantly socialist. Examples of the first type are extremely various and include such movements as Kemalism in Turkey, the early Kuomintang, the Roumanian Iron Guard, or the Japanese 'Young Officer' groups. General Neguib's movement may prove a successful example of this type: it is not yet clear whether Neguib will be a Kemal or a Kerensky.[1] Of the second type the three outstanding cases are the Communist movements of Russia, China, and Yugoslavia.

Once in power, the revolutionaries establish their own political régime and pursue their own economic and cultural policies, which affect the pace and nature of industrialization and the formation

---

[1] It became apparent during 1953 that Neguib was a less powerful figure than Colonel Gamal Abd-el-Nasser, who obtained undisputed supremacy in 1954. Neguib was perhaps a sort of Kerensky, but Nasser appears in 1964 to be a Kemal rather than a Lenin.

of social classes. There are certain obvious similarities between the two revolutionary régimes which are now thirty years old, Bolshevism and Kemalism. Both have modernized their once backward peoples beyond recognition. Both pursued industrialization under State initiative. The Bolsheviks, who started on the not inconsiderable foundations of Imperial Russian industry, have of course gone much farther than the Turks, who started almost from nothing. Both were bitter opponents of organized religion. Both enormously widened the opportunities of education. In particular, the Moslem nations of the Soviet Union, whose cultural level in 1917 approximated to that of the Turks of Anatolia, have made similar quantitative progress in education. The qualitative progress in the two countries is hard to estimate. Both régimes created powerful new armies, recruited from the masses, during a desperate struggle for survival, whether against Russian White armies or a Greek invasion. Through the new army, and after the war was over through the new system of education, brilliant careers stood open to many who till then had vegetated in a swamp of poverty and ignorance. Both countries acquired new bureaucracies, new intelligentsias, and new working classes. In both countries the life of the peasant masses was profoundly changed.

The essential differences between the Bolshevik and the Kemalist system are not social but political and moral. It is, of course, true that in Kemalist Turkey there have always been private businessmen side by side with State enterprise, whereas in the Soviet Union there have been no private businessmen since about 1928. But this difference is insignificant in comparison with the political and moral differences which distinguish mere dictatorship from totalitarianism.

Kemalist Turkey was for thirty years a one-party state. But the People's party of Turkey bore very little resemblance to the Bolshevik party. Communist parties, with their 'democratic centralism', their prohibition of 'fractions', their recurrent purges, and their absolute subordination to the will of a supreme autocrat, have no parallels, not even in Nazi Germany. Communist parties not only seek absolute power but seek it in the name of a doctrine regarded as universally valid for all nations and all lands. The Soviet dictatorship is not only negative but positive. It tells its subjects not only what they must not do – the usual function of all dictatorships of the past – but also what they must do and say and think. Nothing is private; everything is political. Such at least has been the aim of the

Industrialization and Revolution

Stalinist régime, in practice only imperfectly achieved, since human nature in Russia as elsewhere is weak.

Most important of all, in clear contrast to all other dictatorships except German nazism, the Stalinist régime is restrained in the exercise of power by no moral or religious inhibitions. There is no limit to what may be done, or to the time that may be taken to do it, to any man or woman or child to compel them to serve the purposes of the régime as determined by the infallible leaders. '*Raison d'état*' was not, of course, first formulated by Lenin or Stalin. But earlier despots were in fact inhibited by religious or moral scruples, accepted alike by them and their society. The idea of the perfectibility of man by decree, derived from the eighteenth-century utopians, was carried to its logical conclusions by the Russian revolutionary thinkers of the nineteenth century, and the Bolsheviks have done their best to put it into practice. Restrained neither by the institutional checks and individualist habits of Western liberal government nor by the religious sanctions that limited traditional oriental despotisms, the Stalinists have erected the most comprehensive tyranny in history. Nazism was perhaps more cruel, but it was less comprehensive, if only because Hitler did not have time, while fighting his war, to extend his rule to all sectors of private and public life in Germany. Hitler desired to create a totalitarian state, but Stalin succeeded.

The specific totalitarian features which developed in the Soviet Union under Stalin's rule have left their mark on the formation of new social classes. Through collectivization the peasants have been bound to the soil in a new form of serfdom. In the factories the working class, enormously increased in the last twenty years, is ruthlessly exploited by its bosses. This exploitation somewhat resembles that which occurred in the West under early capitalism, but is aggravated by two special factors. One is the inhuman speed of construction, decided for political reasons by a government which recognizes no limit on moral or religious grounds. The second is that the absence of civil liberties and representative institutions makes it impossible for workers or peasants to decide who shall lead them or give them orders.

The ruling class formed by thirty years of Bolshevism and twenty years of Stalinism is a bureaucracy, which includes officers, policemen, civil servants, party bosses, trade union bosses, and managers of factories and 'machine tractor stations'. On its fringe are the decorative aristocracy of highly paid actors, ballerinas, court poets, and literary hate merchants. So are the leading scientists and professors. Below these come the Soviet petty bourgeoisie of teachers, technicians, clerks, and bookkeepers. In official Soviet terminology bureaucracy and aristocracy and petty bourgeoisie are lumped together under the heading 'toiling intelligentsia'. The aesthetic, moral, and political values of the Soviet ruling class are strikingly similar in some ways to those of the Victorian bourgeoisie. There is the same hatred of originality in the arts, the same preference for nice, catchy tunes and pompous public buildings (neo-classical where our grandparents chose neo-Gothic), the same crude puritanism in private life, the same aggressive national arrogance and imperialism. The position of the Soviet manager in some ways recalls that of the rugged individualists of the Wild West in the 'open frontier' days. His skilful use of tact and bluster, of graft and lies and tricks, of intrigue and lobbying would win the admiration of the pioneers and robber barons of West European and American capitalism, could they rise from their graves to behold him.

The difference, which is fundamental, lies in the political framework. Under early capitalism in a liberal political framework the aesthetic heretic could survive, the exploited worker could organize himself, and the subject nation could struggle for political rights. Under Stalinism the prejudices of the dominant social group are enforced by the bullets of the police. Political and social power are indivisible. The Soviet writer or artist who offends official standards is forcibly prevented from pursuing his art until he has publicly abased himself and publicly professed the aesthetic values of his masters. Strikes are counter-revolutionary conspiracy, and striking workers are 'agents of the imperialists'. Members of non-Russian nationalities who defend their national or regional interests against Moscow's will are guilty of treason. Not only is national deviationism in the present a crime: national resistance to Russian armies, even when these were Tsarist, is made retrospectively criminal. The national heroes of the Moslems of Caucasus or Turkestan were reactionary 'mullahs' in the service of British or Turkish imperialism. They did not realize that Russian (Tsarist) conquest was for them an objectively progressive experience, as it promoted their social development. This doctrine recalls the conviction of the Victorians that they were bringing the benefits of civilization to African natives, or of President McKinley that he was lifting up the Filipinos by annexing their islands.[1]

PROBLEMS OF POWER

That Stalinist totalitarianism creates discontent can hardly be doubted. Workers do not like being exploited, and the Russian worker of today, better educated than the Russian worker of 1913, is less likely to be deceived. The peasants have never ceased to offer passive resistance to Stalinism, and the sweeping concessions recently announced by Mr Khrushchev suggest that they are by no means unsuccessful. But the hostility of the masses cannot shake the Government of an industrialized twentieth-century State, least of all if it is totalitarian. More dangerous is hostility within the ruling class.

The Soviet ruling class enjoys great material privileges. But history shows that these do not satisfy a rising social group. Those who need no longer worry about their daily bread have time to worry about other things. Those who have scraps of uncertain power desire full and secure power. Those who have the substance of power desire the trappings and the honours as well. It is improbable that Soviet bureaucrats and managers do not feel these desires. The intellectuals too must be dissatisfied. It is they who feel most acutely the absence of liberty, and who are most aware of the contrast between their material lot and that of the masses. A special category are the intellectuals of the non-Russian nationalities. Since 1917 hundreds of thousands of Soviet Moslems have received the rudiments of a modern education. It is a common fallacy to assume that cultural benefits win the gratitude of colonial peoples, or that colonial nationalism is mainly created by oppression. On the contrary, it is often the best things that colonial Governments do that

[1] This description of the Stalinist régime, written a few months after Stalin's death, still seems to me in 1964 to be essentially true. In the following ten years there have been great changes. Pressure on writers and artists is much milder, but has not ceased to exist. Falsification of history is far less crude but has not disappeared. Persecution and Russification of the non-Russian peoples has been replaced by a much milder form of 'elder brother' patronizing. The powers of the security police have been reduced, and they are more sparingly exercised. Stalin's excesses have been denounced. The standard of living of all classes has risen. In general the era of Khrushchev has been one of relaxation and increased optimism. But the totalitarian (as opposed to merely dictatorial) nature of the Soviet régime remains.

bring them most hatred. It is unlikely that the Soviet Empire is an exception to this rule. Annamese intellectuals owed their education to the French régime, Indian intellectuals to the British, yet this did not make them grateful admirers of British or French rule. Instead of expounding to their own peoples the ideas of the colonial Power, they led their peoples in their struggle for independence. It is unlikely that the attitude of the Uzbek intellectual is different, though the attitude of the M.V.D. to him is certainly different from that of the British Indian police to nationalist leaders. The recurring purges in the political and cultural life of the Soviet republics support this view.[1]

There is as yet no historical example of the overthrow or transformation of a totalitarian régime. Hitler's Reich, which in any case was not yet fully totalitarian even in 1945, was simply destroyed by war. Two countries perhaps provide some indications, though neither had a fully totalitarian régime. They were Turkey and Yugoslavia.

In Turkey the ruling party permitted the formation of an opposition, held a free parliamentary election, lost it, and accepted the verdict of the polls. The victorious Democratic Party extended the freedom of press and association, improved the conditions of the industrial workers, and gave greater opportunities to private business enterprise. More democracy went hand in hand with more capitalism. In all this American influence may have had some part. But essentially it was due to internal social development. The ruling bureaucracy became settled into bourgeois society. With a fairly efficient system of modern education, a fairly competent and honest Administration, and a large number of persons performing the functions of a business class, whether as private individuals or as State officials, bourgeois liberties became attractive. The interest of the Turkish experience is that it shows, first, that a revolutionary dictatorship can modernize a backward people without being Stalinist, or even Marxist: and, secondly, that when a certain level of

[1] Subsequent developments have confirmed this argument. The frequent reorganizations of the structure of command of the Soviet economy by Mr Khrushchev indicate the desire both to satisfy some of the wishes of the managerial class and to prevent this class from obtaining political power. Of the stirring of independent critical thought among Soviet intellectuals, there have been frequent signs, especially since the Hungarian Revolution of 1956. The attitude of the intellectuals of the non-Russian nationalities remains unknown, but purges of party and administrative officials in the Central Asian republics have continued under Khrushchev's rule.

cultural and social progress has been attained it is possible to advance from dictatorship towards democracy.[1]

In Yugoslavia Marxist doctrine has been preserved. Great concessions have been made to the peasants. In 1949 and 1950 collectivization was extended to about a quarter of the arable land of Yugoslavia. In 1953 two-thirds of these collective farms have been dissolved. There has been, however, no appreciable increase in private enterprise in industry or trade. The trend of policy is to decentralize both political and economic administration. The League of Communists, as the party has been renamed, still has a monopoly of political leadership, but an attempt is being made to separate policy from administration, and to entrust the execution of policy not to party politicians but to professional civil servants. The legal code has been reformed, and the supremacy of the law is being reaffirmed. The equalitarian and puritanical aspects of socialism are stressed. The official thesis is that Yugoslavia is elaborating a new form of socialist democracy, different either from Stalinism or from European social democracy.

Either the Turkish or the Yugoslav path, towards liberal capitalism or towards idealist socialism, is conceivable in the Soviet Union. One would expect the former to be more attractive to frustrated managers, the latter to discontented intellectuals. Theoretically change might come in one of four ways – by defeat in war, by a mass rising, by a palace revolution, or by far-reaching reforms introduced from above. Of the first nothing need be said. To most civilized men and women, on both sides of the Curtain, this remedy must seem worse than the disease. The second is almost inconceivable. The M.V.D. not only prevents all overt opposition but also ensures that all organized activity that goes on in the Soviet Union – whether political or not – is controlled by it. Moreover, the forces whose discontent would have to be fused for such a purpose – the educated class, the workers and peasants, and the non-Russian nationalities – are hardly less hostile to each other than to the régime,

[1] This estimate was unduly optimistic. The government of the Democratic Party, led by Mr Menderes, in later years became increasingly dictatorial and repressive. In May 1960 it was overthrown by a military *coup d'état*. Since then Turkish politics have been extremely confused. Nevertheless, in 1964, though great power is held by the armed forces, who act behind a veil of secrecy, and who are themselves divided into factions, Turkey has a new democratic constitution, several political parties, and a press in which matters of policy can be frankly discussed. There are not sufficient grounds for saying that the evolution towards liberty has been reversed.

and the régime's propaganda works tirelessly to keep them disunited.

Palace revolution and reform from above are more probable because they can be undertaken from within the régime. But either a group of successful conspirators or a reforming despot (Malenkov or some other) would soon find themselves up against the obstacles that confronted the reforming Tsar Alexander II ninety years ago. After some years of reform the forces of inertia and reaction in his entourage reasserted themselves, prevented further reform, and deprived of much of their value even those reforms which the Tsar had made. A decisive factor in this return to reaction was the revolt in 1863 of the Tsar's Polish subjects, to whom he had previously made a number of concessions. It may not be fanciful to suggest that in 1953 the revolt of the East Germans and the consequent fall of Beria have played a similar role. If indeed Malenkov ever considered any legal or political reforms, as opposed to much less fundamental economic reforms, it seems obvious that since July he has given up the idea. The social tensions in Soviet society, however, remain, and of these the most dangerous are those affecting the upper stratum, the new educated class, whose aspirations must in the nature of things be political rather than economic. It is from this group that pressure for change – whether through regular channels or by palace revolution – will come.[1]

Exploitation of the working class is a result not of capitalism but of the early stages of the industrial revolution, which may be initiated by capitalist businessmen or by statist bureaucrats. Aesthetic philistinism, tasteless pomposity in architecture, and persecution of originality in the arts thrive in periods of the rise of a bourgeoisie, but this is not less true of State bourgeoisies than of private capitalist bourgeoisies. In so far as the last hundred years of industrial revolution are a period of imperialism, this is due not to the power of private capitalists as such but to the rise of new, self-confident, and aggressive social forces thrown up by industrialization. The State bourgeoisie of the Soviet Union is as imperialist as was the capitalist bourgeoisie of Victorian Britain, and much more imperialist than is the bourgeoisie of any Western imperial or ex-imperial country today.

The problem of human society today is not, as the Marxists would

[1] Malenkov was, of course, ousted from power by Khrushchev in 1955. The Hungarian Revolution of 1956 was for a time a setback to reform. Nevertheless since 1958 Khrushchev has undoubtedly carried out considerable improvements in both economic and administrative policy, and seems in 1964 likely to continue on this course of moderate reform.

have us believe and as many non-Marxists have let themselves be persuaded, economic power but just power. In different societies at different stages of industrial development power may be mainly economic, or political, or ideological, or it may be totalitarian – a chemical compound of all three which differs in quality from all other sorts of power. Abuse of any of the three simple types of power can be checked only by political liberty, without which there can be no social progress. Totalitarian power is the negation of all progress as well as of all liberty.

Nor is the present conflict in world affairs due, as Marxists and doctrinaires of free enterprise alike maintain, to a struggle between 'capitalism' and 'socialism'. The early industrializing capitalism of the mid-nineteenth century belongs to history. Both the early State-initiated industrialization that exists today in 'underdeveloped' countries and the post-industrial societies of the West in which private enterprise still flourishes, face problems quite different from those that beset the society which Marx observed. As for 'socialism', it has two distinct meanings, the one static and abstract, the other dynamic and real. The first is a perfect society, which most socialists agree has not yet been seen on earth but which some perversely identify with the Stalinist totalitarian régime. The second is a movement of men and women struggling for certain principles of social justice and liberty. Unfortunately confusion about socialism the abstraction has gravely weakened socialism the reality. Many Western socialists still fail to understand that their enemy is not just capitalist injustice and tyranny but all sorts of injustice and tyranny. They could learn much from Spanish socialists struggling against Franco's tyranny and even more from Polish socialists who fight for the rights of the Polish workers and the Polish nation against Stalinist exploitation.[1]

The present conflict is not between capitalism and socialism. It is a struggle of Stalinist totalitarian imperialism against its intended victims in Western Europe, the Middle East and India, and against the only Power with whose help they can resist, the United States. But more fundamentally the conflict is between those who believe that power should be separated and limited, in the interest of human freedom and dignity, and those who believe that it should be concentrated and unlimited, in the interest of those who wield it.

[1] These words could have been equally well written of socialists in any other East European country. However, the action of the Polish workers, especially those of Warsaw, in the crisis of October 1956 certainly proved this point.

Russian Revolutionaries

One hundred years ago the word 'revolution' seemed indissolubly associated with France. Frenchmen are still fiercely proud or ashamed of their revolutionary tradition, and it still influences their political thought and action. But today France seems to have yielded her pre-eminence as the land of revolution to Russia. The Russian revolutionary tradition was the offspring of the French, but developed a character of its own. Bolshevism was only one of the branches of a movement which goes back at least to the 1820's.

Professor Venturi's study of Russian Populism deals with the period from 1848 to 1881, when, as he rightly observes, 'all Russian socialism was Populist', that is to say, before the specifically Marxist branch had been clearly differentiated. There is a vast wealth of primary sources on this subject, published partly in exile but mostly in Russia, both between 1905 and 1917 and under the Soviet régime. Signor Venturi has thoroughly studied this material, chiefly in Soviet libraries. He was also well prepared for his task by his knowledge of eighteenth-century France and European socialism. His book is the first comprehensive study in a Western European language of the early period of the Russian revolutionary movement. All Western students of Russia will be greatly indebted to him. His own compatriots are fortunate, and the house of Einaudi is to be congratulated on producing this very large work which, it may be hoped, will soon be made available in English or French.[1]

The main emphasis is on the history of the movement rather than of the ideas, though the latter inevitably receive a great deal of attention. The author is free from any doctrinaire notions of separating history into compartments. When necessary he discusses intelligently and clearly the economic structure of Russia, the policy of the Government, the Polish and Ukrainian nationalist movements,

---

This article was first published in *The Times Literary Supplement*, 12 June 1953.

[1] Franco Venturi, *Il popolismo russo*, Turin, Einaudi, 2 vols. This work was translated into English and published in 1960 by Weidenfeld and Nicolson under the title of *Roots of Revolution*.

the influence of religious sects, and the war with Turkey in 1877, to mention only some of the external factors that affected the revolutionary movement.

While understanding the importance of Russian imaginative literature to contemporaries, and himself familiar with its contents, Signor Venturi insists on the importance of distinguishing between fiction and fact. Nechaev was a real person, Peter Verkhovensky a fantasy. Pisarev was impressed by the character of Bazarov, and some young Russians tried to model themselves on it. But Bazarov never trod the soil of Russia. Signor Venturi clearly has no sympathy for those who hold that Russian history and thought are veiled in esoteric mysteries impenetrable to Western man. He lays especial stress on the links between Russian and European thought, including that of his compatriot Mazzini.

The Russian revolutionary movement started from the intelligentsia. The word is Russian and the phenomenon first appeared in Russia. But later developments in other countries of Southern and Eastern Europe and of Asia have shown that it is in no sense peculiarly Russian. The intelligentsia is a product of modern education. It owes its origin in Russia to the moods of enlightened absolutism that found sporadic expression during the reigns of Catherine II and Alexander I, who laid the foundations of a Russian system of schools and universities. It was reinforced by economic development, which created a demand for modern skills. At first educated persons came almost exclusively from the nobility. Alexander I tried to give opportunities to talented children of humble social origin, but under Nicholas I this trend was reversed. Even so, as the century advanced, increasing numbers of non-noble boys attained higher education. The Imperial Ministers of Education had obscurantist aims but were too incompetent to achieve them.

The educated Russian shared the most advanced culture of contemporary Europe. He could not fail to see the contrast between this culture and the state of his own country. Material backwardness, social oppression, and lack of freedom filled him with shame. Those who came from classes other than the nobility (the *raznochintsy*) felt it more strongly than the nobles, for they had more direct experience of Russian reality. They knew that while they themselves belonged to the mid-nineteenth century, the people from which they sprang lived in the Middle Ages. They also had stronger personal motives for discontent than had their noble fellow students, for various bureaucratic obstacles restricted their careers, or even prevented them from using such skills as their education had given them.

Many of the discontented *raznochintsy* were sons of Orthodox priests. Such, for example were two leading revolutionary writers, Chernyshevsky and Dobrolyubov. The seminaries to which priests' children were admitted were a step on the educational ladder. But the low quality of the instruction and the bullying pedantry of the teachers often bitterly offended the more able pupils. Their unsatisfied religious longings left a vacuum soon filled by revolutionary ideas. Members of the schismatic or sectarian religious groups – which formed perhaps one-fifth of the Russian people – were naturally inclined to disaffection. So were members of the non-Russian nationalities. Poles and Jews, victims of special forms of discrimination or oppression, showed greater sympathy than Russians for revolutionary ideas. Ukrainian nationalism, combined with radical democracy, had made its appearance already in the 1840's. Georgia and Armenia were also beginning to produce a discontented intelligentsia. It was never true that the intelligentsia as a whole, in Russian or non-Russian provinces, actively supported revolution. But ideal and personal motives combined to place the majority of the intelligentsia in opposition to the régime and caused them to prefer the revolutionaries to the Government. Certain flowers and weeds grow only in certain soils. Had not the intelligentsia as a group been alienated from the régime, the professional revolutionary conspirators, a small minority drawn from its ranks, could never have appeared.

The ideas of Saint Simon and Fourier were known in Russia in the 1830's. Alexander Herzen, the first great figure of the revolutionary movement, founded a Saint-Simonist group in 1834, at the age of 22. It was in exile that he became acquainted with the ideas and persons of Proudhon and Marx. These two also made powerful, though different, impacts on Herzen's contemporary and fellow exile, Michael Bakunin. Herzen witnessed, and Bakunin took an active part in, the events of 1848–9. In Russia the years that followed the European revolutions were the darkest period of reaction. A new phase came when, during the Crimean War, which mercilessly exposed Russia's weakness, Alexander II succeeded his father. At this time Bakunin was still in Siberia. But Herzen, from his London exile, and Chernyshevsky, from the columns of the great St Petersburg review *Sovremennik*, profoundly influenced the public opinion which made its appearance in the freer atmosphere of the new reign. Both men welcomed the new Tsar's proclaimed intention to abolish serfdom, and both were disappointed by the policy which slowly put the intention into effect. But the differences in the temperament and ideas of the two men soon outweighed the similarities. Herzen resented Chernyshevsky's attacks on the whole nobility, including its enlightened section. To Chernyshevsky Herzen appeared no longer a great revolutionary, but an ineffectual liberal windbag. Chernyshevsky's visit to Herzen in London in 1859 did not reconcile them. The breach between them is a landmark in the history of the Russian intelligentsia. It marks the victory of the *raznochintsy* over the 'repentant noblemen', of the vitriolic pamphleteer over the writer with earlier standards of courtesy. Chernyshevsky and Dobrolyubov were talented writers and noble spirits. But there is at times an ill-tempered self-righteousness in their writing that set the tone for their successors. Combined in a later generation with the characteristic Marxist imputation of sordid motives, it has culminated in the style of *Pravda* editorials in our own day.

Already in the 1850's Russian Radicals discussed the problem, passionately debated for the next half-century, whether Russia could by-pass capitalism and go straight from its present condition to socialism. Belinsky, the first of the Radical *raznochintsy*, had held that the bourgeoisie had a progressive role to play. Herzen and Bakunin, depressed by the failures of the European bourgeois in 1848, fervently hoped that Russia could escape embourgeoisement. Herzen hoped that the traditional institution of the village commune could be transformed into the basic unit of a socialist society. Chernyshevsky had the same hope, but did not romanticize the commune as it was. He thought that it might help Russia towards socialism, if it was remoulded in accordance with the socialist doctrines of the West. He did not believe that it could be a 'model and symbol of a Russian mission', which would enable Russia to lead Europe on the road to socialism. The opposite view was expressed by his contemporary, the poet Mikhailov, in his revolutionary leaflet *To the Young Generation*:

> We are a backward people, and therein lies our salvation. We should thank fate for not having lived the life of Europe.... We do not want its proletariat, its principles of aristocracy and the State, its imperial power.... Europe does not and cannot understand our social

demands.... We believe in the strength of Russia because we believe that we have been chosen to bring into history a new principle, to have our own say, and not to follow the traces of Europe.

The years 1857 to 1861 were one of the great turning-points in Russian history. They were years of great hope and bitter disappointment. As the discussions and preparations for the emanicpation of the serfs progressed, it became clear that this great reform would be achieved on terms extremely unfavourable to the peasants. The contrast between the promise of 1857 and the decree of 19 February 1861, accounts for the bitterness of the young Radicals, which Herzen in his distant exile could not feel as they did. The terms of the emancipation doomed the peasants to long years of economic misery, from which subsequent reforms came too late to rescue them. They also turned the Radicals into bitter enemies of the Tsar and his régime. It became clear to them that not only the landowners but the whole bureaucratic system was responsible for the sufferings of the Russian people.

These same years were a turning-point in the political field. This was probably the only real opportunity for the introduction of constitutional government in Russia. The anti-liberal dogmatism that has lately become so fashionable in the interpretation of Russian history has confused the issues. There could, of course, be no question of a parliamentary democracy in the Russia of 1861. But central representative institutions based on a restricted franchise could have played an important part, as in eighteenth-century England or nineteenth-century Prussia. A small educated class, partly noble and partly bourgeois, already existed. From its ranks could have been drawn abler and wiser public servants than the bureaucracy could provide. Public debates in a national assembly could have prepared the Russian people for advance towards more democratic government. This course was open to Alexander II. But, blindly loyal to the dogma of autocracy, he rejected it. The estrangement of educated men and women from the whole established order continued, and the mental climate grew ever more favourable to the revolutionaries.

The first revolutionary groups were formed in the 1860's. They could achieve nothing against the State machine. But these groups, which printed leaflets and discussed policies and methods of struggle, were necessary forerunners of the later more efficient conspiracies. Their experience pointed the way, and their sporadic contacts with the exiles in Europe provided them with new ideas. Foremost among the exiles in this stage was Bakunin, who escaped from Siberia and reached London in 1861. To these small groups within Russia Professor Venturi gives much attention, and this is one of the most valuable parts of his book for Western readers, to whom – even to those who are specialists in Russian history – their story is almost unknown. He discusses, for example, the effect on the Russian scene of the Polish rising of 1863, the contact between Polish and Russian revolutionaries which led to the abortive conspiracy of Kazan in 1864, and the mysterious 'Organization' of Ishutin, to which belonged Karakozov, who made the first unsuccessful attempt on the Tsar in 1866.

Signor Venturi also devotes a long chapter to an exceptionally interesting and little-known figure, P. N. Tkachov, the exponent of Jacobinism. Tkachov was much influenced by Marx's economic doctrines. He believed that Russia was on the threshold of capitalism, and that if things continued as they were a class of prosperous farmers and bourgeois would appear. But the experience of Europe showed, he held, that this would be fatal to the cause of revolution. Action could not therefore be postponed.

> *Now*, or perhaps quite soon it will be *never*. To-day circumstances favour us, in 10 or 20 years they will be against us.... If we have no urban proletariat, we have no bourgeoisie either. Between the oppressed people and the State which crushes it with its despotism there is in our country no middle class. Before our workers stands only the struggle against the political power.

Revolution must be the work of a minority of devoted conspirators. The State machine, which they must attack, was much weaker than it appeared. Defeat in war, or peasant revolts, would shake it. The revolutionaries must seize it, and wield it for their own purposes.

Tkachov's influence was not very great inside Russia, but his ideas were largely justified by events. The revolutionary movement became an impressive force in the 1870's. The mass 'going to the people' was not successful: it led to mass arrests and savage sentences. The revolutionaries realized that they must have a secret organization, centrally disciplined. They came to understand the importance of the purely political struggle, as distinct from the wider aim of social revolution. The 'People's Will', created in 1879 by a split in the 'Land and Liberty' party, devoted all its efforts to the assassination of the Tsar. It outwitted the vast imperial police, and got its man. But it could not seize power, nor cause the system to collapse. Its story has been told in English, particularly in David Footman's excellent *Red Prelude*.[1] But even those who have studied the subject will find much interesting detail in Signor Venturi's last 400 pages. They are especially interesting on the role of the incipient industrial working class in the movement.

The course of the revolutionary movement in Russia was very unlike that of European socialism or trade unionism. It is not surprising that contemporary European observers should have regarded Russian experience as unique and have attributed this to some qualities inherent in the Russian national character. But today this view is less justifiable, for many features of the Russian experience have repeated themselves in 'underdeveloped' countries in Eastern Europe and Asia. It is even possible to sketch a pattern of revolution in non-industrial societies, of which Russia provides the first historic example.

This pattern has three stages. In the first stage the movement consists only of small groups of intellectuals, who have no mass support at all, and who discuss means of applying to their country the radical ideas which they have imported, prefabricated, from the West. In this stage (*kruzhkovshchina* in Russian terminology) the ideas have become known before the social conditions to which they are related have come into being. In the second stage the revolutionary intellectuals win their first mass support, and they find it in the places where it is both physically and mentally most accessible – in the cities. But in non-industrial societies a combination of professional revolutionaries and urban workers cannot suffice to destroy or to capture the State power. This is possible only in the third stage, when leadership and restricted mass support are reinforced by large-scale mass support, which can only be found in the villages. But peasant support can hardly be won so long as the State machine functions normally. In normal conditions the revolutionaries are denied access to the person of the peasant by the police, and to his mind by the peasant's own traditional and religious loyalties. The revolutionaries get their chance only when an external blow shakes the State machine.

In the last seventy years this has usually meant war. Tkachov's analysis was sound as far as it went. The Russian State machine was fundamentally weak, but not quite so weak as he thought. It lasted

[1] Cresset Press, 1944.

longer, and more blows from outside were needed than he had expected. The war of 1877-8 helped the 'People's Will', the war of 1904-5 nearly overthrew the autocracy, and the war of 1914-17 brought it down. In a country whose social structure is balanced, and in which society and the State machine are interlocked at all levels, the régime can survive even defeat in war: Germany in 1918 is the classic example. But in a country which is socially 'underdeveloped', and where the State machine is simply something imposed on the people from above, defeat in war is likely to bring the collapse of the régime, and to give the revolutionaries their chance. In the resulting chaos, the ablest revolutionaries will beat their rivals.

Russian development in the years 1848-81 fits this pattern. The 1860's were the period of *kruzhkovshchina* with no mass support. By the end of the 1870's the second stage had been reached. The first mass support – it was still very small – was found in the working class of St Petersburg and of some southern cities. A premature onslaught on the State machine led to the destruction of the movement. When revolutionary action revived at the end of the 1890's, the working class was a much more important force, though still far too weak to give a real hope of victory. In the disorders of 1905 the revolutionary movement was passing from the second to the third stage, but the autocracy was still strong enough to beat back the attack. In the summer of 1917 the third stage was finally reached, and in the following period Lenin vanquished his rivals.

Other 'underdeveloped' countries show similar sequences. In Yugoslavia the second stage was reached in the years 1919-20 but the struggle ended in defeat. The Communists, forced by police pressure back into the *kruzhkovshchina* stage, could leap forward into the third stage when the German invaders destroyed the State machine of the old Yugoslavia, which they themselves had previously been too weak to break or seize. In China the year 1927 saw a combination of the second and third stages. The massacre of the workers in Shanghai deprived the Communists of their first mass support, which had been from the urban proletariat. But as the revolutionary tide swept through the provinces in 1926-7, this brought the Communists peasant support, of which they were able to preserve some remnants in the following years. The disintegration of the State machine in large parts of the country enabled Mao Tse-tung to build up his own State within the State, and many years later to spread the third stage of revolution over China. Less sensational, but not less relevant, examples can be found in other lands, and by no means solely in Marxist movements.

This is not to deny the specific features of the Russian movement. Indeed, because it was the first movement on this pattern, it greatly influenced the leaders of others. Chernyshevsky, Bakunin, Ishutin, Tkachov, and A. D. Mikhailov are unquestionably Russian. Those who study them should, as Professor Venturi does, examine both those features which unite them to the stream of European thought and action, and those which distinguish them. Among the latter perhaps the most important was the influence of religion – Orthodox schismatic, and sectarian. Many writers, including Signor Venturi, have noted its existence, but a thorough study of the interconnexion between religious and revolutionary ideas in nineteenth-century Russia has yet to be made. It is obviously unlikely that any Soviet scholar will handle this theme in a convincing manner. It is a good subject for some Western historian. That the subject of the Russian revolutionary movement before 1881 is not yet exhausted implies no reproach to Signor Venturi. He has produced the most thorough survey yet written, penetrating and readable, with an admirable balance between biography, theory, and action. Specialists in the Russian field will be grateful to him, and those who wish to understand the background to the disturbances of our age will do well to consult him.

Hitler's Revolution

The vast literature that already exists on Hitler is mainly concerned with foreign policy. Hitler's régime and the process by which it was established have attracted less study, and for the most part of lower quality. One reason is that since 1945 problems of revolution and of totalitarian government have been understood chiefly in terms of Communism, to the exclusion of other types. Another is that an understanding of Nazism and Fascism is still obscured by the survival of some of the quasi-Marxist slogans and half-truths of the 1930's. The Nazi revolution has been little studied as a revolution. Indeed there is a certain unwillingness to admit that it was a revolution at all. This can be explained partly by the fact that no revolutionary seizure of power, in the classical sense, took place; partly by a belief that it was not a real revolution because the 'social system' was not changed. The last point is, of course, no more than a quarter-truth. It is true only in the formal sense that there was no systematic transfer of property from one 'class' to another. Jews and Nazi Party bosses presumably do not qualify as 'classes'. But if the drastic transformation of the relations of all social, religious and political groups to one another, which resulted from Hitler's rise to power, did not amount to a 'social revolution', it is hard to see what those two words can mean.

The other side to Hitler's victory was the collapse of the Weimar Republic, which is the subject of a new and exhaustive study by the young German scholar, Dr K. D. Bracher.[1] This, too, has been much obscured by myths and half-truths. Pre-eminent among these is the myth of the 'betrayal of the working class' by the Social Democrats in 1918–19. The truth is that in 1918 the German working class supported the Social Democrats, and did not desire a revolution of the Leninist type. The Congress of Deputies of Workers' Councils, freely elected by German workers, which opened on 16 December

---

This article was first published in *The Times Literary Supplement*, 20 June 1956, under the title 'The Weimar Collapse'.

[1] Karl Dietrich Bracher, *Die Auflösung der Weimarer Republik*, Stuttgart, Ring Verlag, DM. 27.80.

in Berlin, voted itself out of existence by a large majority. The Spartacist revolt of January 1919 never had the slightest chance of success. The Social Democrats used the army, staffed by officers of the old régime, to restore order. Noske, the man chiefly responsible for this policy, may indeed be criticized both for the policy and still more for the way in which it was applied. But the argument that German democracy was doomed as soon as Luxemburg and Liebknecht were killed and Ebert came to terms with the Reichswehr does not deserve serious consideration. Another fourteen years were to pass before the Weimar Republic was dead, and they were eventful years.

Each of the main factors that operated in this period – the 'Bourgeois' parties, the Socialists, the Communists, President Hindenburg and his circle, the army, the regular bureaucracy and the Nazi movement itself – receive careful consideration in Dr Bracher's work. Rather less than half is devoted to a survey of the trends of the 1920's and to a sociological analysis of forces. The second part of the book, rather more than half, is a narrative of the events of the period of crisis, 1930–3. The author is consciously aiming at a balance between a traditional historical approach and a fuller use of the methods of the social and political sciences, which hitherto have perhaps been somewhat neglected by German scholars. He has dug deeply into the voluminous original sources, and approaches his task in a refreshingly objective spirit. It is to be hoped that he will follow this excellent work by a similar study of the second stage, the consolidation of Nazi power after January 1933.[1]

Revolutions in the twentieth century have been of two main kinds, which may be described as a frontal assault on the citadel of power, and capture of the citadel from within, with the complicity of part of the garrison. Hitler obtained power from within. Once installed, he used the machinery of government, which had passed into his grasp intact, to carry out a revolution that overlooked no sector of society.

The closest parallel to Hitler's revolution, both in the seizure of power and in the use of power, is the Communist revolution of 1948 in Czechoslovakia. The Nazi revolution and the Russian Bolshevist revolution seem at first sight poles apart. Their

[1] Dr Bracher published in 1960 a second volume entitled *Die nationalsozialistische Machtergreifung* (Köln-Stuttgart, Westdeutscher Verlag), which deals with the events of 1933 and 1934.

circumstances were indeed very different. Yet a comparison between them is not without significance.

In Russia the impact of a disastrous war brought the collapse of a régime that had long been hated by a large number of its subjects, especially the most educated, and which had given abundant proof of its inability to lead the nation or even to make good use of its most loyal servants. The Russian bureaucratic machine was something imposed vertically from above on its subjects, almost wholly lacking the horizontal links with the different strata of society which form the strength of a modern State. Outwardly imposing in peacetime, it cowed its subjects: they may not have loved it, but they obeyed. Military defeat shattered it: heavy as cast iron, it was also as brittle. When it broke, society itself began to decompose.

In Germany the horizontal links between State and society were numerous and strong. They resulted from advanced industrial development, efficient means of communication, and above all mass education of a generally high quality, three factors of which only the first beginnings were visible in Imperial Russia. In 1918 military defeat had not brought a collapse of the German State. In 1930-2 economic depression brought poverty, unemployment, fear, and fury in abundance, but the machinery of government continued to function. In Russia from February to October 1917, disintegration was continuous and accelerated. In Germany in the slump years, for all the screams of hate and the march of private armies, there was no such headlong rush into chaos.

Some similarity can, however, be found in the paralysis of will among nearly all the politicians, and especially in the highest places of all. Dr Bracher speaks of a *Machtvakuum*, a vacuum of power. The Social Democrats had given up in 1930: instead of playing a part in events, they preferred to protest against cuts in social insurance. The Communists performed dervish dances, driving themselves into frenzy with incantations of magic dogma, unrelated to anything that was happening in Germany. The incantations were not even of their choosing: they were provided ready-made from abroad. The Centre Party was held together by the will-power of Brüning, grimly pursuing a course of austere virtue, grimly indifferent to the passions of the crowd, to whom he would not deign to explain himself. Around the aged President the courtiers and the generals played their little games. Admittedly even this falls short of the vacuum of power around the Empress Alexandra and Rasputin.

The parallel is closer when one compares the relationship of Hitler to the German Right-wing groups with the relationship of Lenin to the Russian socialist parties in 1917. Kerensky, Tseretelli, and the rest disliked Lenin, but fundamentally they regarded him as one of 'theirs', misguided but still a revolutionary, on their side of the barricade. Of this loyalty of socialists to each other and to the revolution, Lenin had not a trace. To him, Kerensky and Tseretelli were as much enemies as Nicholas II and Kornilov. He exploited their illusions and their sentimentality to destroy them. Something of the same mentality existed among the German enemies of socialism and democracy. They did not like Hitler as a man, and they resented his party's bid for power. But fundamentally they thought of him as one of 'theirs', a German patriot, a conservative, a believer in order, one who would reassert the challenged authority of the Prussian officer, the businessman and the bureaucrat. To Hitler, they were objects of contempt and hatred. He would exploit bourgeois values and their pathetic vanities to achieve supreme power, then enslave them, drive them wherever his thirst for conquest led him, destroy those few who at last opposed him, and in the end destroy the whole nation.

The Russian socialists at least tried to resist when it was too late, and many thousands perished. The German Right never resisted at all. The heroic failure of July 1944, was the work of individuals, not of any of the organized groups that had existed in 1932.

Lenin and Hitler are not usually compared. Hitler was a vainglorious demagogue and conqueror. Lenin was a demagogue too, and if he was not a conqueror it was not for lack of trying. Personal vanity he lacked; his was the profounder conceit of himself as history's chosen instrument. The two men's work led to different results. Hitler's to the ruin and partition of Germany, Lenin's to the industrial greatness of Russia and the reign of Stalin. But in one thing they were alike: in their inflexible determination to achieve sole unlimited power. They were the two totalitarian pioneers of the twentieth century, the two founders of a power structure that made nonsense of conventional categories of party, class, or creed.

Lenin's triumph has been surrounded with a legend of historical inevitability. Fortunately no such claim has been made for Hitler. Certainly Dr Bracher's narrative provides no basis for the belief that

Hitler's Revolution

Nazism was bound to win. On the contrary, the blunders, intrigues and vanities of certain individuals, especially of Hindenburg, Schleicher, and Papen, played a decisive part.

The slump created the misery on which revolutionary movements thrive. But in a slump the proletariat is weak: when millions are unemployed, workers' organizations break down. In such conditions parties based chiefly on the working class have little chance of power. In Germany the Communists gained some ground at the expense of the Social Democrats, but their success was dwarfed by that of the Nazis, who knew how to exploit all types of discontent, won a large following among workers as well as in other classes, and enjoyed sympathy in the highest circles.

Hitler wisely resisted pressure from his party to use force. He knew his private army could not stand up to the Reichswehr, and he believed he could get power by legal means. Among President Hindenburg's advisers opinions were divided between two policies. One was to rule by dictatorship, the other to obtain a parliamentary majority based on the Nazi Party but denying Hitler full power. The first course commended itself to Papen, the second to General von Schleicher. Hindenburg himself was re-elected President in April 1932, by the votes of the moderate Left. But far from feeling any gratitude or loyalty to his supporters, he was determined to make himself acceptable to the Right, which had voted for his rival, Hitler (36·7 per cent. of the votes cast in the second poll, to Hindenburg's 53 per cent.).

Schleicher's first important help to Hitler was given on 10 May. General Groener, the Minister of Defence, had decided to ban the Nazis' private army, the SA. Schleicher informed him that the army no longer had confidence in him, and Groener resigned. Two weeks later Hindenburg dismissed Brüning. The new Chancellor, Papen, dissolved the Reichstag and on 20 July suppressed the Social Democratic Government of Prussia, which offered no resistance. The Communists jeered at the Social Democrats, but did not take, nor were indeed in any position to take, action of their own. The general election of 31 July gave the Nazis 37 per cent. of the poll. The Reichstag met only once, on 12 September, voted almost unanimously against Papen, and was dissolved. In the next election, on 6 November, the Nazis' vote fell to 33 per cent., while the Communists' rose from 9 per cent. to 11 per cent. Papen proposed to continue government by decree, ignoring Parliament, but now

Schleicher intervened for the second time to the advantage of Hitler. He told the President that Papen's plans involved a serious danger of civil war, and that as this might even be accompanied by a Polish invasion the Army could not guarantee order. Hindenburg therefore dismissed Papen and made Schleicher Chancellor on 2 December.

Schleicher's political plans were based on co-operation with the moderate elements in the Nazi Party, led by Gregor Strasser, the head of the party organization. But when Hitler rejected Strasser's proposals, Strasser resigned from the party, and made no attempt to split its ranks. Schleicher was unable to form a strong Government, but the Nazis, too, were losing ground in the country. Hitler was saved by Papen who, determined to revenge himself on Schleicher, suceeded in arranging a coalition with Hitler as Chancellor, while the Army was made secure by Hindenburg's appointment of General von Blomberg as Minister of Defence.

This story has been told before, for example in Mr Alan Bullock's biography of Hitler. But Dr Bracher provides much interesting detail. One might mention his thorough analysis of the various elections of 1932, his account of the Papen–Hitler meeting at the house of the banker Schröder on 4 January 1933, and a memorandum by General von Hammerstein on the attitude of Schleicher on 29 January, which Dr Bracher publishes as an appendix.

The collapse of the Weimar Republic and the triumph of Hitler are not just important events in the history of Germany. Their study provides the best evidence yet available on the roots of totalitarianism in an advanced industrial society. Their significance extends to other countries than Germany and other periods than the 1930's.

Two: Eastern Europe after the War

The Danube States in 1946

YUGOSLAVIA

Yugoslavia is going through a revolution which is rapidly transforming it into a State of the Soviet type. The revolution began during the Partisan war and was to a large extent a spontaneous movement of the common people. The war was fought not only against the foreign invaders and various Yugoslav quislings, but also against the old régime of corruption and dictatorship from which Yugoslavia had suffered for many years. The common man, and especially the peasant, desired a complete break with the past, a New Deal based on social justice and on the right of every citizen to take part in the government of his country. If this desire had not been widespread, and if the peasants had not given their support to Marshal Tito in the belief that he stood for these aims, the Partisans could never have survived the first two terrible years of the struggle. The Germans would have destroyed them long before the first allied help reached them in the autumn of 1943.

It is also true that from the beginning the war of liberation was led by the Communist Party. The Communist leaders knew very well what kind of revolution they wanted and have worked consistently to achieve their aim. This has been still more obvious since the liberation than it was during the occupation. The situation in Yugoslavia at the end of the war in many ways resembled that of Soviet Russia at the end of the civil war. Formidable tasks of reconstruction lay ahead. The Yugoslav Communist leaders saw in the experience of the Soviet Union the best guide for their actions. They have followed Soviet practice in their political, economic, and cultural policy.

The Yugoslav Constitution is closely modelled on the "Stalin" Constitution of the Soviet Union. Yugoslavia is not officially called a Soviet State and is unlikely to receive that title in the near future. The 'People's Republic' is based on a pyramid of 'people's committees', which form the administrative organs of the State in

---

This paper was first published in *The Times* in eight articles between September and November 1946.

village, town, county, and province. But the functions of the committees correspond closely to those of the soviets in the U.S.S.R.

Just as the Russian soviets arose naturally from the Russian revolutionary movement, so the Yugoslav 'people's committees' arose from the necessities of the Partisan war. Their first duties were to ensure supplies for the armed forces and to organize essential administrative services in areas liberated from the invaders. Few of their leaders were experienced members of the old Yugoslav bureaucracy. Most were new men, who won the confidence of the people by personal qualities shown in the fulfilment of concrete tasks. Many of these men were given other jobs, sometimes much more important jobs, when the whole country was liberated. Administrators had to be found to fill their places and also to occupy those left empty in the areas which had remained under enemy occupation until the end of the war. This was done by nomination. Local elections will take place before long in Yugoslavia, but they will not undo the trend of the last two years. The 'people's committees' have been changed, as the Russian soviets were changed twenty years ago, from genuine organs of local government into instruments of a centralized system rigidly controlled from above. The control is exercised through the Communist Party.

The Communist Party dominates the 'People's Front', the single political organization of present-day Yugoslavia. The Front contains people who belonged in the past to many different parties, but it is not a coalition. Several minor parties (Republicans, dissident Croatian Peasants, and others) belong to it, but have little scope for separate party activity. Unlike the Communist parties of most European countries, the Yugoslav party has not published officially the names of the members of its central and local committees. There is little public mention of Communist Party activities. The most prominent leaders are well known, though the exact functions which they perform within the party are not in all cases obvious. The lower ranks are kept as secret as possible. The Communist leaders regard the Front as an organization for the 'political education' of the whole people. They consider the old party system outmoded and wrong, and do not intend to allow its restoration. During the old régime a large part of the nation, especially the poorer peasants and the workers, were in fact if not in theory, excluded from political life. Under Communist leadership the Front is intended to bring these people into politics, to mould this amorphous mass into a

Communist shape. The Front corresponds in fact to the 'Communist and non-party block' of the Soviet Union.

Results have varied from one region to another. In the backward and impoverished provinces of Bosnia, Montenegro, Dalmatia, and Macedonia they have been fairly successful. There the average man probably has a more genuine opportunity than before of influencing government in the matters that most affect his daily life. In Serbia and Croatia this is much less the case. There, economic and social conditions were always better, and even under the old dictatorship there was a good deal of political freedom. Several different political parties and ideologies had firm traditions and numerous supporters. It is in those areas that the 'democratic centralism' of the people's committees has won least support.

Yugoslavia is thus ruled by a Communist Party which has outwardly merged itself in the People's Front, but in fact controls both the Front and the State machinery by appointing its own members to key positions in both. In particular, the posts of secretary of local branches of the Front and of secretary of people's committees in province, county, and town are usually held by members of the party. Equally important is the Communist control of the armed forces. A small number of officers from the old regular army joined the Partisans during the war, but the great majority were indifferent or hostile. Some were prisoners of war until 1945; some belonged to the Serbian or Croatian quisling armies; and some simply remained inactive at home. All three categories have been excluded from the present army. Its soldiers are conscripts from the whole nation, but all positions of command are occupied by trusted supporters of the régime. The generals are members or sympathizers of the Communist Party, and the junior officers and N.C.O.s mostly won their rank during the Partisan war. The army's loyalty is further ensured by the institution of political commissars based on the Soviet model. The commissars proved themselves brave and efficient during the war and contributed greatly to the maintenance of morale in the face of exceptional hardships. Their task is now to spread 'political education' among the soldiers.

The old police apparatus was thoroughly unpopular among the Yugoslav people, and many of its members were guilty of collaboration with the invaders. During the war the Partisan leaders began to create a new police, and the work has been completed since the liberation. Routine police duties are performed by the uniformed 'people's Militia'. The political police, formerly known as O.Z.N.A. ('Organization for the Defence of the People'), is now called the 'State Security Administration' (U.D.B.). It is not, as in the Soviet Union, a separate Ministry, but is combined with the militia under the Minister of the Interior. The Minister, General Alexander Ranković, is one of the most powerful men in the country. The strength and activities of U.D.B. are kept as secret as possible. It has a reputation for efficiency and ruthlessness.

A further powerful weapon of the Communists is the institution of public prosecutors, which is also copied from the Soviet Union. The Federal Public Prosecutor is elected by a joint session of the Houses of the Federal Parliament. He appoints prosecutors for the federal republics, who in turn appoint prosecutors for provinces and counties. The task of the prosecutors is to ensure the execution of the laws by Ministries and subordinate authorities. They are responsible only to the Federal Public Prosecutor. They are empowered to intervene in legal proceedings in course and to demand the annulment of legal decisions passed by the courts or administrative authorities. They can take action on the basis of complaints or denunciations from any citizen. It is still too early to say how this institution will work, but its potential importance is obvious.

Against this power system created by the Communist Party there can be little effective resistance. In a declaration given to a special correspondent of *The Times* on 14 November 1945, Marshal Tito stated that he expected an opposition to crystallize within the People's Front and that he 'would like to see the opposition lead a full political life'. He added that he meant by this 'those who oppose us honestly'. In the session of the Federal Parliament which ended last month the well-known Serbian Agrarian leader, Dr Dragoljub Jovanović, made some criticisms of the Government's laws on co-operatives and on the Public Prosecutor, and of the Government's foreign policy. Dr Jovanović has been known for twenty years as a man of the Left and suffered for his opinions under the pre-war dictatorship. Though he did not himself fight with the Partisans he was always their friend, and after the liberation he joined the People's Front and occupied a high position within it. Within a few days of his critical speeches Dr Jovanović was deprived by majority vote of his seat in the Serbian Parliament. He will doubtless lose his seat in the Federal Parliament when it reassembles in the autumn. The Faculty of Law of Belgrade University was

The Danube States in 1946

compelled to deprive him of his professorship. Finally, on 11 August, a packed meeting was held in Belgrade of alleged delegates of his People's Peasant Party, which formally expelled him from its ranks. Dr Jovanović was the first man to offer opposition from within the People's Front. His fate is in no way inconsistent with Marshal Tito's statement to *The Times*. The operative word in that statement was 'honestly'. It is the Communist Party which decides what opposition is 'honest'. Any opposition which does not satisfy the party's definition must be crushed, by whatever means are most convenient, and the party has a wide choice of means.

Another matter in which the Yugoslav Administration has followed the Soviet example is the nationalities question. The attempt of the old Serbian politicians to impose their domination on Croats and Macedonians, and the struggle of the latter against Belgrade, were one of the main factors which made democracy impossible in Yugoslavia between the world wars. After the 1941 partition, Pavelić's Croatian fascists massacred tens of thousands of Serbs in Bosnia, while the Bulgarians expelled large numbers from Macedonia. It was to be expected that after the war the Serbs would take revenge by further bloodshed. The prospects of the survival of a Yugoslav State seemed most uncertain.

Ever since 1919 the Yugoslav Communists have favoured a federal system for the country, in which each nationality should have equal status. When they created the Partisan army in 1941 they began to put their principles into practice. Their propaganda insisted that the only enemies were the invaders and their quislings of whatever nationality they might be. Serbian and Croatian chauvinists alike served the invaders. The Serbian and Croatian peoples were brothers and must fight the common battle together. As time passed this propaganda won thousands of converts. It became, in fact, clear that Ustashe and Chetniks were collaborating not only with the invaders but with each other. At the same time Croatian and Serbian peasants joined each other in Marshal Tito's forces. In Bosnian Krajina, for instance, where in 1941 the worst massacres of Serbs had occurred, Serbs and Croats were, in 1943, fighting side by side against Germans, Ustashe, and Chetniks.

After their victory the Communists put their nationalities policy into legal form in the Constitution. Yugoslavia is now divided into six federal republics, corresponding to the sixteen Soviet Republics of the U.S.S.R. The three most important republics – Serbia,

Croatia, and Slovenia – are inhabited by peoples of clearly defined national character. Macedonia, for thirty years the object of bitter rivalry between Serbian and Bulgarian nationalities, is now given republican status, and its people are officially considered a separate nation. The degree of national consciousness of the Macedonians is a matter on which opinions are divided. It must, however, be admitted that the new policy is a constructive attempt to end a quarrel which has three times brought war to the Balkans and oppression to the people of Macedonia.

The fifth republic is Montenegro. The proportion of Montenegrins among the leading Yugoslav Communists is high, and they have always insisted on the separate nationality of their people. On this point scepticism is more justified than in the case of Macedonia. The sixth republic is Bosnia. Here there is no question of a separate nation. Bosnia is inhabited by Serbs, Croats, and Muslims, of whom the latter, though strictly a religious community, possess special cultural characteristics which amount almost to distinct nationality. As the three groups are inextricably intermixed, it would be impossible without grave injustice to give the province to either Serbia or Croatia, or to divide it between them. Separate republican status therefore seems the best solution.

In addition to the six republics the Voivodina is an autonomous region (corresponding to the autonomous Soviet republics of the U.S.S.R.) and the Kosovo Metohija district is an autonomous province (a unit which also exists in the Soviet Union). Both are included in the Federal Republic of Serbia. The Voivodina is the Danubian province and is inhabited by Serbs, Croats, Hungarians, and various smaller national groups. The Kosovo Metohija district borders on Albania and is largely inhabited by Albanians.

The Communists saved Yugoslavia from a bloody civil war on racial lines, which would have been inevitable if Mihailovitch had come to power. Today there is little discrimination on national lines. A man does not lose his job or go to prison because he is a Serb or a Croat. Nationalist feeling still exists, but it is waning and receives no encouragement from the authorities. There are laws against the propagation of national hatred, which are severely enforced. Even among the enemies of the Government the conviction that the old national feuds were a mistake is spreading. This change is the most constructive achievement of the new system.

The actual practice of federalism is more doubtful. Strict limits are set to the home rule of the federal republics by the system of 'democratic centralism', which enables the Communist Party to control the whole State machinery. Some republics enjoy more freedom than others. Slovenia and Macedonia have the advantage of distinct languages. The Macedonians, after thirty years of oppression from Belgrade or Sofia, are especially sensitive to any external interference, and the Federal Government, which wishes to encourage the sense of Macedonian nationhood, has shown much tact in its dealings with them. Bosnia, too, has enjoyed a good deal of autonomy. The needs of material reconstruction are greatest in Bosnia. For a long time the poor state of communications compelled the Bosnian Government to act on its own initiative. The results confirmed the confidence of the Belgrade authorities, who have done a lot to help Bosnia.

The autonomy of Serbia and Croatia is much less certain. One unexpected consequence of the war needs emphasizing. The greater part of Yugoslavia is divided geographically into two zones, the rich plainlands and low hills of Serbia and Croatia, and the forests and barren mountains of Bosnia, Montenegro, and Dalmatia. Between the world wars, political power was concentrated in Serbia, and economic power was divided between Serbia and Croatia. The mountain areas were neglected. During the Second World War it was the mountain areas which gave the greatest number of recruits to Tito's forces. A high proportion of senior officers, political commissars, and civil administrators are today Bosnians, Dalmatians, and Montenegrins. It was also these areas which were most nearly destroyed by fighting and need most help in reconstruction. The populations of Serbia and Croatia, which most escaped destruction, now have to pay for the restoration of the other provinces. The positions are reversed. Many Serbs and Croats resent this economic burden and the increased political power of the mountaineers, whom they regard, not without some justification, as men of inferior education and ability.

It is not easy to estimate public feeling towards the present Government. Economic conditions have greatly improved during the last year. This is largely due to U.N.R.R.A. supplies. The experience of other countries has, however, shown that supplies are of little help if they are not efficiently distributed. In this respect the Yugoslav authorities have a good record, which is confirmed by responsible U.N.R.R.A. officials in the country. Inflation has been prevented. The main communications have been restored. Industry is gradually recovering, and essential goods are beginning to reach the villages from the towns. The Government is going energetically ahead with plans for the industrialization on which the future welfare of the country depends.

The improvement is generally admitted, but this does not mean that people are contented. The peasants resent selling the greater part of their crop to the Government at fixed prices. They are not satisfied by recent measures, increasing the proportion available on the free market and reducing the price of agricultural tools and other manufactured goods needed in the villages. The maize and fodder harvests have been seriously damaged by drought. The industrial workers also have cause for discontent. Though they are given priority in food rations and in the purchase of various goods, their standard of living remains low. They are subjected to pressure to make them do various forms of 'voluntary' overtime. The system of 'socialist competition,' based on methods used in the Stakhanovite movement in the Soviet Union, forces the last ounce of energy from the worker as ruthlessly as any capitalist employer of the past.

These things cause discontent among peasants and workers. But discontent is not the same thing as political opposition. The Yugoslavs are patient and patriotic. They realize that many of their difficulties are inevitable consequences of the war. They are willing to put up with hardships in order to rebuild their country.

Probably more discontent is created by the lack of political freedom, the monopoly of power by the Communist Party, and the flood of propaganda which invades every village in the country and every minute of people's lives. When the day's work is over the worker or official must attend a meeting of his trade union to discuss at length the wickedness of British Imperialism, or the sufferings of Indonesia or China. Next day he must attend a 'spontaneous' demonstration to demand the liberation of Trieste or the overthrow of Franco. The schoolteacher or professor must attend a course in Marxism, prepared in accordance with the latest anthology selected in Moscow. Every town is covered with slogans and posters. Not only the intellectuals of the old school but the simple citizen and peasant suffer in this stifling atmosphere.

Many things which are now wrong in Yugoslavia will improve with time. As new administrators are trained the abuses of the bureaucracy will be reduced. To speed this process a special institution, the State Control Commission, has been created. It is modelled on the former 'Workers' and Peasants' Inspection' (now Ministry of State Control) of the U.S.S.R. Its duties include coordination of the work of Government departments, investigation of acts of injustice, and replacement of incompetent by sound officials.

There will be many improvements, but certain things will not change. The Communist Party will not relax its grip. First priority will always be given to considerations of power. This is in accordance with Communist doctrine, which holds that no plans for economic development and for the raising of the standard of living can be achieved except by the unchallenged leadership of the revolutionary vanguard, the Communist Party. Everything must therefore be subordinated to the strengthening of the party. The Yugoslav party is confident of its own strength and of that of the Soviet Union, which it believes will back it unconditionally. With many million Soviet bayonets behind it, it feels able to ignore all opposition. In return it will stand by the Soviet Union whatever surprises the international situation may bring.[1]

BULGARIA

September 9, the second anniversary of the Bulgarian revolution, by which the Fatherland Front seized power, was marked by the proclamation of a People's Republic, for which the plebiscite of the previous day had given a large majority. The Fatherland Front was formed during the war by the Communist, Agrarian, Socialist, and Zveno parties. It provided the political leadership of the Partisan movement, and brought the Bulgarian Army into the war on the allied side. The Partisans fought throughout the spring and summer of 1944 against the forces on the pro-German side, and if they achieved little it was not for lack of courage. The army fought bravely and efficiently in Yugoslavia and Hungary for the last seven months of the war.

There is no doubt that the Fatherland Front represented in

[1] Only two years later came the breach between Yugoslavia and the Soviet Union. However, the initiative came from the Soviet side. No evidence that has appeared up to now (1964) suggests that there had been any intention on the Yugoslav side to cease supporting Soviet foreign policy in all fields of international politics.

September 1944 the overwhelming majority of Bulgarians. High hopes were held of a new era of democracy and social justice. During the following two years, these hopes have been to a large extent disappointed. The first party to secede from the Front were the Agrarians. Their leader, Dr G. M. Dimitrov, came into conflict with the Communists soon after his return from exile in the Middle East in September 1944. He then maintained that the Agrarians, as representatives of the peasant majority of the Bulgarian people, were the largest party in the country and should have a policy of their own. In his opinion, the Communists were using the Fatherland Front to further their own aims and were holding the other parties prisoners within it under the pretext of 'national solidarity'. His independent line soon won him the enmity of the Communist Party and of the Soviet occupation authorities.

Dimitrov was accused of sabotaging the war effort against Germany and of being a 'foreign agent'. The latter expression referred to his past co-operation with Britain, whose action in Greece in the winter of 1944 caused genuine alarm in Bulgaria. The result of the campaign against Dimitrov was that he was compelled in January 1945, to resign the secretaryship of the party. His successor, Petkov, was ousted at a packed congress of the party by the supporters of a pro-Communist wing led by Obbov, who thus obtained control of the party. Petkov resigned from the Government in August together with three other Agrarian leaders. The fiction of Agrarian representation was preserved by the followers of Obbov, but the majority remained loyal to Petkov.

The Socialist Party was similarly split in May 1945. A pro-Communist wing led by Neikov, with the help of the police, forcibly took possession of the party offices and newspaper. Neikov's followers also seized by force the Socialist Co-operative organization. The independent Socialists remained in opposition under the leadership of Pastuhov and Lulchev. Since August 1945, the opposition Agrarians and Socialists have been allowed to publish newspapers which, though severely censored and frequently suppressed for a few days at a time, still manage to appear. Perhaps the best indication of the respective strength of the Government and opposition factions of the two parties is given by the circulation of their papers. The pro-Government Agrarian and Socialist organs sell between 7,000 and 15,000 copies, the opposition papers over 100,000.

The existence of opposition papers should not be considered proof that the opposition enjoys freedom. In August last three out of fifteen members of the Socialist central committee and seven out of twenty-two members of the Agrarian 'Presidium' were in prison or concentration camp. The veteran Socialist leader Pastuhov received a five year prison sentence in February for an article criticizing a speech to the Bulgarian Army by the Communist leader George Dimitrov. This Dimitrov, the hero of the Leipzig 'Reichstag fire' trial organized by Goering in 1933 and later Secretary of the Comintern, who returned to Bulgaria this year, is now the leading figure in the present régime. He should not be confused with Dr G. M. Dimitrov, the Agrarian leader, mentioned above. Dr G. M. Dimitrov, who was condemned to death by the pro-German Government of Filov in 1942, has the unusual distinction of having also been condemned *in absentia* by the present Government to twenty years in prison, on the unconvincing charge of defeatist propaganda during the 1944–5 campaign of the Bulgarian Army against the Germans. He is at present in exile for the third time.

The opposition intends to contest next month's elections for the Constituent Assembly. Neither its leaders for independent foreign observers in Sofia consider it likely that it will be allowed to win many votes.

The fourth party of the original Fatherland Front, Zveno, draws its support mainly from the professional class and from army officers, both regular and reserve. Its most striking personality is General Velchev, who organized *coups d'état* against the Agrarian Government of 1923 and the Centre Government of 1934, and was also concerned in the revolution of 1944. At first a party of dictatorship, Zveno has adopted a more democratic programme, which its leaders like to compare with that of the British Labour Party. Zveno remained happily within the Fatherland Front until this summer, when General Velchev, as Minister of War, began to resist the increasing control of the army by the Communists. Then a campaign against him began in the Government press. The Obbov Agrarians recalled his action against the Agrarians in 1923. The Communists accused him of co-operation with Mihailović during the war. He was denounced for giving evidence in favour of Dr G. M. Dimitrov at the latter's trial.

In June a new law transferred the powers formerly held by the War Minister to the Cabinet as a whole. Velchev was relieved of his duties on grounds of health.[1] Another distinguished officer, General Kiril Stanchev who, though not a member of Zveno, has long been closely associated with it, and who was the chief organizer of the 1944 revolution, is in prison. Several leaders of Zveno, including the Prime Minister, M. Gheorghiev, remain in the Fatherland Front, but any tendency to independence within the official party has been removed.

Communist control is now almost as complete in Bulgaria as in Yugoslavia. Though the old democratic constitution is nominally in force, the administration is directed by the Communist Minister of the Interior, Yugov, who appoints governors of provinces, heads of counties, and mayors of towns and villages. A new constitution will be made by the Assembly which is to be elected at the end of October. This may or may not copy the Yugoslav or Soviet Constitution, but will doubtless ensure that the constitutional theory is brought more closely into line with Communist practice than is at present the case.

The Bulgarian Army has to be greatly reduced in accordance with the peace terms. This opportunity has been used to remove as many as possible of those officers whose loyalty to the new régime is not certain. The dismissed officers include many who did well in the war against Germany in 1944-5. Key positions are held by Communists, of whom the most important are Generals Kinov and Kozovski. Kinov served for many years in the Red Army, and Kozovski, who had a good military record in the Spanish Civil War, has also undergone training in Russia. Kinov is Chief of Staff, Kozovski head of the political administration of the Army, the department which controls the political commissars. The commissars are officially entitled 'assistant commanders'. They are second-in-command of units down to battalion level. In matters affecting the very wide field of 'political education' they take their orders only from their superiors within the department.

The police, now called Militia, are controlled by a Communist and come under the Communist-led Ministry of the Interior. The uniformed police officially number about 12,000, but are believed by well-informed people to be at least four times more numerous. A recent decree created a 'Frontier Militia', also under the Ministry of the Interior, to which men will be transferred from the Army. The

[1] Velchev subsequently made his peace with the Communists, and was appointed Bulgarian Minister in Switzerland. He later broke with the régime and died in exile.

duties of this force will doubtless correspond to those of the former 'Frontier Troops of N.K.V.D.' in the Soviet Union. The secret police of Bulgaria is the State Security Section of the Militia, whose members do not wear uniform. It includes men who have received special training in the Soviet Union.

Political prisoners are of two kinds. Prison sentences are given only after trial. They usually come under the Law for Defence of the People's Power. Crimes under this law include making 'statements which might impede economic life', 'creating mistrust in the Government' and 'spreading opinions which harm relations with a friendly State'. People may also on a direct order of the Minister of the Interior be removed without trial to a concentration camp. A recent law also empowers the Minister to mobilize for compulsory labour and 'democratic re-education' any 'idle' persons. The Minister is the judge of what is idleness and what is 'constructive employment'. Mobilized persons are released after six months, but if after an interval they cannot find 'constructive employment' they may be called up again.

The most important remaining means of Communist control are the trade unions. These undoubtedly obtain material advantages in food and clothing rations for workers. They also engage in political propaganda. Workers who do not conform to the required political line lose their employment and their special rations. Public officials and teachers also belong to trade unions, which energetically further their 'democratic re-education'.

Communist control on the lines described above has made rapid progress, especially since the unexpected return in July of General Biryuzov, the head of the Soviet Control Commission, who had made his official good-bye in the spring. The increased tempo may be due to the departure of the Red Army from Bulgaria anticipated in the peace treaty. The Soviet Government may indeed feel that the presence of its own troops is no longer needed, since its Bulgarian friends are so firmly in power. The plebiscite of 8 September brought no surprises. None of the parties supported the monarchy. Yet it has a symbolic importance. 'People's Republic' is the title given to those states which have most nearly approached the Soviet model. By the proclamation of 9 September Bulgaria has been formally received into the same select club as Yugoslavia, Albania, and Mongolia. It is a reward for the progress made during two years of Eastern democratization.

ROUMANIA

Roumania is passing through the same sort of 'revolution from above' as Bulgaria. The process has been slower, and the methods used have been somewhat different, but the aim is the same.

The Roumanian Government is based on the 'National Democratic Front', an alleged coalition of Left-wing parties. But whereas the Bulgarian 'Fatherland Front' was at one time a real alliance of parties, the Roumanian N.D.F. was always an artificial creation. It was put in power by Mr Vyshinsky in March 1945, when the German counter-offensive in Hungary made it essential for Moscow to have a 'reliable' government. But when the danger had passed the N.D.F. remained in power. It is entirely controlled by the Communist Party, whose members hold the Ministries of the Interior, Communications, and Justice, besides several under-secretaryships in other Ministries. Two other parties, the Ploughmen's Front and the National Popular Party, are tools of the Communists.

The Ploughmen's Front was founded in 1934 in southern Transylvania by peasants who were dissatisfied with the hesitant policy of the old National Peasant Party. Though the Front was prevented by police pressure from extending throughout the country, nevertheless within its home area it was a genuine radical peasant movement run by peasants. The only non-peasant connected with it was the present Premier, Dr Groza, who was more an adviser than a leader. After August 1944, the Front made progress, attracting the poorer peasants in many parts of the country. Left to itself, it would have become an important factor in Roumanian politics. But the Communists, determined to use the Front to weaken the old Peasant Party, flooded it with their members and their propaganda and forced its growth in regions where until then it had no real basis. It soon became obvious that the Ploughmen's Front had become a mere rural branch of the Communist Party, run no longer by its old peasant leaders but by the Communists.

The National Popular Party was created by the Communists to attract to the régime progressive elements of the middle class. It contains a number of younger men of firm democratic convictions, who opposed the pre-war dictatorship and did some minor underground resistance during the war. These men are aware of the abuses of the present régime, but feel that it still deserves support,

The Danube States in 1946

as it stands for social progress, while the opposition parties represent only an outworn past. But in their haste to build up the National Popular Party against their opponents, the Communists flooded it with every sort of raw recruit or unscrupulous opportunist. Quantity killed quality. Today the National Popular Party, like the Ploughmen's Front, is a complete failure.

Another group of Government supporters are the dissident Liberals of M. Tatarescu, the present Foreign Minister. Their only prominent personality is their leader, a clever opportunist with a dictatorial past, which can be used against him if ever he shows hesitation. At present he is serving the Communists with the same devotion with which he served ex-King Carol from 1933 to 1940.

The remaining Government party is that of the Social Democrats. They were of small importance before 1944, but have recently won support from the growing non-Communist section of the working class and from part of the professional class. Their leaders cooperate unconditionally with the Communists, but most of the members prefer an independent policy. The cleavage between pro- and anti-Communist Socialists is not, however, so clear as in Bulgaria.

The Roumanian administrative apparatus is unchanged in form, though there have been extensive changes in personnel. The prefects of counties are nominated by the Ministry of the Interior. They are sure to be persons approved by the local representatives of the N.D.F., that is, of the Communist Party. The same is true of the mayors of towns and villages. The gendarmerie and police are organized on the pre-war model, but at least the key positions have been given to men more or less trusted by the régime.

The old political police – the political section of the *Sigurantsa* – still exists; but its activities are supplemented by those of a new body, the Special Security Service, directed by the leading Communist Bodnarash, the Secretary of the Prime Minister's Office, who is generally regarded as the real ruler of Roumania. It is a curious coincidence that Bodnarash is of the same ethnical origin as the late leader of the Fascists (Iron Guard), Codreanu. Both men had a Ukrainian father and both came from the north-eastern province, Bucovina. Bodnarash's Security Service is more efficient and ruthless than any of its predecessors. It makes sudden arrests and holds its prisoners without trial in one of two prisons over which it has complete control. They are believed to be organized in accordance with the latest methods of the Soviet police.

As in Bulgaria, the reduction of the Army in accordance with the peace treaty is being used for a political purge. Officers considered unreliable are dismissed, even if they are technically outstanding and have good records from the eight months' war against Germany in 1944-5. A special feature of Roumania is two political units formed of former prisoners of war 're-educated' in Soviet camps. They are named after the revolutionary heroes Tudor Vladimirescu and Horia, Closhca and Crishan. They are known as 'divisions', but their numbers possibly exceed those of a division, as they have provided large numbers of recruits to the purged gendarmerie and police and to the political commissar department of the Army. Yet they still exist as separate formations within the Army. The political commissars are officially known as the department of 'Education, Culture, and Propaganda'. They are organized in much the same way as the commissars in the Bulgarian Army.

Though they hold powerful means of control, the Roumanian Communists do not feel secure. The Communist Party suffers from what is described as a 'crisis of cadres'. Convinced and loyal members of the party probably do not exceed a few hundreds. The remainder are attracted by material inducements and by threats. Civil servants faced with unemployment join the party under pressure. Former Iron-Guardists join partly because they like extremism and violence and partly because if they do not they can be accused as 'war criminals'. Members of national minorities join because they hope to obtain Government protection. Mention should be made of the Jews, some of whom see an opportunity for revenge for the persecution of past years. But it cannot be easy for the Communist leaders to run a team of Jews and anti-Semite toughs.

The two old or 'historic' parties, National Peasants and Liberals, have been nominally represented in the Government since the Moscow decisions of December 1945. In fact their representatives have no power in the Cabinet, and the whole Government propaganda machine is used to pour abuse on their leaders. Each party has a newspaper in Bucarest, but none in the provinces, and distribution outside the capital is obstructed in various ways. The two newspapers are fairly heavily censored, but it must be admitted that they are allowed to criticize Government policy.

The promise made by the Groza Government after the Moscow

agreement, to hold free elections, does not seem likely to be fulfilled. When the opposition parties attempt to hold a meeting in a town, they are attacked by armed bands of Communists brought up in lorries. In an incident of this sort at Pitesti in August, M. Penescu, the General Secretary of the National Peasant Party, was wounded and one of his friends killed. At Alba Iulia in the same week several prominent leaders of the party in Transylvania were beaten in the street. In villages opposition meetings cannot be prevented, as the peasants are solidly behind the opposition, and the Communists cannot find men to serve them. But party speakers who go from town to village are waylaid on their return and beaten. In all cases the police refuse action against the aggressors. The closest historical parallel is the first two years of the Fascist régime in Italy. There, too, other parties were officially allowed to exist, but their followers were beaten and murdered by Fascist toughs while the police looked on.

No visitor to Roumania can long remain in doubt of the overwhelming popular support for the opposition. Whether the Government entirely deserves its unpopularity is another matter. It has carried out a land reform and has restored trade unions, which have undoubtedly brought material benefits to the workers in spite of their abuse for political purposes by their Communist leaders. These are not negligible achievements. Yet the fact remains that the Government is hated, for the general economic misery (greatly increased by a terrible drought, for which only Nature is to blame, but which has destroyed the vital maize harvest), for the burden of the Russian army of occupation, and for the corruption and brutality of the Administration, which have increased even in comparison with earlier dictatorships. On the other hand, M. Maniu, the veteran leader of the National Peasant Party, is more popular than ever in his long career. His past mistakes and weaknesses are forgotten. He stands now not for any programme or ideology but for the idea of national independence. He is the symbol of the Roumanian nation. And because he and his friends know this they will fight the coming election, whatever the cost in human lives. M. Maniu is a brave man. He has no illusions about the methods his opponents will use. But he feels that today he cannot compromise and that if he goes down in the struggle it will have been worth while.

This is perhaps the most tragic moment of Roumania's tragic history. Never did a country so much need radical social reform.

Yet the extortions of the Red Army, who remembered the devastated villages and cities of Ukraine, and the misdeeds of the Communists, who remembered how past Roumanian rulers had maltreated them, have largely discredited the ideas of the Left. Today most Roumanians are aware of only one issue – whether their nation will survive. For their part, the Russians, feeling the fierce flame of Roumanian nationalism, foresee a revival of Fascism, supported by 'foreign imperialist intervention'. They cannot forget that Roumania is the back door to the invasion of their own country, and therefore fear to give it up. Yet the longer they stay, or maintain by force their servile nominees, the greater is the hatred and unrest. There seems no way out.

TRANSYLVANIA

Between Vienna and the Black Sea live two non-Slav nations, Roumanians and Hungarians. The greater part of each nation occupies the plainlands of the middle and lower Danube, separated from each other by the eastern Carpathians. The two nations mix in Transylvania, the plateau province which lies in the bend of the Carpathians, between the two plains. The Roumanians and Hungarians cut off the Czechs and Poles in the north from the Yugoslavs and Bulgarians south of the Danube. They have many common interests and striking similarities of national character. Hitherto they have been divided from each other by the quarrel for the possession of Transylvania.

Roumanians form more than half the population of Transylvania, and the Hungarians are about half as numerous as the Roumanians. The remainder is made up of Germans, Jews, and other small minorities. For 1,000 years Transylvania was ruled by Hungarians, sometimes as part of the Kingdom of Hungary, sometimes as a more or less independent principality. During this period the Roumanians had few national or individual rights. After 1918 the province was given to Roumania, and it was the turn of the Hungarians to be second-class nationals. In 1940 Hitler and Mussolini, by the 'Arbitration' of Vienna, cut the province in two, dislocated its economic life, and satisfied neither side. In 1946 it has been once more handed to Roumania. It is clearly less unjust to give it to the more numerous than to the less numerous nation. But no settlement can be considered good which makes no provision for the treatment of the minority.

It should, of course, be realized that considerations other than the welfare of its people are bound to influence the fate of Transylvania at a general peace settlement. Transylvania is the gateway from Central Europe to the Russian steppes. That is why in 1940 Hitler, thinking of his planned invasion of Russia, gave the Carpathian line to Hungary. Whatever the political sympathies of the Hungarian nation and Government, Hungary was geographically at the mercy of Germany. By extending the Hungarian frontier eastward Hitler was extending his own frontier. In 1946 exactly the same considerations have induced the Soviet Union to back the Roumanian claim. There is no natural frontier from the Iron Gate to the Urals, and Roumania is geographically at the mercy of Russia. By extending the Roumanian frontier westward Mr Stalin is extending his own frontier towards the heart of Europe.

The fact remains that Transylvania is a country of mixed nationalities, and that, whatever its formal international position, it can have no peace or prosperity until these nationalities are equally treated. This fact was ignored by the semi-feudal Hungarian régime before 1918 and by the nationalist dictatorships of Roumania from 1918–44 and Hungary from 1940–4. There are some indications that it has been recognized by the Roumanian Government of 1946.

There is no doubt that the present Roumanian Prime Minister, Dr Groza, has been for many years a convinced champion of Roumanian–Hungarian friendship. Himself a Transylvanian, he wishes the province to be the common home of both nations and a 'bridge of friendship' between the two States. That is also the official policy of the Roumanian Communist Party, as expounded by its General Secretary, Gheorghiu-Dej, who recently rebuked one of his party colleagues, the Minister of Justice, Patrascanu, for a too nationalistic attitude. Moreover, the policy of equal treatment has not remained on paper only. According to the leaders of the political party of the Transylvanian Hungarians, the Hungarian People's Union, there are now 1,680 Hungarian primary schools in Transylvania, contrasted with 765 before the war, and 127 secondary schools contrasted with 67. And whereas before the war these schools were supported by the Hungarian community themselves, they are now supported by the Roumanian State. There is also a State-supported Hungarian university for Transylvania, part of which is situated in Cluj (Kolozsvár) and part in Târgu Mureş (Márosvásárhely). In predominantly Hungarian areas, as in the three Székely counties of the south-east, the public officials from the prefect downwards are predominantly Hungarians. These facts entitle the Roumanian Government to claim that it has given concrete proof of its goodwill.

Unfortunately it cannot be said that much progress has been made towards the reconciliation of the two nations. Both are dissatisfied with the present situation. The Roumanians remember the oppressive treatment they received from the Hungarian administration in North Transylvania after 1940. They claim that many of the officials who then came from Hungary have remained and have obtained protection by joining the Communist Party. In general the knowledge of defeat and the presence of an army of occupation have created a mood of extreme nationalism among the Roumanian people. This reflects itself in hostility to the foreigners in their midst, the Hungarians. But perhaps the chief cause of anti-Hungarian feeling is simply hatred of the Roumanian Government.

The present dictatorship of the Communist Party is hated for many different reasons, and therefore everything it does is unpopular. Its policy toward the Hungarians is disliked not so much for its own sake as because of its authors. The result of these various causes is a widespread belief among Transylvanian Roumanians that the Hungarians enjoy a privileged position, that the dictatorship is a dictatorship by Hungarians against Roumanians, and that they will have no peace until 'they are rid of the Hungarians'. This point of view is to some extent upheld by the opposition parties. Government supporters attribute to M. Maniu the intention, should he ever attain power, of expelling the Hungarians in mass on the Czechoslovak or Polish model. This accusation is probably a calumny. But it is true that among M. Maniu's supporters (who form the great majority of Transylvanian Roumanians) there is much talk of the impossibility of a peaceful coexistence of the two nations and of the need for an exchange of populations.

The Hungarians also have reason for discontent. The policy of equal treatment has not everywhere been put into practice. Government funds for Hungarian schools arrive late. Official posts dependent on certain Ministries controlled by politicians of nationalist tendencies (notably Finance and Justice) are often given to Roumanians even in Hungarian districts, while in districts of mixed population Roumanians almost always predominate. These are minor grievances, and an improvement is admitted in comparison with the past. Another cause of complaint is the predominance of

Communists in Hungarians affairs. The Hungarian People's Union has a political monopoly. It deals with the Roumanian Government in matters affecting Hungarian interests and is supported by the Hungarian population in the absence of any alternative. But its leadership is in Communist hands, and this is resented. The main cause of Hungarian discontent is uncertainty for the future. The Hungarians are grateful to M. Groza's Government, but they know well that it is detested by the Roumanians and does not represent them. The Groza Government may go, but the Roumanian people will remain, and Roumania has undertaken no formal international commitment which could oblige another Government to treat Hungarians fairly.

Transylvania is worth study as an example of the inter-relationship of internal politics, ideology, nationalism, and great Power strategy. The relations of Slav with non-Slav, and of the great Power of the East with those of the West, influence and are influenced by the Transylvanian question. Transylvania is fitted in every way to be a 'Central European Switzerland'. It has a special geographical position, strong historical traditions of its own, and in spite of all evidence to the contrary there is much mutual sympathy and sense of common interests among both its nations. But there are two conditions without which a 'Swiss' solution is impossible. These are that both Roumania and Hungary should have governments which represent and can freely express the will of their peoples, and that a serious effort should be made on all sides to bring about a closer unity of all the nations and countries of the Danubian Basin. Both these conditions are today as far from fulfilment as they were at the outbreak of war.

During the first months after victory the Soviet Union seemed to be pursuing a policy of Danubian unity. Soviet policy appeared to be based on the belief that the Danubian peoples, in gratitude for their liberation by the Red Army and for the social transformations carried out with the support of the Red Army, would enthusiastically co-operate with Russia. And if they were all to be friends of the Soviet Union, it was desirable that they should make friends with each other. During this period Soviet policy encouraged reconciliation between neighbouring nations. But hopes were not fulfilled. The undisciplined behaviour of Russian troops, the economic consequences of occupation, abuse of power by Communists, international tension, all contributed to create anti-Soviet feeling in all

Danubian countries. Realizing that the Danubian peoples were not their friends, the Soviet leaders realized that they no longer had an interest in furthering their reconciliation with one another. It was easier to fall back on Pan-Slavism and on the diversion of Roumanian nationalism from the eastern frontier to the west.

In Transylvania and throughout the Danubian Basin international co-operation is as much a dream as it was in the Hitlerian era. The problems remain the same. If they proved intractable in the past, it is unlikely that they can be wished away in the future.

HUNGARY

Any British visitor's estimate of the present state of Hungary must depend on the direction from which he arrives in the country. If he comes straight from London to Budapest he will be depressed by the war damage, the economic hardships, and the general uncertainty. But if (like your Correspondent) he comes from Roumania he will have just the contrary impression. He will note the energy with which the people of Budapest are rebuilding their city. He can buy newspapers and periodicals expressing widely different opinions on controversial subjects. Above all he will be suprised by the vigorous intellectual activity displayed both in print and in conversation. In comparison with the mental sterility and haunting fear prevalent in the Balkans, Hungary seems an oasis of culture and liberty.

This comparison is essential for an understanding of the Danubian situation as a whole. It should not, however, be taken to mean that Hungary has not her troubles. In fact she is faced with grave problems in internal politics, in economic life, and in foreign policy.

The Hungarian Government is a coalition, and unlike Roumania and Bulgaria, a real coalition. The two most important parties are the Communists on the left and the Small Farmers' Party on the right. The Communists won 17 per cent. of the votes in free elections a year ago, which is much more than their Roumanian comrades could hope for. They are supported by a section of the industrial working class and won a number of peasant votes, particularly in the eastern counties, where radical opinions have been strong since the last century. They have also welcomed into their ranks a number (nobody knows how many) of former Hungarian Nazis ('Arrow Cross'). They are ably led by Matthias Rákosi, who languished sixteen years in a Hungarian prison for his opinions and spent the war years in the Soviet Union. He and several other prominent leaders of the party are Jews.

The Social-Democrats, who won 20 per cent. of the votes, are stronger than the Communists in the industrial working class of Budapest, where trade union tradition is firmly rooted. The present Socialist leaders co-operate unreservedly with the Communists, though there is opposition to this within the party ranks. The third and smallest party of the left are the National Peasants. The Communists attempted to use this party against the Small Farmers' Party in the same way as the Ploughmen's Front was used in Roumania. But whereas the Ploughmen's Front was a peasant body without a head, the National Peasant Party is just the opposite. Its leaders are a group of brilliant intellectuals whose ideas do not conform to any ready-made pattern. While continuing to co-operate with the other left parties, they have resisted Communist 'penetration'. They have thus remained a small party with little mass support, but have kept their independence.

The three left parties together polled slightly over 40 per cent. at the elections, while a little less than 50 per cent. went to the Small Farmers' Party. The Small Farmers won the majority of the peasants' and the whole of the middle-class vote. Their supporters also included many who would have voted for the extreme right if they had had the chance. This last point is used by the left parties as an argument to show that the Small Farmers' Party has 'fascist' tendencies. There seems in fact little ground for suspicion of the democratic convictions of the party's present leaders, particularly since the expulsion from its ranks early this year of twenty prominent members of its right wing. The Prime Minister, M. Ferenc Nagy, himself a peasant, has gone far in co-operating with the left. He is even criticized by some of his own followers for being too conciliatory. According to a well-informed Hungarian source, the left parties, with 45 per cent. of the votes, control 79 per cent. of the posts in the Administration and 69 per cent. of the posts in the police, the Communists alone having 52 per cent. of the latter. Many supporters of the Small Farmers' Party feel that M. Nagy and his predecessor as leader of the party, the present President of the Republic, M. Zoltán Tildy, could have prevented this by a firmer policy at an earlier stage. They hope that steps can now be taken to undo it.

It cannot be said that the coalition is working smoothly. There is constant friction in big and small matters. Individual Ministers treat their ministries as private satrapies for their party rather than co-ordinate their work in a general Government policy. The Communists and Small Farmers exchange accusations and insults in public. It is frequently said that 'this cannot last', and yet somehow it has lasted, and may well last a long time yet. Neither the left block nor the Small Farmers are confident of their ability to rule alone. Reconstruction needs the united efforts of all. In the last resort almost every one prefers the present situation to a breach.

Many Hungarians genuinely believe that their country is ruled by a ruthless Communist dictatorship. They point out that the Communists hold the ministries of the Interior and Communications; that the Political Police and the Frontier Guards (modelled like their Bulgarian counterpart on the Soviet 'Frontier Troops of the N.K.V.D.') are almost wholly in Communist hands; and that 'political education' on Communist lines is being introduced into the remnants of the Army. But the Political Police has fewer powers, and Communist control has generally gone less far than in neighbouring countries to east and south. The personal attitude of the Hungarian Communist leaders differs, for instance, from that of their Roumanian comrades. Whereas the latter hardly attempt to conceal that they are ruling by force as representatives of Soviet policy, the former seem genuinely willing to co-operate on a basis of equality with other Hungarians. Whether this is because the Hungarian Communists are better patriots than the Roumanians, or merely because Moscow considers Hungary strategically less important, is a matter of opinion.

The economic situation has improved, but is still difficult. The stabilization of the forint has so far been successful. The inflation enabled the Government to carry out a measure of essential industrial reconstruction at small cost. During this period miracles of endurance were performed by the Hungarian workers, who accepted heavy sacrifices in the national interest. Now the strain has been appreciably relaxed, and the new currency has some real purchasing-power, but the price of deflation is being paid in unemployment. More than 30,000 are already out of work in the building trade. The future stability of the forint must depend largely on whether there will be a black market in agricultural goods after the harvest. A serious problem is the disparity between industrial and agricultural prices. Farm goods have been allowed to rise only to twice the pre-war prices, whereas some industrial goods required by the peasants have risen as much as six times. This is largely the result of factors beyond the Government's control, but it causes discontent among the peasants which may become politically dangerous. A campaign is being carried on for the reduction of industrial prices through lowering of costs of production. Industry suffered greatly from removals of machinery. The equipment moved to the U.S.S.R. will never be recovered, but it is hoped that some of that seized by the Germans will eventually be restored. For instance, machinery from the Manfred Weiss works required for the manufacture of agricultural machines is still in the Western zones of Austria, and Hungarian rolling stock is scattered about the railways of Germany.

A year ago Hungarians understood that their country had been beaten. Probably few doubted that it would revert to the Trianon frontiers. But since the beginning of 1946 a more optimistic note appeared in the press and public speeches. The visit of M. Nagy and M. Rákosi to Moscow in April was a landmark. On their return it became widely believed that the Soviet Government would support at least part of Hungarian claims on Roumania. When at Paris nothing of the sort occurred there was bitter disappointment. The new settlement will be worse than Trianon, for the proposed expulsion of 200,000 Hungarians from Slovakia, explicitly defended by Mr Vyshinsky, will be a serious economic burden on impoverished Hungary.

The memory of the past is a dark shadow over Hungary. The unbending hostility of the allies in 1919 caused the downfall of Count Károlyi's democratic Government. The 'injustices of Trianon' were used for twenty years by the semi-dictatorial régime of Horthy to divert attention from domestic problems and develop hatred against neighbouring countries. The word 'democracy' is being again identified by the action of the victorious Powers with national humiliation. The lesson is already being driven home in the speeches of the conservative, courageous, and popular Primate, Cardinal Mindszenty.

The parties of the left, though feared by many Hungarians as aggressors, consider themselves on the defensive. Remembering 1919 in Hungary and 1932 in Germany, the Socialist leaders feel that, whatever the faults of the Communists, they must co-operate with them to save the unity of the Left. There is little prospect of a revival of the Arrow Cross Nazi movement, but extreme nationalism, anti-Semitism, peasant hatred of the towns, and political Catholicism, might easily combine with the widespread distrust of the Communists and of the Russians to produce a Clerical-Fascist movement similar to that of Dollfuss. The evolution of the Austrian Christian Social Party between 1920 and 1934 is an ominous warning for the Hungarian Small Farmers' Party of today.[1]

In contrast to Roumania and the Southern Slav countries, it can be said of Hungary that, in spite of difficulties and mistakes, a real attempt is being made to build a democracy capable of maintaining friendship with both the Soviet Union and the Anglo-Saxon powers. Whether it will succeed will depend, at least in part, on the West.

SOVIET POLICY

In all the Danubian countries today internal political and economic life is overshadowed by international policy. All are directly or indirectly dominated by the Soviet Union. Their future depends on their own relations with Moscow and on Moscow's relations with the other Powers.

Soviet policy in the Danube States since the German defeat has been guided by three aims. The first is to prevent their future use as bases for aggression against Soviet territory. This, in the Soviet view, requires not only military guarantees but the complete destruction of the political power of the old ruling classes. The pre-war rulers of allied Yugoslavia, as well as of enemy Bulgaria, Roumania, and Hungary showed themselves implacable enemies of the Soviet Union, and this the Soviet leaders have not forgotten. They have therefore systematically assisted the forces working within these countries for the overthrow of these classes and have themselves intervened where those forces have been too weak.

The second aim is the achievement of far-reaching social reforms. Here self-interest and idealism coincide. It is to the interest of the

[1] So it seemed in 1946. In 1964 it looks differently. The Austrian People's Party, the successor to the Christian Social Party, has abandoned its fascist tendencies, and since 1945 has shared power, in constantly renewed coalitions, with the Socialists. Austria is in fact today the outstanding example of Catholic-Socialist co-operation. When for a few days in 1956 the Hungarian people shook off Communist rule, and a multi-party democracy was restored, it looked for a time as if the Austrian model of co-operation between Catholic peasants and Socialist workers would be renewed. But the Soviet counter-revolution by military invasion, on 4 November 1956, put an end to such hopes.

The Danube States in 1946

U.S.S.R. that there should be internal stability in the Danubian countries, and this is only possible with big social changes. At the same time the Soviet leaders, and the simple Red Army soldier, certainly feel it their mission to bring social justice to these benighted lands. The Russian troops were taught to think of themselves as liberators and expected to be greeted as such by the Balkan peoples.

The third aim is to compensate the Soviet people at the expense of the vanquished. In the opinion of Soviet leaders, not only must the beaten enemy atone for as much as possible of the damage he caused in the Ukraine, but there is a moral obligation on all the new Danubian governments to assist the reconstruction of the Soviet Union. Only the heroic efforts of the Red Army, they argue, saved the Danubian peoples from German Fascism and its quislings and gave the new men the opportunity of power. The price of social revolution on the Danube was paid by thousands of shattered Soviet villages and factories and millions of dead and homeless Russian citizens. The economic resources of the liberated Balkan countries must therefore be largely used to hasten Russian recovery.

The strain is, of course, heaviest in the defeated enemy States. Roumania and Hungary must pay heavy reparations for several years to come. Further clauses in the armistices, which provide for the restitution of goods removed by them from Russian soil during the war, for the maintenance of Soviet troops occupying or crossing their territory, and for the transfer to the U.S.S.R. of German property in their territory, have been liberally interpreted and represent an added burden considerably greater than the total sum of reparations proper. Moreover, apart from deliveries under these clauses, the Red Army during the first months of occupation removed large quantities of livestock, machinery, and various kinds of manufactured goods. Finally, both Roumania and Hungary have concluded commercial treaties with the U.S.S.R. which are extremely favourable to the latter. A special feature of these treaties is the formation of joint trading companies, which possess a large share in Roumanian timber and Hungarian bauxite and monopolize river and air transport in both countries. The Soviet–Roumanian and Soviet–Hungarian oil companies are less important, as the chief petrol concerns are controlled by Western capital,[1] but they may

[1] Western oil interests in both Roumania and Hungary were expropriated a few years later.

play a bigger part in the future, since they have far-reaching rights over new discoveries.

Bulgaria has escaped more lightly. As she did not invade the U.S.S.R. she does not have to pay reparations. But the requisitions of the first months and the expense of the Red Army occupation have been heavy. Yugoslavia is an allied State, but the Yugoslav Government has not shirked its duty of contributing to Soviet recovery. Though the Yugoslav partisans liberated most of their country themselves, they have had good reason to be grateful to Moscow for diplomatic support on several occasions. The Yugoslav contribution is a commercial treaty whose terms are kept secret. Enough is, however, known to make it clear that the prices of Yugoslav goods are extremely low and those of Soviet goods extremely high.

The contrast between the second and third aims of Soviet policy has not escaped the notice of the Soviet leaders themselves. The Danubian peoples at first welcomed the Red Army, in joy at the expulsion of the Germans and in hope of social justice and freedom. The inevitable economic decline which followed liberation was bound to cause disillusionment, which the Soviet authorities have been concerned to prevent from being turned against themselves. This they have attempted to do by extensive propaganda, by radio, press, films, posters, and demonstrations. Special mention should here be made of the societies for cultural relations with the U.S.S.R., which are active in all four countries.

This propaganda extols the superiority of the Red Army man over the soldiers of all other armies in discipline and kindness. But the peasants and workers of Roumania, Hungary, and Bulgaria (though not of Yugoslavia) have seen the Red Army man with their own eyes and think differently. As they have not seen devastated Russia and do not know the personal and social background of the Russian soldier, they make no allowances. They are merely infuriated by propaganda which their own experience belies. The propaganda emphasizes the unparalleled generosity of the U.S.S.R. in demanding as reparations only a small part of the cost of the damage inflicted by the invading armies. But the Danubians know that reparations deliveries are priced in dollars at the 1938 level, which means that the sum required is almost double what it seems on paper. The propaganda stresses Soviet 'economic help'. But the Danubians know that the quantity of Russian goods which enters

The Danube States in 1946

their countries is negligible in comparison with that which leaves it for the U.S.S.R., and is heavily paid for.

The argument about "economic help" is worth emphasis, for it is widely used in both allied and enemy countries. Every bale of raw cotton which crosses the Danubian frontier from the U.S.S.R. is officially described as 'help', and the public is given the impression that it is a gift. Actually it is paid for at unfavourable prices. The development of trade between the Danubian countries and the U.S.S.R. is most desirable in the interests of both, but commercial deals are not acts of philanthropy. To represent them as such is not only dishonest but foolish, for too many people know the truth.

Propaganda has harmed the Soviet cause. The understandable severity of a victor whose own land has suffered now appears to the Danubians the studied cruelty of a hypocritical and malevolent exploiter, determined to reduce them to utter destitution and slavery. Every Russian action seems a crime, every word a lie. At the end of the war the Danubian peasants and workers saw in the Russians their liberators. A large part of the intelligentsia (a decisive element in these countries) was strongly pro-Soviet. Many had lost their old love for the West, which had patronized the corrupt and oppressive ruling classes, had made the Munich pact, and – as seen from the Danube – had played so small a part in the victory over Hitler. These men looked instead to Russia, whose people and history resembled their own, and whose leaders stood for social justice and had freed Europe from the German monster.

There was immense goodwill towards Russia, and her enemies kept silent. Within a year, by the bad discipline of their troops, by their economic pressure, by their tactless intervention in internal politics, and by their crude and unconvincing propaganda, the Russians destroyed this goodwill.

Soviet propaganda continues to speak of the devotion to the U.S.S.R. of the 'broad popular masses' and the 'best sons and daughters of the people', but neither the rulers in the Kremlin nor the soldiers on the Danube are deceived. They know they are hated and bitterly resent it. They consider themselves generous liberators, and cannot understand the ingratitude of the liberated. Puzzled and unhappy, they seek an explanation. And the only answer can be the secret activity of 'reactionary cliques', supported by the 'Western imperialists'. It is the sinister policy of 'certain foreign Powers' that is to blame.

Having decided on this explanation, the Russians have little difficulty in proving it to themselves. The centralized Soviet system increases the effect. Once the Soviet officer or official knows that his superiors desire reports on Western imperialist intrigues and reactionary plots, he provides them with zeal. The most insignificant events are given deep meaning. Casual social contacts of Western diplomatists are part of a deep political plan. A chance remark of any irresponsible Danubian malcontent is proof of the intentions of the American Government. A political prisoner is repeatedly interrogated on his subversive contacts with the British, and if in boredom or desperation he invents some fantastic story it is accepted as serious evidence. Once the profound conviction of devilish Western scheming is created nothing can remove it.

The Russians are obsessed with the fear of being dupes. They will not be taken in by any professions of friendship by Westerners. They know better. They will, in fact, believe any story from any source provided that it is discreditable to their allies. And they cannot understand that this is a form of naïveté in reverse.

Although much has changed in the countries of south-eastern Europe since Hitler's day, one thing has remained – the attitude of official propaganda to Britain. It is a striking experience, on returning after five years, to meet so many of the same slogans which were once used by the organs of Filov, Stojadinović and Gigurtu at the bidding of their common teacher, the late Dr Josef Goebbels.

Britain is still the plutocratic and reactionary Power which exploits and oppresses Indians and Africans, which prepares wars, and which gets other nations to do all the fighting. The most violent attacks are to be found in Yugoslavia, where the main theme is the British Administration in Trieste. But the defeated enemy States do not lag far behind. Usually they quote the Soviet or Yugoslav press, but they make their own comments as well. A Roumanian paper in September published an insulting article on the Australian delegation at Paris. The Bulgarian Communist George Dimitrov has denounced British imperialism in language which would suggest to any uninformed person that Bulgaria was a victorious Power and Britain a defeated Fascist enemy.

There are undoubtedly genuine grounds for discontent with British policy. One is the apparent protection of Balkan 'war criminals'. It is true that the Yugoslav authorities use this expression

The Danube States in 1946

in a very broad sense. There are, however, certain individuals now living in territory under British control who can only be regarded as quislings. Such are the Serbian General Damjanović, who served under *Wehrmacht* command, and the Serbian Orthodox priest Djujić, who led a band of Chetniks in close collaboration first with the Italians and then with German and Ustasha forces. All Yugoslavs, whatever their political views, are amazed at the disappearance of the Croat Fascist chief Pavelić, the organizer of King Alexander's murder in 1934 and the author of the bestial massacres of Serbian and Jewish men, women, and children in 1941-2. The Yugoslavs cannot understand how the allied security services have failed to find this assassin.[1]

Another complaint is the retention in the Western zones of Germany and Austria of property removed from Danubian territory by the retreating Germans. Hungarian livestock is used by German peasants, to whom Hitlerism brought prosperity, and invaluable industrial machinery from Budapest factories is kept idle, though desperately needed at home. A third complaint is the reluctance of the British to recognize the help given by some Balkan countries in the allied war effort. The Roumanian and Bulgarian armies materially assisted the defeat of the Germans in Central Europe in 1944-5 and incurred respectively some 60,000 and 30,000 fatal casualties. Whatever the faults of the present Roumanian and Bulgarian régimes, public opinion in both countries feels that the two peoples deserve some credit.

These and other grievances are embroidered and exploited by the present régimes to work up hatred against Britain and the United States. Nevertheless, in all the Danubian countries today the Western Powers are more popular than ever before. But sympathy for the West is of various kinds. Those who know and admire Western forms of democracy are only a small minority. They include some of the finest brains among the intelligentsia, and some peasants and workers who have spent years in the United States, the British Dominions, or France. A second category are the millions who suffer from poverty or fear, to whom the phrase 'Western democracy' is merely a vague symbol of a better life. Many of these had similar emotions about France after 1918, Nazi Germany in the early thirties, and the U.S.S.R. in 1944. Now they pin their hopes on the

[1] Even in 1964 the mystery remains unexplained. Pavelić somehow escaped to the Argentine, where he died peacefully some years later.

'Anglo-Saxons', of whom they know no more than they did of the others.

A third category are those who look to the West, not from cultural affinity or political idealism, but simply because they hope that the Western Powers will expel the Russians by force from their countries and restore the old social and political system. These people can legitimately be described as 'reactionary cliques'. They make great efforts to convince the British that they are their friends, and their compatriots that they enjoy British confidence. It would be a tragic mistake if British policy were in fact based on these people. There is not much evidence that this is the case. But the present Governments are inclined to accept at their face value the boastings of the reactionaries.

Special mention should be made of the Catholic Church. It stands, of course, for the connexion with Rome and the West and fears the spread of Communism and of Russian domination. It has not only lost much property in the recent land reforms, but is threatened in its cultural and spiritual influence. Catholic schools have been closed in Yugoslavia and suffer from lack of funds in Hungary. Many of the accusations against Archbishop Stepinac of Zagreb were unconvincing, and his sentence was savage. But concern for his fate does not justify the identification of the Catholic Church with 'Western democracy'.

In Croatia and Hungary the Church has stood throughout the centuries for certain civilized values which are the common heritage of the West. But it cannot be said that it has ever favoured democracy, whether political or economic. And during the recent war, though Stepinac and Mindszenty, both men of the extreme right, did protest on several occasions against particular actions of Germans and Fascists, other priests behaved quite differently. Indignation at the reluctance of the Vatican to take disciplinary action against priests involved in Ustasha crimes is by no means confined to supporters of Marshal Tito.

Relations between the Soviet Union and the West in the Danubian Basin are only part of the greater problem of their relations throughout the world. The chief topic of conversation among Danubians is whether there will be a new war. Few desire it, even among those who have lost everything and face a future of prison, forced labour, or permanent unemployment and under-nourishment; for it would mean the final destruction of their countries. But many believe that it is inevitable.

Danubian optimists argue, like their friends in the West, that Russia needs peace for reconstruction and that she possesses within her frontiers such economic resources as will enable her by years of toil steadily to raise the standard of living of her people. She needs no territorial expansion, but wishes only to secure the main approaches to her soil from west and south.

The pessimists argue that Russia has thrown away these natural advantages by deciding to devote her resources principally to armaments and heavy industry. And the cause of the decision lies in the unshakable conviction of the Soviet leaders that peace with the non-Soviet world is impossible. Conflict has been decided long ago, by the ineluctable laws of history, and the task of Soviet statesmanship is to prepare for it and as far as possible to choose the place and time. The pessimists are not impressed by Mr Stalin's recent reassuring statements. They argue that though the Soviet rulers may indeed wish to avoid war now, it is only for the purpose of gaining time to consolidate their hold over Eastern Europe, to incorporate its natural and industrial resources in their economy, and to draw upon its 100,000,000 inhabitants for the Soviet Army of the future.

The Western traveller to the Danubian countries can only note these points of view. The questions which they raise cannot at present be answered. The obviously genuine friendliness for and interest in foreign countries shown by Soviet officials encountered on the journey prove nothing of the intentions of Soviet policy. The Danubian picture remains confused. The ruling minorities possess great constructive qualities. Unlike the pre-war régimes, they understand their countries' basic social problems. They have ambitious plans for the future and sincerely intend to carry them out. That they have so far achieved little is due mainly to economic difficulties inherited from the past, but partly also to their preoccupation with questions of power.

On the other hand, though the opposition leaders merit respect for their honesty, courage, and patriotism, they, too, have grave faults, which it would be folly to overlook. They are almost entirely negative, have no constructive social and economic programme, and are almost insanely nationalistic. From these movements a new Fascism could easily grow. The present leaders of the opposition parties are genuine democrats. There is, moreover, no evidence that any Fascist underground organization today exists. Nor is the restoration of the power of big landowners and capitalists a practical prospect.

But the rise of a new Fascism, based on the bureaucratic middle class and part of the peasantry, and inspired by anti-Semitism, clericalism, and extreme nationalism, is by no means improbable. If such a development occurs, it will be in no small measure the fault of the Communists themselves, whose unrelenting thirst for power has driven them to eliminate or discredit the non-Communist democrats, who were strong in the first months after Germany's collapse, and would have been their natural allies had they not arbitrarily decided to divide the nation into two categories – their servants and their enemies.

Czechoslovakia in 1947

THE CZECHS BETWEEN EAST AND WEST

Of all the countries in the 'Eastern zone' of Europe, Czechoslovakia alone has hitherto succeeded in maintaining friendly relations with the Western Powers as well as with the Soviet Union, and in keeping a balance in her internal affairs between political freedom and social change. Her recent decision, at the dictation of Moscow, to reject the invitation to the Paris conference[1] which she had previously accepted, raised the question whether Czechoslovak democracy can survive in a divided Europe. A brief survey of the situation created during the last year will make the issues clear. Let us consider first the Czech lands of Bohemia and Moravia, and then the rather different circumstances of Slovakia.

In the elections of May 1946, which all observers agree were fairly conducted, the Communist Party won nearly 40 per cent. of the votes in the Czech lands. It is therefore not surprising that the Communists should play a leading part in Czech politics. With very few exceptions they have behaved in a constitutional manner.

Communists are at the head of the Ministries of the Interior, Agriculture, Internal Trade, Information, and Social Welfare. The Political Police, which comes under the Interior, is largely controlled by Communists, but its powers are, both in theory and in practice, less extensive than in neighbouring countries. Certain sections of the Ministry of Defence are also to some extent 'penetrated' by Communists, but these by no means always get their way. The Education Department of the Army, though subject to political influences, is, nevertheless, not a mere organization of Communist political commissars, like the corresponding departments in the Balkan countries.

Under the vigorous direction of the Minister of Information, Mr

---

This article was first published in two parts in *The Times*, September 1947.

[1] This conference was summoned in July 1947, following General Marshall's speech and Mr Bevin's response, in order to discuss the economic needs of Europe. The Czechoslovak Government accepted the invitation to the conference on 7 July, but after pressure from the Soviet Government it declined on 10 July.

Kopecky, one of the most dynamic personalities of Czechoslovak politics, the Prague Radio has been made into a sort of pocket borough of the Communist Party. There is some uncertainty as to the respective duties of the Ministries of Information and Education. Schools and universities come under Education, but youth organizations come under Information. After the liberation an organization called the Union of Czechoslovak Youth (S.C.M.) was set up, in which the Communists had from the beginning a dominant position. During the course of the following year the non-Marxist parties set up youth organizations of their own, but S.C.M retains its title and enjoys a privileged position which is a source of much controversy.

One of the most striking features of the 1946 election was the large number of votes won by the Communists in rural areas. The pre-war Agrarian Party had been banned because of the 'collaboration' of its leaders. To many peasants it seemed that the Communists, backed by the powerful Soviet Union, were the 'coming party'. They therefore voted for them, not from compulsion but from 'peasant slyness', or in the hopes of protecting themselves from the accusation of 'collaboration'. But probably the largest category of Communist supporters among the peasants were those who had received German property in the border regions. Many former landless labourers or dwarf holders now own well built and furnished German farms with fine cattle, pigs, and equipment. The distribution of this property was controlled by the Communist Minister of Agriculture, Mr Dyurish, and his able Communist assistant, Engineer Kotyatko.

The gratitude of the new owners to the Communists has been less than expected. Once possessed of land they quickly shed the revolutionary enthusiasm they had shown as labourers. A further sobering factor was the discovery that the repayments due from them to the State would be a serious burden for a long period of years. Now the Communists wish to carry out a further reform, to redistribute land in the purely Czech areas. This is naturally opposed by the more prosperous peasants. The policy of Mr Dyurish has recently been strongly attacked in the Agricultural Committee of Parliament, and there have been hostile meetings of peasants in the countryside, which the Communists attribute to the influence of former members of the banned Agrarian Party.

The expulsion of 3,000,000 Germans, now almost complete, was a vast enterprise which has utterly transformed Bohemia. Through their control of the Ministries of Interior and Agriculture, the Communists created for themselves in the border regions a party State within the State. Inevitably the former German inhabitants suffered hardship, but Czech public opinion considered that this was well merited. Greater misgivings were caused by violence and injustice committed in these areas by Czechs against Czechs. These were discovered and denounced with great courage by the Czech press. It would of course be wrong to attribute all abuses to the Communists. If Communist misdeeds have attracted more attention than those of members of other parties, this is mainly due to a popular reaction against the sanctimonious complacency, common to the Communist parties of all countries, with which they arrogate to themselves a monopoly of the civic virtues.

In 1945, when Czechoslovakia was full of the liberating Red Army forces, the Czech Communists could have seized complete power, and chose not to do so. The responsibility for this choice lay with Gottwald, the party leader and present Premier, a trained Communist of many years' experience, and a good Czech patriot,[1] whose policy is to achieve his party's aims in a manner acceptable to the Czech people. The Czech Social Democrats collaborate closely with the Communists, but maintain an independent organization. There is some evidence that opinion in the factories is swinging away from the Communists towards the Socialists. Relations between the two workers' parties are not so good at the lower levels as at the top. In some provincial cities, where Communists won a relative but not an absolute majority of votes, it has happened that Socialists joined with representatives of the other parties to elect a non-Communist as mayor. Even in the national Parliament Socialists have voted against Communists.

The National Socialist Party draws its main support from the professional class and small officials, but also has a following among industrial workers and peasants. It somewhat resembles the old French Radical Party. It stands for political democracy, with a smattering of socialism, is somewhat anti-clerical (though less than before 1938) and strongly nationalist. The vagueness of its

[1] It was widely believed among non-Communist Czechs at this time that Gottwald, a man of personal amiability, was 'more Czech than Communist'. In 1948 this proved to be untrue. Gottwald was a ruthless leader who played the *faux bonhomme*. Whether he was a 'patriot' is of course a matter of opinion. He himself would doubtless have argued sincerely that Czech patriotism required agreement with the Soviet Union in all matters.

programme is largely compensated by the high quality of its leadership. It is the second strongest party in the Czech lands.

The People's Party is not specifically confessional, but is mainly supported by the Catholic peasantry and intelligentsia, and is stronger in Moravia than in Bohemia. It has benefited from the fine record of priests during the German occupation, which has freed the Catholic Church from the stigma of being 'Austrophile' and 'anti-national' from which it suffered in 1918. The party now stands for a progressive social policy, similar to that of the M.R.P. in France. Its leadership is less impressive than that of the National Socialist Party, but it has an able team of younger men who are already making their mark.

The four parties have hitherto co-operated satisfactorily within the Government, though none has sacrificed its own point of view and all have criticised each other frankly in Parliament and press. All four accepted the nationalization policy. It is no doubt true that there is a section of Czech opinion which lies to the right of any of the parties, and thus has no political representation. But this is not a very large or important section. Abuses have not been completely eliminated, and there are still people in prison who have not had a trial. But great progress has been made towards stability since 1945.

A factor not easily estimable but of immense importance has been the influence of President Beneš. His prestige and popularity among the Czech people are enormous. No living European statesman, except Mr Stalin, has so many years' experience of leadership in domestic and international politics. A devoted pupil of the late President Masaryk, he has always maintained that neither political nor social democracy can exist without the other. Almost unique among pre-war leaders in his appreciation of the strength of the Soviet Union, he has never failed to stress his country's cultural links with the West. He has always preferred cautious to sensational methods, but events have usually proved him wiser than his impatient critics.

Will all this now change? The Government's decision not to go to Paris appears to have created widespread dismay in Prague. The great majority of Czechs desire the alliance and friendship of Russia, but all except the Communists are against breaking their old ties with the West. The non-Communists together have a majority in Parliament. But if they were to use their majority, the Communists could use the trade unions, which they control, to create economic collapse or civil war. The country is almost completely surrounded by Soviet troops. Events in Hungary have shown that even to think of out-voting the Communists in Parliament at a future date is defined in Moscow as 'a treasonable plot against democracy'. If on the other hand the non-Communists, in order to preserve the present degree of political freedom, continue a 'co-operation' with the Communists which every day becomes more one-sided, they risk becoming identified by their friends in the West with a specifically anti-Western policy. Then the time will come when the Communists, no longer deriving any advantage from their 'co-operation,' will summarily eject them and set up a one-party system.

The Czech leaders have shown in the past much courage, patience, and wisdom, and the Czech nation is justly famed for its political intelligence. All are well aware of the dangers, and will try their best to avoid them. Whether they will succeed neither they nor their friends in other countries can now foresee.

NATIONALISM IN SLOVAKIA

Slovakia, which from 1939 to 1945 under the semi-fascist régime of Monsignor Tiso was formally an 'independent republic' and in fact a vassal of Nazi Germany, is once more united with the Czech lands. This was decided in 1944 by the exiled Government of President Beneš and the leaders of the Slovak anti-German rising of that year. The Czech statesmen recognized the separate nationhood of the Slovaks, who were to be represented by a provisional Parliament known as the 'Slovak National Council' (S.N.R.), with executive departments headed by 'Trustees'.

Since the summer of 1945 these organs have in fact ruled Slovakia. Unfortunately, however, their formal status has not yet been exactly decided, and this is the main factor delaying the new constitution of the Czechoslovak Republic. To all Slovaks the S.N.R. and its Cabinet of 'Trustees' are more than a mere provincial Government. The Czech and Slovak Communists, with the example of the U.S.S.R. in mind, would like to give Slovakia approximately the status of a Constituent Republic of the Soviet Federation. If there is no demand on the Czech side for a separate Czech Constituent Republic to correspond to the Slovak, then, they say, there should only be two authorities in the country – a Central Government in Prague for the whole State and an autonomous Government in Bratislava for Slovakia only.

This view is opposed by the Czech non-Marxist parties, and especially by the National Socialists, on the grounds that it would be 'dualism', a word which has unfortunate associations in view of the experience of Austria-Hungary from 1867 to 1918. They propose instead three 'Land Governments' for the historical 'lands' of Bohemia, Moravia, and Slovakia. The Communists reply that this would create an unnecessary bureaucracy and would correspond to no real need, as Moravians are in no way nationally distinct from Bohemians, whereas Slovaks differ from both. In order to meet the admitted desire for fuller self-government in the Czech lands the Communists propose the creation of a new unit, the 'province', intermediate in size between the traditional 'land' and the 'county'. This they claim would be more suited to real economic and administrative needs.

The controversy is complicated and obscure, and none of the three groups – Czech nationalists, Slovak nationalists and Communists – is entirely sincere with each other. The Communists strongly urge full recognition of Slovak demands, but in practice support centralization. In this they are influenced partly by Soviet practice (which combines regional cultural autonomy with rigid political centralization), and partly by Slovak internal political development. During 1945 the Communists were firmly in the saddle in Slovakia, but the elections of May 1946, gave them only half as many votes as the conservative Democratic Party. There have been no elections to the People's committees (the organs of local government in county, town, and village), but these were filled by nominees of the parties in 1945 and then reshuffled in accordance with the results of the Parliamentary elections in each constituency a year later.

The present position is that the Democrats hold the majority of the posts, but the Communist Party is strongly represented in the Prague Government owing to its success in the Czech areas. Much confusion is caused by the fact that in certain cases the 'Trustee' at the head of a Department in Bratislava belongs to a different party from the corresponding Minister in Prague. For instance, Information is represented by a Communist in Prague and a Democrat in Bratislava, while Education has a National Socialist in Prague and a Communist in Bratislava.

The Education Department is one of the most important in Slovakia. Catholic influence has always been very strong in the schools, and this is certainly one of the chief reasons for the lack of success of the left among the Slovak peasants. The Communist 'Trustee,' the poet Novomesky (who was one of the three delegates sent to London in 1944 by the leaders of the rising), has the task of changing as rapidly as possible the spirit of Slovak education. He is helped by the fact that the war-time Tiso Government, itself strongly Catholic, brought all the schools under State control. But now that a Communist is in charge the Church is distrustful of Novomesky's plans for 'democratizing the schools'.

There is little evidence to show that the Communist minority rules Slovakia, that Catholics are persecuted, or that the Slovaks are exploited by the Czechs. But the fear of all three is undoubtedly widespread. Non-Communists can express their views without danger, but hesitate to do so, lest it be held against them in the event of a change of government or of a new war which is a universal bogy throughout Eastern Europe. In general, the non-Communists are far less willing to take risks in Slovakia than in the Czech lands, though their position is stronger. The Catholic Church also fears the future. There have always been two political tendencies within its ranks of which approximate foreign parallels would be the Fascism of Dollfuss and the progressive democratic movement of the M.R.P. in France. The first dominated under Tiso, and still undoubtedly has a large following, though the second is making progress. The existing political parties do not fully represent Catholic opinion. The Democratic Party leadership contains Catholics, but most of its leaders are Protestants (who form some 20 per cent. of the population). The Freedom Party, created shortly before the elections of 1946, has a more definitely Catholic character. It appears to be gaining ground at the expense of the Democrats, and on the whole stands for a more conservative policy.

The three problems of Communism, Catholicism, and Czech-Slovak relations were all raised by the recent trial and execution of the quisling ex-President Tiso. Formally Tiso committed treason, for he played an important part in the disruption of the Republic in 1938. Moreover, as head of the 'independent' Slovak State he could not disclaim responsibility for political persecution and atrocities committed by the authorities subordinate to him. In particular, when in 1944 the Slovak Army rose against the Germans, Tiso urged the people to help the Germans to suppress the rising, and in fact Slovak Fascist armed formations (the so-called 'Hlinka

Guard') obeyed these orders. So Tiso was as guilty as several quislings from other countries who have suffered death.

But it was not a question only of justice. Tiso remained popular in Slovakia. The period of 'independence' had been one of economic prosperity. Many argued that no other course was open to Tiso in March 1939, because the only alternative then was the partition of Slovakia between Germany and Hungary. As for his action in 1938, that was not treason because Tiso owed allegiance not to the Czechoslovak Republic but to the Slovak nation. Every sort of excuse was made for Tiso. He was put in a quite different category from the other quislings. So strong was popular feeling that many Slovaks who had every reason to hate him argued that he should be spared on grounds of political expediency.

Nevertheless Tiso was executed. Both the Czech and the Slovak Communist parties insisted that the man who committed the sacrilege of sending troops against the Soviet Union must die. Among the Czechs the National Socialists felt that he must be punished as a traitor to the State, and the Social Democrats as usual followed the Communist lead. President Beneš acted constitutionally in rejecting, on the advice of his Cabinet in Prague, the appeal for clemency which was supported by the Slovak Democratic Party. This party in many ways resembles the Small Farmers' Party in Hungary. Its ranks include the same mixture of peasants and businessmen, bureaucrats and school teachers, Catholics and Protestants, reformers and reactionaries. It would probably not be hard to 'implicate' some of its leaders in indiscretions which could be represented as a 'conspiracy'. The fierceness of recent Communist attacks against the Democrats has caused fears that some such manœuvre is being prepared. The destruction of the Democratic Party in Slovakia might well be the thin end of the wedge for the liquidation of the Parliamentary régime in Czechoslovakia as a whole. Even now the smouldering national quarrel is a source of great weakness as it enables the Communists to divide the 'non-Marxists' against each other.

Wise men in both Prague and Bratislava understand this. They know that there can be no 'independent Slovakia' today, that if Slovakia were separated now from the Republic it could only be in order to become a member of the Soviet Union, and that that is the last thing which Slovak nationalists and Catholics desire. Such men have high hopes of the industrialization of Slovaks under the Two

Year Plan, which will in time provide jobs for the poverty-stricken peasants of over-populated mountain villages. If only international peace can be assured, and meanwhile practical economic results be achieved, then they believe it will be possible to win the Slovaks definitely for the Czechoslovak Republic. But the followers of the late Tiso rejoice in each further development of the tension between the West and Russia, for they hope that a new war will restore a Slovak State which they will control.[1]

[1] The fears expressed above for the future of democracy in Czechoslovakia were unfortunately soon confirmed by events. The Communists in fact made a determined political onslaught on the Slovak Democrats in the autumn of 1947. This was not successful, but it proved but a dress rehearsal for the main Communist attack, which came in February 1948, and resulted in the destruction of multi-party government and its replacement by Communist dictatorship of the type already established in the rest of Eastern Europe.

Greece in 1948

Greece has always been a poor country, and no other except Yugoslavia suffered so much from the ravages of guerrilla action and enemy reprisals. Now, three years after the armistice, civil war is raging and fear paralyses the whole economy.

Greece's troubles are due partly to certain basic structural weaknesses, partly to mistakes made by her politicians and their Western advisers, but mainly to the international balance of power, which the Greeks can but slightly affect by their own actions.

The visitor to Greece is at once struck by the paradox that though plenty of goods are being imported prices remain high and stocks unsold. One reason is the insecurity of communications outside Athens. Another is that, having no confidence in the currency, the merchants hoard, preferring to sell a little at large profit and keep the rest in reserve. Perhaps the greatest scandal of post-war Greece – which Government supporters as well as critics admit – is the power of the big importing merchants, who are closely linked with some of the industrialists.

There was a time when these men, through their good connexions with the banks, obtained credits and used them not to import raw materials for industry but to buy gold, which they then sat on. It is true that gold is not held only by rich men. In the general distrust of the drachma, even poor people use spare cash to buy a few gold sovereigns as a reserve. But the action of the big gold buyers was different in kind. They have used their power unscrupulously for their own profit, and have ruined Ministers who have tried to check them. Today credits cannot be so easily obtained, and stocks of goods rather than gold are hoarded.

The main points of the policy which the American advisers are recommending to the Greek Government are increase in revenue, stability of wages, and restriction of credit.

Three-quarters or more of Greek taxation receipts come from indirect taxes. This unjust system is maintained not simply because

---

This article was first published in the *Manchester Guardian*, 23 October 1948.

the rich are powerful but because the machinery to change it does not exist. In practice only visible property is heavily taxed. A moratorium on rents has the effect that house-owners get something like pre-war incomes while prices have immensely increased. This measure is of undoubted benefit to the poor, but it is paid for only by an arbitrarily chosen section of the pre-1940 rich, many of whom now suffer real hardship. Taxes on business are theoretically heavy, but in practice they are largely evaded. The widespread belief that many big businessmen keep two sets of books is confirmed by experts, Greek and foreign. A great deal of wealth is not kept in bank deposits at all, and the fiscal machine is not capable of finding hoards of gold. And underpaid tax-collectors can often be persuaded not to try too hard.

In these circumstances the only way to increase revenue in the short term is to concentrate on indirect taxes, which can be collected. The American advisers are conscious of the social implications, but at present see no alternative. Meanwhile they are pressing for reforms in methods of business accounting and in the organization of the fiscal machine, which they hope within a few years will make possible the introduction of a just system of direct taxes. Until then, reform legislation would, they believe, be empty demagogy.

The maintenance of wages at their present level means hardship for many workers. The American economic experts are well aware of this, but are convinced that, as in the past, an increase of wages would only be followed by a rise in prices and would not benefit workers. They believe that when it is made clear that in spite of all pressure there is to be no concession on the wages front, recent speculative price increases will be removed to the advantage of all.

Various changes have been made in credit policy. Rates of interest must not exceed 12 per cent., whereas until recently they were as high as 35 to 40 per cent. The commercial banks have been compelled to keep considerable deposits at the Bank of Greece, which has caused them to call in loans. As a result of the credit shortage hoarders have been obliged to sell gold for drachmas. The price of gold has appreciably fallen. It is hoped that this tendency will continue and bring prices down.

Greece's balance of payments is still in a precarious state. The general lack of confidence has caused a reduction in remittances from Greeks abroad, and most of the war-time earnings of Greek ship-owners – including insurance payments for losses – have not returned to Greece. These two items formed a large part of the pre-war balance. The largest single export before 1941 was tobacco, half of which was taken by Germany and Central Europe. Attempts to recover the German market have not been successful. One reason is that Germany has little at present to offer Greece. Another is that the Western zones are smoking American tobacco. This fact is a cause of great embarrassment to the Americans in Greece and a powerful propaganda weapon for the Communists. Reduction of the area under tobacco is no solution, as there is no other crop suitable which would pay as well.

The immediate aim is to bring Greece back to the 1938 level. But if that is achieved the task will only have begun. For Greece was in 1938 a poor country, suffering from the universal plague of Southern and Eastern Europe, agricultural over-population, intensified by the influx of refugees from Asia Minor in the nineteen-twenties, which the Greek economy never really absorbed between the wars. More than any Balkan country, Greece needs economic planning. The E.C.A.[1] programme includes important projects for the development of water power. This is indeed the best hope for the industrialization of Greece. Processing of farm produce, more intensive extraction of minerals, and light industry based especially on aluminium do offer fair prospects if electric power is made available.

Many years will pass before much can be realized, and it will depend not only on American aid but on Greek ability. Greek planners can be found. Some of the younger experts both in and outside Government offices are at least as able as the corresponding people in the Soviet-dominated 'planned economies' to the north. But they are faced with formidable obstacles – the incompetence of the bureaucracy, the indifference of the elder politicians to all except party intrigues, and, of course, above all else the disastrous civil war.

Poverty and injustice are the result partly of the war and partly of the more distant past, and it is mere demagogy to argue that they can quickly be put right. Nevertheless, if the Greek people are asked to bear terrible sacrifices and to do without improvements for the immediate future they may at least expect to be told what is being planned for their welfare when the civil war is over, and they may reasonably require that leadership should be in the hands of people

[1] Economic Cooperation Administration, the American organization set up under the Marshall Plan.

who can be trusted to carry out such plans as soon as possible. Unfortunately it is doubtful whether either of these two conditions at present exist.

The present Government of Greece is based on the Parliament elected in the spring of 1946. Observers from the three Western Great Powers pronounced these elections free and fair. People's Party (or Populists) won an overwhelming majority, and would probably do so again if there were new elections. Towards the end of 1947, on American advice, the Government was broadened to form a coalition, including the second party in the country, the Liberals, whose ninety-year-old leader, Mr Sophoulis, became Prime Minister.

Neither Populists nor Liberals bear much resemblance to parties in Britain. Their traditional dispute – Monarchy versus Republic – is stale, and neither has a modern programme. The Populists have always been strongest in the Peloponnese, and the Liberals in the north and especially among refugees from Asia Minor. Both parties largely depend on personal and regional influences. This is especially true of the Populists, who are rather a loose collection of undisciplined individualists than a party. An example of lack of discipline is the leaders of the official trade unions, Mr Makris and Mr Patsantsis, both members of the party, who abused each other in public in the most extravagant language without anyone thinking this a matter of concern to the party.

At present the Populist have the lion's share of the power. They are of course entitled to it as victors in the elections. On the other hand the Liberals argue that if the Government is to be a coalition they must have a share of real power, not just be a window-dressing to give democratic respectability to a Populist Government. In fact, a struggle for position goes on within the Cabinet and the Administration. Ministers fill their departments as far as possible with members of their own party, and efficiency suffers. An example is the division of power between the Ministries of Interior and Public Order. The former, held by the extreme Right-wing Populist Mavromichalis, appoints the 'nomarchs', whose powers correspond to those of French prefects. The latter, held by the Liberal Rendis, is responsible for the police in Athens and the gendarmerie outside.

Civil liberties in Greece cannot be judged by British standards. The Communists have declared war on the Greek State, and cannot therefore expect the same treatment as other citizens. Certain democratic liberties do exist. The press criticizes the Government, sometimes in violent terms, both from the extreme Right and from the Left centre. Small opposition parties, such as those of Papandreou and Canellopoulos, can meet and organize. The regular law courts maintain high standards. Offences involving help to the rebels are, however, dealt with by courts martial. It is difficult to see how this could be avoided in a state of civil war, but the powers of courts martial may be, and in practice perhaps are, in some cases abused.

The weakness of Greece's political system has always been its bureaucracy. Officials are underpaid and can only support their families by increasing their pay from irregular sources. The great increase in the cost of living since the war has made this traditional problem more acute perhaps then ever in Greece's history. A second evil is over-centralization. Even minor decisions are referred to Athens. Ministers' ante-chambers are crowded with people of all classes and from all parts of the country asking for help in matters which should have been decided weeks before in their own village. The Government has adopted on American advice a scheme of administrative decentralization which, if really carried out, will be a useful reform.

Since 1945 a British Mission has been helping the Greek Government to create a non-political gendarmerie. Unfortunately, as its leaders are well aware, a 'non-political Greek' is at the best of times a rare creature, and the last three years have not been good times. A special training college prepares young recruits who are considered to have attained a high professional standard. The senior officers are the survivors of the Right-wing fringes of the 30's, and some also served under Axis occupation. To instil a 'new spirit' into them is no simple task. From the beginning the gendarmes have been the first target of the rebels. In the eyes of the Communists the Greek soldier is a misguided conscript, but the gendarme is a Fascist volunteer, a member of the Western imperialists' Gestapo, to be exterminated. It is understandable that the gendarmes, never likely to be sympathetic to the Communists, should have a special hatred for them after the casualties they have suffered. Inevitably they have been more lenient to Right-wing bandits than to the Communists.

Unfortunately very few Greek gendarmes or police officials have a clear idea of what a Communist is. They are flooded with denunciations. How are they to distinguish the real subversive agent from the victim of personal spite or of irresponsible busybodies? Knowledge of Communist mentality, methods and doctrine are needed. But a Greek police official who tried to study these things would soon find himself denounced as a 'Communist'. Meanwhile, indiscriminate arrests and long detention of suspects only serve to increase the volume of discontent and to swell the ranks of Markos.[1] Ministers and senior officials realize this, but have not yet found a way to stop it.

Criticism of the Government comes from two main directions. Some clamour for 'strong government', which might mean dictatorship, civil or military. They put their hopes in the bitter mood which is reported to prevail among the fighting soldiers, who complain of the intrigues and luxury of Athens and talk of 'cleaning it up' when they come home. Others demand a more radical Government, which should attempt by social and administrative reforms to win over from the rebels all who are not 100 per cent. Communists. They argue that the present régime is 'the iron curtain in reverse', that, as in Bulgaria of the Fatherland Front, a police guarantee of 'political reliability' is necessary for employment, and that the people are being progressively alienated and demoralized.

No better Government could be obtained with the present Parliament. Critics argue that it is no longer representative, that new elections should be held, or else a non-Parliamentary Government of 'better men' be formed. 'First the British, then the Americans, have been in charge of Greece,' they say. 'They have got to find a better team.' But in order that the Americans should advise the King to dissolve Parliament they must be convinced either that new elections are possible and would give a different result, or that the present situation is quite insufferable and that a group of men is available who not only better understand the

[1] Markos Vafiades was chief political commissar of E.L.A.S. (the Communist-led resistance movement) in Macedonia under the occupation, and became the military leader of the Communist rebellion in 1946. In December 1947 the rebels announced the formation of a 'democratic Greek Government' in 'the free mountains of Greece'. Markos was its Premier and Minister of War. In February 1949 Markos was removed from this post, presumably on the grounds that he had been closely connected with the Yugoslavs (who until Tito's excommunication were the chief suppliers of the Greek Communist forces).

country's needs but are capable of putting their policy into practice. So far they do not seem convinced of either. Moreover, they find it difficult to distinguish among the critics those who urge 'democratization' in order to strengthen popular resistance to Communism from the 'fellow-travellers' whose aim is a 'Kerensky régime' to prepare seizure of power by the Communists. Thus, for lack of a clear alternative, it is likely that the present régime will continue. It must be admitted that this prospect plunges in despair some of the ablest and most patriotic men in Greece.

When in 1946 the Greek Communists for the second time took to the hills, whether this was arbitrarily ordered from the Kremlin or was a measure of defence against persecution by right-wing bands, or was the result of both, they set themselves to reduce Greece to chaos. No honest observer can doubt that they have been remarkably successful.

Outside the cities of Athens and Salonika, Attica and the Corinthian isthmus, there is no real security on the mainland of Greece. The rebels are, of course, strongest in the north. After a long battle they were forced to abandon the Grammos mountain fastness, but most of their forces slipped into Albania, and the Vitsi massif farther east is the scene of a new battle. They are strong in Thrace, assisted by the Bulgarians. At the end of September rebels entered the town of Larissa, in the Thessalian plain. There are groups in various mountains of Central Greece. The rebel forces in the Peloponnese have notably increased during the summer, profiting no doubt from the fact that the main Greek forces were concentrated against Grammos. Railway tracks and roads are frequently mined, including side roads never used by the Army but only by peasant carts. Villages are attacked, houses burned, and men killed or removed. Terror and demoralization are the aim.

The cadres of Markos's army are trained Communists – the officers and political commissars. These seldom let themselves be taken alive. The majority of the rebel prisoners taken by the Greek Army declare that they were forced against their will into the rebel forces. Obviously every prisoner has an interest in making his captors believe this. But there is no doubt that the rebels have conscripted large numbers both to fight and to labour. They have also removed children to the countries under Soviet influence. Some of these were no doubt voluntarily sent by Communist parents, and some of the parents who bewail their loss to the Greek authorities may either be repenting of an action performed voluntarily or be hiding their feelings for their own protection. But there is no doubt that considerable numbers of children have been removed against their parents' will.

The peasants in rebel-infested areas are indeed to be pitied. Whatever they do, they can expect only trouble. If they refuse help to the rebels the rebels will shoot them; if they help the rebels the Government forces will punish them. Centuries of Turkish rule and native despotism have taught all Balkan peasants to conceal their feelings, nowhere perhaps so much as in Macedonia. It is thus difficult to know what the people think. But without doubt the Government forces are less ruthless than the rebels. One result may be that those who stay in their villages obey the rebels as they fear them more. But another result has been the flight of enormous numbers of refugees to the cities. In Macedonia and Thrace there are nearly 350,000 of these and in the rest of Greece over 200,000. Most have lost their homes, many have lost relatives. Among them are families which were driven from Asia Minor in the twenties by the Turks, from their new homes in 1941 by the Bulgarians, and are now in flight for the third time within a generation. To house and feed them is a heavy burden on the authorities, and in spite of heroic efforts it is only possible to give them the barest necessities. They are now being urged to return to areas cleared by the Army, but there is little response. Until it is clear that the rebels will not come back yet again the refugees have no confidence.

It is hard to say how much support the Communists enjoy outside the fighting areas. Villagers who go out at night to mine roads in rebel-free areas do so from conviction. Among the workers of Piraeus, Salonika, and Kavalla there must be some sympathizers. Communists were once strong in the trade unions, and their influence will not have been destroyed by administrative purges of leaders. The present unions have the benefit of British and American expert advice, but they cannot be considered representative. Their leaders do not inspire unlimited confidence and have been able to do little for the workers owing to the economic conditions described earlier. Still, there has been little sign of Communist activity in the towns, and the Markos radio recently 'dissolved' the illegal Communist leadership in the Athens area for its failure to organize recruits and supplies for the 'Democratic Army'.

University graduates and village schoolmasters have played a part in the Greek Communist movement. Among these are not only 'white-collar unemployed' with personal grievances but also men of real education, concerned for their country's future and seeing no way out of the economic swamp save by revolution. They may not be numerous, but it would be foolish to underestimate their intellectual ability, sincerity, or courage. In general the majority of the Greek people are against Communism, as much for nationalist as for ideological reasons, but the Communist minority is not 'insignificant' either in quantity or in quality.

The aid given to rebels by the northern neighbours has been abundantly proved by the United Nations committee (U.N.S.C.-O.B.), with its able teams of observers from six countries. Arms and food are sent, and defeated rebel bands cross the frontiers to rest and re-equip. Even in the distant Peloponnese arms have been landed by ship and dropped from the air. A specially provocative form of assistance is to place rebel artillery a few feet inside the Greek frontier, so that the Greek Army cannot return the fire without its shells falling on the other side. The rarity of incidents is due to the extreme restraint of the Greek command. If the Greek generals were the bloodthirsty monarcho-fascist monsters depicted by Communist propaganda they would long ago have responded to the aggression from the north in the same spirit. The only recent incident was in mid-September, when a Yugoslav battalion marched into Greek territory and was driven back in disorder by a Greek company.

Even with much better leadership, economic, social, and political reforms would still be a labour of Sisyphus as long as civil war continues. And though during the last year the Greek Army has greatly improved, the task is too great for it. Even if its numbers were doubled, with equipment at least up to its present standard, it is doubtful whether it could seal off a frontier 500 miles long, nearly all consisting of rugged mountains. The majority of the Greek people, though determined not to yield to Soviet-supported Communism, passionately long for an end to war, which in various forms has already lasted eight years. Economic and military help from the West has not been enough. Some Greeks believe that a more courageous policy of reform would, by winning away many of Markos's followers, bring peace nearer. But all non-Communists are agreed on one thing – that the chief cause of Greece's troubles is international. Cannot something be done, they ask, to reduce the danger from the north?

Ever since the collapse of the Ottoman Empire in Europe one of the vital factors in Greece's foreign policy has been her relations with her Balkan neighbours – Albania, Bulgaria, and Yugoslavia.

It is customary to think of Greece as a purely peninsular country, a small maritime State whose interests are bound only to the Mediterranean Powers. But this is only half the truth. Since 1913 Greece has been also a continental State. The Greek nation includes not only the olive-growers of the Peloponnese, the merchants of Athens, and the sea-farers of the island but also the tobacco-growers of Thrace and the farmers of Macedonia. The second city of Greece lies near the mouth of the Vardar, the natural outlet from Central Europe to the Aegean.

These simple geographical facts have not yet been thoroughly understood by the educated class of Greece. Before the war many Greeks had business and personal contacts with France, Britain, Germany, and the United States, but very few troubled to know the peoples with whose countries there was a direct land frontier: they were barbarians 'not worth knowing'. For their part, the educated classes of the north Balkan countries, who also overvalued their contacts with Paris, Berlin, London, or Rome, looked on the Greeks, with equal stupidity, as 'corrupt unwarlike degenerates'.

To most Greeks the Albanians are not a nation at all but a miscellany of plundering tribes whose leaders owe what little culture they possess to Greece. Southern Albania is 'Northern Epirus' and should be a Greek province. The Bulgars are the 'eternal enemy'. It is forgotten that Greece made an alliance with them in 1912 against Turkey. To suggest that Bulgaria has been and can be a danger to Greece only when she is used by Germany or Russia is almost blasphemy. Still more unpopular is it to point out that the Bulgarians behaved no worse during the occupation than did the Italians, let along the Germans; or that the Bulgarian people was the chief sufferer from the dictatorship of Boris and Filov, and is now from the terror of Dimitrov.

Every Greek nationalist must call the Bulgars a race of criminals and argue (even if he does not really believe that anyone will listen to him) that Plovdiv (Philippopolis) should be in Greece. To the Serbs Greek nationalism is more indulgent. These two nations fought together in 1913, 1916, and 1941. Yet their alliance was based on little more than diplomatic convenience. There was no warm friendship or even mutual understanding. Greeks always feared Serbian ambition to control Salonika, and the recently published papers of Ciano show that they were not wrong.

Since 1941 there has been more understanding in Athens of the importance of the Balkan neighbour. There was the ill-fated Yugoslav–Greek treaty of 1942, intended by the exiled Governments as a first step towards a Balkan Federation. More recently Mr Pipinellis, Under-Secretary for Foreign Affairs and one of the most influential men in the present Greek régime, wrote before his departure to the present meeting of the United Nations a series of articles in which he claimed that Greece had always favoured Balkan Federation and remains faithful to this aim. He even maintains that ideological hostility does not necessarily preclude cooperation between States which have common interests, and he believes that there is a basic community of interest for all Balkan nations in preserving their independence of any Great Power pressing southwards from the Danube plain.

Inevitably the Tito–Cominform dispute aroused great attention in Greece. When Mr Pipinellis wrote of common interests in spite of ideological differences it seems likely that he was thinking of Yugoslavia. Certainly there is no sign of a more friendly attitude to Greece on the part of Tito. But equally certainly there are new facts in the Balkan situation of which Greece must take account.

It is a fact that there is a complete breach of political and economic relations between Yugoslavia and Albania. Albania now has no friendly neighbour and depends for all relations with the outside world on sea communications with the Soviet Union. These must pass through the Straits and round the Peloponnese, and it is doubtful whether many Soviet ships can be spared for the purpose. The second fact is that the old rivalry between Yugoslavia and Bulgaria for Macedonia has broken out again. The honeymoon period, in which both Governments recognized the right of the Macedonians to separate nationhood within the framework of a federal Yugoslavia, is over. Under cover of rival solicitude for the Macedonians outside their respective territories, 'Great Serb' and 'Great Bulgarian' petty imperialisms are reviving. Now that Moscow has dictated, for ideological reasons, a breach between Belgrade and Sofia, relations cannot remain coldly hostile but must become steadily worse. These two facts can be of real benefit to Greece, provided that the diplomacy of the Western Powers can exploit them.

The Western Powers, of course, have some experience of Tito's 'gratitude'. Considerable military supplies in war, and U.N.R.R.A. aid after victory, were repaid with insults and with the blood of American pilots shot down and a British officer murdered on the Austrian frontier. If the Western Powers helped Tito again they would doubtless require some guarantees. It seems only too likely that if Tito were to accept Western help it would only be in order to raise his own value in the eyes of the Soviets, to convince them that it was worth their while to accept his friendship on his own terms. Should the Kremlin show itself willing to do this, he would again betray the West.

Thus co-operation between the West and Yugoslavia would rest not on mutual confidence but on a mere temporary community of interest. Yet if Tito continues his present policy of hostility to the whole world, he must know that he faces disaster. It is no use to declaim, as in a recent speech, that the Yugoslav people will fulfil its Five-Year-Plan alone, unjustly boycotted by the 'People's Democracies' and yet refusing to deal with the 'imperialists'. Rhetoric will not build electric power stations. The implacable men in the Kremlin will never make peace with unrepentant heretics, and Tito does not seem disposed to a recantation which would mean political, and perhaps also physical, extinction. Therefore Tito's proud independence cannot last for ever. This the Western Governments must realize, and should prepare themselves accordingly.

If Yugoslavia could be detached from the Soviet block the Albanian problem could be solved with little international danger. The Greek Army would then have to hold only the Bulgarian frontier. This it is strong enough to do while at the same time cleaning up the rebel forces in the interior. Otherwise, enormous funds will be needed to prop up the Greek economy and to train and equip a much larger army. It may be that material aid will in any case have to be increased. But the Western Powers cannot ignore the additional method of 'political warfare' in the northern Balkans.[1]

[1] During 1949 Yugoslav aid to the Greek Communists diminished and then came to an end. As a result it was possible for the Greek Army to win the Civil War in 1950. Thereafter reconstruction and economic development in Greece went ahead fast, though it is also true that in 1964 there is still great poverty, and there are still terrible unsolved economic problems.

Three: Communism in Eastern Europe

The Hungarian Tragedy

HUNGARY, 1945-56

Hungary has had three major revolutions in her modern history – in 1848, 1918, and 1956. The Revolution of 1848 was a rising of the nation against foreign rule, in a pre-industrial age: it was a movement of landed gentry, intellectuals, and peasants. The Revolution of 1918 was a rising of the industrial working class against the old social order; but armed conflict with neighbouring nations (Roumanians, Slovaks, and Serbs) turned it into a national movement, and for a time, though its leaders were Communists, gave it the support of officers, bureaucrats, and intellectuals. In the Revolution of 1956 the social and national factors were fused: it was a rising of the workers against exploitation, of the intellectuals against thought-control, and of the whole nation against the Soviet imperialists.

The Communist régime created by Mátyás Rákosi, which was overthrown in October 1956, was the result of the occupation of Hungary by the Soviet Army in 1944-5. Soviet occupation followed defeat in the Second World War (Hungary was Hitler's last ally in the field), and the collapse of a Fascist reign of terror organized by Hitler's last disciples. To understand the Rákosi régime, one must begin by considering the cause of Hungary's involvement in the war and the nature of Hungarian Fascism.

Hungary joined the Axis in order to regain as much as possible of the territory which she had lost in 1920. The historic Kingdom of Hungary had been a multi-national State. The original Magyars came from the Eurasian steppes to Central Europe in the ninth century. They have preserved their language, which is not Indo-European; racially they became mixed with the Slavs and Roumanians who lived in the Danube Valley and the Carpathians before their arrival. St Stephen, the first Christian King of Hungary, declared: *Regnum unius linguae uniusque moris imbecille et fragile est.* Racial intolerance was not regarded as a virtue in the Middle Ages. After the Turks had conquered Hungary in 1526, and then

---

This article was first published as the introduction to *The Hungarian Revolution*, edited by Melvin J. Lasky, Secker and Warburg, 1957.

been expelled at the end of the following century, the country's ethnic composition became still more complicated. But the birth of modern nationalism in the nineteenth century affected not only the Magyars but also the Slovak, Roumanian, Croatian, and Serbian subjects of Hungary. Louis Kossuth, the revolutionary leader of the Magyars in 1848, ignored the national claims of these other peoples: consequently they supported the Habsburgs in repressing the Revolution. When Hungary obtained something approximating to 'Dominion Status' under the Compromise of 1867 with Austria, the Budapest Governments had another chance to win the loyalty of the non-Magyar peoples. Again the opportunity was missed. Slav and Roumanian nationalism became an increasingly serious danger not only to Hungary but to the whole Austro-Hungarian Monarchy. When the Monarchy was defeated in war in 1918, the nationalities broke away from Hungary and joined the new Republic of Czechoslovakia and the greatly expanded kingdoms of Roumania and Yugoslavia.

The revolutionary Government of Hungary in October 1918 tried to win the nationalities by offering the autonomy which the old régime had refused. But now the nationalities were as intransigent as the Magyar rulers had been. Their determination to secede, and to take with them large areas inhabited by Magyars, was one of the main factors which caused power to pass into the hands of the Communists in Budapest. The short-lived Hungarian Red Army was in the end overpowered by the Roumanians. The peace treaty of Trianon not only gave the nationalities independence from Hungary, but also transferred about one third of the Magyar nation (three million persons) under foreign rule. This was bitterly resented by all Magyars. It is of course true that the discontented included landowners who had been deprived of estates, and bureaucrats who had given up jobs in the lost territories. But the repudiation of Trianon was more than the revolt of privileged classes: it was the profound feeling of a whole nation. Undoubtedly, however, this national feeling benefited the old ruling class and the political Right wing. Nationalist indignation was used to divert effort from internal social reform. In foreign policy, Hungary sought any protector who would espouse her irredentist cause. The first patron to appear was Benito Mussolini; the second, Adolf Hitler. By associating herself with the Axis, Hungary recovered territory from Slovakia in 1938, Ruthenia in 1939, part of Transylvania from

Roumania in 1940, and the Bácska from Yugoslavia in 1941. The price of the last acquisition was, first to allow Hitler's troops to pass through Hungary to attack the Yugoslavs, and three months later to join Nazi Germany in war against the Soviet Union.

Association with the Axis inevitably strengthened Fascism within Hungary. It has often been asserted that Hungarian Fascism was a creation of landowners and capitalists. But this is not true. The dominant political outlook of Hungarian landowners, up to 1944, was a sort of Whiggish liberalism. They were reactionaries in social policy, but they preached and practised a large measure of personal political freedom. As for the capitalists, they were mostly Jews, and naturally disliked Fascism and Nazism.

In any case the power of the Hungarian landowners has been exaggerated. Certainly they were supreme in the countryside, both economically and politically. But the government of the country, and the determination of its policies, were largely in the hands of a bureaucratic middle class, many of whose members were children or descendants of landed gentry, but who had little connexion left with the villages. The growth of industry in the 1930's also drew Magyars – as opposed to Jews or members of the German ethnical minority – into business. Here they found themselves in competition with the older business class which was largely Jewish, and this provided a strong new motive for anti-Semitism. The Hungary of 1867–1918, whatever its faults in other fields, had shown a remarkable toleration to Jews. Certainly there were Magyars who expressed dislike of Jews on vague religious or cultural grounds, but Jewish citizens enjoyed equality before the law, in practice as well as in theory. The first anti-Jewish violence appeared in the White Terror of 1919–20, which followed the defeat of the Communist revolution. But in the 1930's economic causes revived it, and it was deliberately fostered by Fascist groups and by agents of Nazi Germany.

It was in the growing middle-class of Magyar bureaucrats, and to some extent among intellectuals and the new business element, that Hungarian Fascism had its main strength. These were the strongholds of Fascism: the odd aristocrat, or half-Jewish capitalist of Fascist sympathies was an exception. Fascism also had a certain mass base. Some Hungarian Fascists agitated for a land reform, and so won some popularity with the peasants. There were also Fascists working among miners and factory workers. The Hungarian Fascists were thus a strong force, and they had an important influence on the intellectual and moral climate of Hungarian political life from the mid-1930's onwards. But they remained in opposition until the last month of Hitler's war.

The Hungarian régime between the world wars, associated with the name of Admiral Horthy, who as Head of State took the title of Regent for a King who never returned, was certainly reactionary, and its methods were often cruel, but it was not Fascist. Even the demagogic General Gömbös, Prime Minister from 1932 to 1936, who dearly loved Fascist phrases and rhetoric, rejected anti-Semitism. Later Governments introduced half-hearted measures of economic discrimination against Jews in order to please Hitler. But these were not harshly executed. It must be admitted that the oligarchic reactionary rulers of Hungary during the Second World War preserved greater liberties for their subjects, even for Social Democrats, than the rulers of any other country in Hitler's Europe, neutral Switzerland and Sweden of course excepted. This came to an end with the direct military occupation by the German Army in March 1944. The Government which followed, a curious mixture of Germanophile generals, time-serving bureaucrats and real Fascists, dishonoured Hungary by deporting to German extermination camps about 600,000 Jews, about half of whom were from Trianon Hungary and half from the territories recovered between 1939 and 1941. It is only fair to say that Horthy tried to prevent this, and that in October 1944 he made a last, pathetically ineffective, attempt to bring his country out of the war, as King Michael had done in Roumania two months earlier. The Nazis deposed him, and installed a puppet régime under the most radical of all the Fascist leaders, Ferenc Szálassi. For a few months this man subjected Hungary to a reign of terror. But now the war was drawing to an end. In the spring of 1945, after a terribly destructive siege, Budapest was taken by the Soviet Army, and the Germans were driven out of the whole country. Szálassi's forces fled with them. Nazi executioners were replaced by the liberating Soviet Army, which soon distinguished itself by the thoroughness with which it robbed and raped the defenceless population.

In 1945 Hungary was completely at the mercy of the Soviet conquerors. Many factories were destroyed, and many of the rest were idle for lack of materials or labour. Agricultural work had been interrupted by the war, and a large part of the livestock had been slaughtered or driven westward by the retreating Germans. The

Administration had ceased to function. Many civil officials and still more Army officials had fled to German territory. There was a nominal Hungarian Government, led by General Béla Miklos, who had obeyed Horthy's order in October 1944 to surrender to the Russians. It was recognized by the Soviet, United States, and British Governments. But in fact the only real authority was the occupying Soviet Army. It could have imposed any régime that it wished.

But at this moment the Soviet leaders did not set up a Communist régime. It is true that they brought with them a number of Hungarian Communists who had been in exile in Russia, of whom the two most important were Mátyás Rákosi and Ernö Gerö. These men at once proceeded to reorganize the Communist Party, which can hardly be said to have existed in Hungary since 1919. At most it was a tiny conspiratorial sect, which in 1944 had conducted a little, brave, but ineffective underground activity against Hitler. Its main leader inside Hungary was a young man named László Rajk. This small organization was now taken over by Rákosi and his emigré team. They rapidly enlisted all the recruits they could find, mainly opportunists and careerists, with a large sprinkling of Fascists hoping to save their skins. But Moscow's official policy at this time was the 'Grand Alliance' in foreign policy and the 'Popular Front' in internal politics. It was therefore premature to hand full power to the Communist Party. Rather, it was necessary to have in Hungary a coalition of democratic parties. These had to be rebuilt, or built for the first time, and each had to have its own organization. The Soviet authorities therefore encouraged, and even practically helped, the available political leaders to set up their machinery, side by side with the Communists.

Potentially the most important was the Smallholders Party, which drew its support from the peasants, who formed slightly more than half the population of Hungary. Between the wars this party had not been very successful, because until 1939 the ballot had been open in rural constituencies, and the gendarmes had always effectively stopped political propaganda, other than that of the Government party, in the villages. The Smallholder leaders were mostly intellectuals of the middle class, their views varying from liberal conservatism to semi-socialist radicalism. During the war the peasant influence within the party had somewhat increased with the foundation of the Peasant Union, a part-economic and part-political organization headed by Ferenc Nagy.

The second party, with a smaller mass base but a longer history and better organization, was the Social Democratic Party. Founded in 1892, it had little opportunity of parliamentary influence under the restricted franchise before the First World War. In 1918 military defeat and the political collapse of the old régime swept the Social Democrats to power, but almost at once they were crippled by the split which gave birth to the Communist Party. During the Communist régime of March–August 1919 the party was reunited, but under Communist leadership. After the White Terror had given way to the respectable oligarchy of Count Bethlen (Premier, 1921–31), the Social Democratic Party, once more shorn of its Communist wing, was able to operate legally again. There was now universal suffrage, and with a secret ballot in Budapest the Socialists were able to return a few members of Parliament. The trade unions were under strong socialist influence. The Social Democrats enjoyed political freedom under the Horthy régime right up to the German occupation of March 1944. In the first post-war years four factions could be discerned in the party. The right wing, led by Károly Peyer, corresponded roughly in its views to the British Labour Party. The centre, led by Anna Kéthly and Antal Bán, might be compared with the left wing of British Labour. It was in favour of co-operation with the Communists, but believed that Social Democrats should remain a separate party. The left, which included the post-1944 head of the party, Arpád Szakasits, favoured fusion with the Communists. Finally the fourth group consisted of agents of the Communist Party or the Soviet Government, such as György Marosán, who later figured in the Kádár quisling 'Government'.

A third party, small but interesting, was the National Peasant Party. It was derived from a group of young intellectuals who in the 1930's had attracted attention by their carefully documented and moving studies of the condition of the Hungarian peasantry. Like the Russian *Narodniki* of the 1870's who had 'gone to the people', these writers had lived among the peasants and had got to know the human side of the problem as well as the statistics of land distribution or grain production. They were known as 'the village-explorers.' They were socialists and revolutionaries, but not Marxists. Later they became split, one wing became quite subservient to the Communists, while the rest simply retired from political life. In October 1956, however, most of these men reappeared as active revolutionaries, and formed the nucleus of the new 'Petöfi Party'.

Together with the creation of party organizations in 1945 went the rebuilding of a State machine. A National Council composed of representatives of the four parties served as a temporary Parliament, and there were local councils similarly composed at a lower level. At all levels the Communists had greater power than their numbers or popularity could justify, but it would be too much to say that they controlled the machinery of government. However, even at this stage they paid special attention to the newly created police force and to the Ministry of the Interior, in which they placed their men in key positions. They also did their best to arrange that those entrusted with important positions by the other parties should be persons subservient to the Communist Party, and even to push their own agents into leading positions in those parties. Here they had some success, especially with the Social Democrats. But on the whole the three other parties at this stage were genuinely independent. It was clear to all that the Soviet Army was master of the country, and no wise person dared publicly to criticise Bolshevik Russia. But it was still hoped that Hungary would be left internal freedom, and that when the peace treaty was signed the Soviet Army would retire.

One of the first acts of the coalition Government was a sweeping land reform. Though carried out in a hurry and in unfavourable economic conditions, it was welcomed by the peasants and by all persons of democratic convictions. It was indeed long overdue. The domination of the agricultural scene by a small number of landowners, with immense personal power over the peasants, was an intolerable anachronism in the twentieth-century. There had been no substantial redistribution of land in 1919, and the victory of the old ruling class over the Communists had postponed reform indefinitely. On the eve of the Second World War, less than 1 per cent. of owners of land possessed slightly less than 50 per cent. of the arable land. The agricultural population of Hungary included a rural proletariat of more than three million persons consisting of estate servants, landless agricultural labourers, dwarf holders, and tenants. Under the 1945 reform about four and a half million acres of arable land were distributed among 660,000 peasant families. The Minister of Agriculture responsible for the reform was a Communist returned from Moscow, Imre Nagy. The Communists were determined to claim for their party the credit expected from the reform. It is doubtful whether they had much success but Nagy personally did win some popularity.

The economic situation was disastrous. To the ravages of war were added plundering by the invaders, the cost of maintenance of the Soviet army of occupation, and the formal reparations claims under the peace treaty. The Soviet authorities were able to interpret the armistice clauses to their own advantage, and vast quantities of goods were removed. The result of these various factors was the worst inflation known in financial history. Money was valueless. The urban population lived from mid-1945 to mid-1946 on the verge of starvation. The reconstruction of Budapest was in effect performed by slave labour; but it was a slavery which the whole population accepted as a patriotic duty. By the summer of 1946 the factories were working again, and the harvest was fairly good. In August a new currency was introduced. For this heroic period of reconstruction, too, the Communists, and especially their economic boss Gerö, tried to take the credit. But it was the achievement not of a party but of the whole nation. And if the Communists' Soviet bosses had been less exacting, it would have been completed sooner.

In October 1945 a free parliamentary election was held, the first in Soviet-occupied Europe.[1] The Smallholders Party had an absolute majority of the votes (57 per cent.), while the Social Democrats and Communists each had 17 per cent. and the National Peasants 7 per cent. But the majority party was not allowed to form a homogeneous Government. The Soviet commander, Marshal Voroshilov, had only given his consent to an election based on free competition between the parties on condition that all agree to maintain the coalition. Moreover the Smallholders were obliged to give the key post of Minister of Interior to a Communist, first to Imre Nagy and soon afterwards to László Rajk.

Despite the presence of the Soviet Army, the sinister manœuvres of the Communists, and the economic hardships, the year 1946 was also a time of freedom and of promise. The peasants were freed of the large estates, and there was hope of a new prosperous agriculture based on the patient labour of millions of smallholders and the natural wealth of the Hungarian earth. The workers were freed of the capitalists, and hoped for a new socialist industrial society in which they would be the leading force. The intellectuals were freed of the mental strait-jacket of the oligarchic and the Fascist

[1] The only other example was in Czechoslovakia in May 1946, and in this case there was no Soviet Army in the country. The courage of the Hungarian voters in the presence of the Soviet troops was all the more impressive.

eras; they could express and develop their social and political ideas, and could hope for a new flowering of Hungarian literature and art. All who believed in friendship with the neighbouring small nations, fellow-victims with Hungary of Hitlerism, now hoped that after decades of sterile nationalism and small-state imperialism on all sides, a new era would begin. The events of 1945 could hardly be described as a revolution in the sense of 1848 or 1918, for their origin was occupation by a foreign Power rather than insurrection from within. But there was a passionate desire for a new life, a powerful explosion of new social and intellectual forces, a great promise of better things to come. No one who visited Hungary in these months could fail to note it.

Yet every one of these hopes was betrayed. Agriculture was neglected and the peasants treated as enemies. The workers were placed under a new yoke, of Communist managers more exacting than the old capitalists. Intellectual liberty lasted only a year or two, and was replaced by totalitarian dogma. The sincere desire of the Hungarians for friendship with their neighbours was spurned. None were more chauvinist than the Czechs and Slovaks, in whom for many years Hungarian democrats had placed special hopes. They looked for the spirit of the great President Thomas Masaryk, but they found that the spirit of Horthy had moved from Budapest to Prague. As for the 'liberating' Power, it was not interested in 'friendship'. Hungary was to become another Soviet colony, another Uzbekistan. In 1945 many Hungarians who were not Communists hoped that the Soviet liberators would help them make the revolution their country needed. Instead the Soviet conquerors destroyed the revolution which Hungarians had tried to make.

The Soviet and Communist offensive against the beginnings of Hungarian democracy reached its climax in 1947. The main object of attack was the Smallholders Party. Already in the previous year the Communists had forced this party to expel some of its most courageous parliamentary members. The security police manufactured a treason conspiracy to compromise the leadership. In February 1947 the party's Secretary-General, Béla Kovács, was arrested by Soviet M.V.D. troops and disappeared. The resistance of the real peasant representatives was broken, and a few fellow-travelling intellectuals were pushed into leading positions in the party by Communist pressure. The same was done to the National Peasant Party. Several prominent figures in both parties escaped abroad.

Communist propaganda made much of the argument that the Smallholders were a 'reactionary party' because former Fascists supported them. It is, of course, possible that Fascists, and perhaps still more, persons of Right-wing views, had voted for the party in 1945. It is also undoubtedly true that Fascist toughs not only voted for, but became members of, the Communist Party, and were welcomed in it. But the character of a party is determined not by its casual voters but by its whole membership and organization. The Smallholders were a thoroughly democratic party, representing the peasants who formed more than half the Hungarian nation. The Communists could not endure that such a party should possess an absolute majority of the seats in Parliament. The only element of truth in Communist assertions that the Smallholders Party was 'conspiring' is that some of its members were talking of using their parliamentary majority to end the coalition and form an homogeneous Government. In any democratic country, such action is perfectly constitutional. This is in fact what happened in the summer of 1947 in France and Italy; the Communists were expelled from the Government coalitions, which continued to rule without them, with the necessary constitutional majority. This would have happened in Hungary, too, if the Soviet Army had not been there. It is sometimes suggested in the West that the Communists in Eastern Europe showed themselves more intelligent than their democratic rivals, because they outmanoeuvred them in the coalitions: the clever Communists proved more than a match of their stupid partners. This is said especially of Rákosi in Hungary. But it is not true. Certainly Rákosi is a clever man. But his partners were not stupid, and he did not deceive them. They knew perfectly well what his aims were. They could not prevent him, because they had no power. He could rely on the Soviet Army for help. The fate of Béla Kovács was the decisive proof. Later the Communists themselves admitted this. Rákosi boasted in 1952 that he had dealt with his partners one by one, cutting them off 'like slices of salami'. Jozsef Révai, another leading Communist, stated in 1949: 'Our force was multiplied by the fact that the Soviet Union and the Soviet Army were always there to support us with their assistance.'[1]

---

[1] As Antal Bán has recorded in *The Curtain Falls* (London, 1951): 'Pushkin, then the Soviet Ambassador in Hungary, once remarked in the presence of the writer: "We have shed our blood for Hungary and we do not want to loosen our grip on her."'

The Hungarian Tragedy

In 1948 the Communists finally subdued the only other important political party, the Social Democrats. Already in 1946 the old leadership of the party had been removed by persons willing to co-operate closely with the Communists. But there were differences as to the degree of co-operation. Most of the leaders, and the great majority of the active members, insisted on keeping their party organization independent, while a minority advocated 'fusion' with the Communist Party, which in practice could only mean seizure by the Communist bosses of the whole organization of the fifty-year-old Socialist Party. The opponents of 'fusion', Antal Bán and Anna Kéthly, were defeated by the intrigues of the Communist agents within their party, supported by the terror of the Communist-controlled security police, and were expelled from it in February 1948. In June 'fusion' took place. It is interesting to note that the champions of 'fusion' lived to learn their errors. Arpád Szakasits after a brief period as President of the Republic, was arrested. Even the Soviet agent György Marosán spent some years in prison.

Hungary now had a one-party totalitarian régime. The security police had the same vast powers as in the Soviet Union. The formal structure of the Hungarian State was adapted to the Soviet model. All means of communication, from broadcasting to the schoolroom, were used for Marxist-Leninist indoctrination and the glorification of Hungary's imperial master, Joseph Stalin.

The Communist Party itself was not safe from persecution. The breach between Yugoslavia and the Soviet Union in the summer of 1948 was followed by a campaign against 'nationalist deviation' throughout Eastern Europe. In Hungary the chosen victim was Laszló Rajk. Whether Rajk had in fact especially close connexions with Tito is uncertain. It is certain that he was never in exile in Moscow, that he played some part in resistance inside Hungary in 1944, that he did not belong to Rákosi's 'Muscovite' band, and that Rákosi disliked him. At his public trial in September 1949 Rajk confessed to various quite unbelievable crimes and was hanged. Of all the East European treason trials, that of Rajk came closest to the Soviet models of 1936–8.

The execution of Rajk was accompanied by a purge in the party, and this continued for several years afterwards. The victims included numerous Communists who had had no connexion with Rajk, and several of the left-wing Social Democrats who had betrayed their party to the Communists in 1948. Among the first was the Communist János Kádár,[1] and among the second the renegade socialist György Marosán, both of whom reappeared in sinister roles in November 1956. An impression of the scope of the purge at the highest level of the party can be obtained from the turnover in membership of its Central Committee. Of 92 persons who were elected members of the Central Committee at the party congresses of 1948 and 1951, 46 had been removed by 1954. This is a turnover higher than in any other East European Communist party except that of Czechoslovakia. The purge was spread out in time, for of the 46 removals 20 took place between 1948 and 1951 and 26 between 1951 and 1954.

Communist treatment of the peasants followed the Soviet model, though at a slower pace. Hungary offers exceptionally favourable conditions for intensive small farming and peasant co-operatives. The large estates were well adapted to cereal production, but small holdings could do better with more valuable crops—fruit, vegetables, meat, and dairy produce. Processing industries could have excellent opportunities. Hungary has far better physical conditions than Denmark, and could build up an excellent export trade in both fresh and canned foodstuffs. This would have required encouragement to peasant initiative, and State aid to genuine co-operatives, to be run by the peasants themselves. But all this is incompatible with Communism. According to Stalinist dogma, peasants are enemies. The only long-term solution is to transform them into agricultural workers, and agriculture itself into a complex of large industrial enterprises, organized according to factory discipline. Until this is possible, the peasants must be held down by physical force and exploited economically. They must pay for the process of industrialization. Above all no peasant initiative must be tolerated, least of all any co-operative initiative. Collective farms, based on the model of the Soviet *kolkhoz*, which is first and foremost a political coercive institution, an instrument of party rule, must be introduced. Collectivization of agriculture was announced as an aim of policy in Hungary in July 1948. By 1952 about 30 per cent. of Hungary's arable land was in either collective farms of State farms. The general level of agricultural output remained backward, and an obstinate struggle continued between the passive resistance of the peasants and the repressive measures of the Government. Not only the peasants,

[1] This is a mistake. Kádár had in fact been a close friend of Rajk.

but the whole nation suffered from this dogmatic policy, which deprived Hungary's economy of a source of great potential wealth.

The Government's main effort went into industry. Here results were undoubtedly achieved, but at high cost. Capital goods industry, especially engineering and chemicals, received dogmatic priority over consumers' goods. In the bauxite and oil industries the Soviet Government had a direct share through the 'joint companies', formed in 1945, to which the Soviet 'contribution' consisted of confiscated 'German assets'. Later the Soviet authorities claimed special rights in the development of uranium ore in Hungary. Soviet trade policies accentuated economic exploitation by fixing prices that underrated Hungarian and overrated Soviet goods. In 1951 the targets of the Hungarian First Five-Year Plan were increased by 60 per cent. (from fifty-one milliard florint to eighty-five milliard), as part of the increase of heavy industry throughout the Soviet bloc in connexion with the Korean War. The burden was borne both by the peasantry and by the workers. The extent to which the standard of living declined during these years cannot be accurately measured from the few ambiguous figures that were published. There is no doubt, however, that the workers suffered great hardship, with long hours, ruthless pressure for higher output per hour, and wages of low purchasing power. The trade unions existed, as in the Soviet Union, not to protect the workers against their employers, but to impose on the workers the will of their masters, the bosses of the Communist Party. By the end of 1952 a good deal of new industrial capacity had been created, and the numbers and level of skill of the industrial working class had notably increased, but the national economy was in a desperate state.

Intellectual and religious freedom were crushed. The Communists prided themselves on their achievements in education. The number of university and technological students enormously increased, and these were mostly children of workers or peasants, who would have found it very difficult to get a higher education under the pre-1945 régime unless they were quite exceptionally able. This extension of opportunity is a real achievement. The quality of the education they received is an open question, but in the physical sciences and technology at least it was usually good. The Communists set themselves the task of creating a new 'toiling intelligentsia' to replace the narrower educated class of the past, and judged by the numbers educated their efforts were successful. They hoped that this new intellectual *élite* of worker and peasant origin would be the most loyal element of the nation. They spared no efforts to indoctrinate them with Marxism-Leninism. Indoctrination took place also in the schools. Not a single Hungarian child escaped it. The results disappointed the rulers in October 1956.

Religion was, of course, denounced by the whole propaganda apparatus. Religious instruction was gradually eliminated from the schools. The churches were allowed to perform religious ceremonies, but were excluded from any social activity. The most dramatic conflict between Government and Church was the arrest of the Catholic Primate, Cardinal Mindszenty. The cardinal never concealed his dislike of the Communists. During the war he had bravely opposed the German Nazis and the Hungarian Fascists. After 1945 he denounced the Communists. He was also a passionate Hungarian nationalist, and was bitterly indignant when the Government accepted the restoration in the peace treaty of the Trianon frontiers. In the summer of 1948 the nationalization of Church schools brought the conflict between him and the régime to an acute stage. He was arrested in December, accused of treason, and brought to trial after five weeks of torture and isolation in prison. He confessed to the charges made against him, and was condemned to life imprisonment. Two years later Archbishop Groesz, the leading Catholic bishop after the cardinal's removal, was also arrested, tried, and confessed. The Protestant churches too were purged of their outstanding leaders, replaced by more pliant persons.

A new period began in July 1953. This was a result of the death of Stalin, the riots in Pilsen, the East German rising, and the fall of Beria. Rákosi gave up the Premiership to Imre Nagy, and contented himself with the post of First Secretary of the party, over which he firmly maintained his grip. Nagy announced a new and milder policy. This coincided with the milder régime promised in the Soviet Union by Stalin's successors. In this 'New Course' Hungary went further than any other East European country. More attention was paid to the needs of agriculture, and peasants were allowed to leave collective farms. Where a majority of members wished to dissolve a collective farm, they were allowed to do so. It appears that in the following months about one-tenth of the farms made use of this right.[1] Nagy also released from prison many of those arrested

[1] The proportion of peasant households which left collective farms – but without the collective farm itself being formally dissolved – was about 30 per cent.

The Hungarian Tragedy

during the purges of the preceding years. He allowed the families who in 1951 had been deported from Budapest to return. This was less helpful than it seemed, for these people – mostly members of the former bourgeoisie – found that their apartments and possessions were occupied by persons who refused to give them up. But at least they had the right to leave their place of exile. Nagy also reduced the pace of industrial development and promised to pay more attention to consumers' goods. The economic results of the Nagy policy were not very substantial, but the generally milder political atmosphere was welcome. It was, however, only reluctantly accepted by Rákosi, presumably under pressure from Moscow. He awaited his opportunity to reverse the trend. This came with the fall of Malenkov in the Soviet Union in February 1955. On 18 April it was announced that Nagy had been removed from the Central Committee of the party as well as the premiership. His agricultural policy was stated to have been wrong, and a programme of further collectivization was announced. Nagy was also accused of having underrated the importance of heavy industry and of having built up the People's Front (a mass organization completely controlled by the Communist Party) as a rival to the party itself. As Nagy's successor in the premiership Rákosi chose a young and obedient follower named András Hegedüs.

Rákosi's new supremacy did not last long. Already the reconciliation between Khrushchev and Tito in the summer of 1955 was an ominous sign, for he could have no doubt of Tito's hostility. The denunciation of Stalin and of the 'personality cult' at the Soviet party's 20th Congress in February 1956 was a further blow. Rákosi fought hard. He even had the effrontery to announce that the Rajk trial had been a 'miscarriage of justice', and to denounce the 'personality cult', while he himself, the organizer of the trial and the object of the cult, remained in power. But eventually, on 18 July, he had to give up his position as First Secretary. He was, however, able to secure the appointment as his successor of his closest collaborator Ernö Gerö, second only to himself in Stalinist rigidity and subservience to Soviet policy.

The removal of Rákosi was immediately brought about by Soviet orders. Mikoyan himself was in Budapest when it was announced. It was also undoubtedly a result of pressure by Tito. But internal forces in Hungary had played their part. The most active element were the intellectuals, and especially a number of Communist writers within the officially sponsored Writers' Association. Writers released from prison during Nagy's premiership exercised a large influence behind the scenes. The Petőfi Club (named after the revolutionary poet who had played a leading part in 1848) was formed during the Nagy period. It provided a forum for literary discussions which soon took a political character, and which drew in many young people, including university students. At the Petőfi Club the demand for the return of Nagy to power was openly expressed. During the summer political criticism increased in the Hungarian press, especially in the organ of the Writers' Association *Irodalmi Ujság*. In September the Writers' Association held its congress, and elected a new committee. The exponents of the party line, who had managed the Association in the past, were not re-elected, and several persons who had recently emerged from prison became members. At the end of the month came the public reinterment of Rajk, attended by a vast crowd, which was clearly less concerned to pay homage to the former Minister of the Interior, responsible in his day for many acts of violence and injustice, than to express its opposition to the régime still in power. Then in mid-October came the crisis in Poland, which provided the immediate occasion for action.

The events of the Hungarian Revolution, which began with the demonstration of 23 October 1956, have been described by many eyewitnesses. Certain general comments on the events may be of interest.

The Hungarian Revolution of 1956 has some obvious points of resemblance to that of 1848. In both cases the first action came from the intellectuals. The students of 1956 were treading in the steps of Petőfi.

The Revolution of 1956 also ended in the same way as that of 1848-9, with the re-establishment of a hated régime by Russian military force. A hundred years ago this took longer: the Austro-Hungarian war lasted ten months, the Russian intervention three, while the whole revolution and war of 1956 was over in less than one month. Things move faster in the twentieth century. After 1849 it took eighteen years to convince the Habsburgs that it was impossible to restore the past: this process is unlikely to last as long in our time. One important difference between 1849 and 1956 is in the behaviour of the Russians. Tsar Nicholas I was a reactionary despot, but he was an honourable and comparatively humane man.

His troops fought only against Hungarian soldiers, and prisoners of war were not maltreated. The Austrians committed atrocities after the Russians were gone, and hanged some of the prisoners whom the Russians had handed over. In 1956 the Russian commanders executed prisoners, massacred civilians and treacherously arrested Hungarian generals whom they had invited to negotiate. They did not leave the activities to the Kádár puppet Government: they preferred to undertake them themselves.

The neighbouring small nations did not fight against Hungary in 1956 as they had done in 1848–9 and in 1919. Certainly the Hungarians gave them no excuse, for during these weeks there was no sign of nationalist claims against Slovaks, Serbs, or Roumanians. On the contrary repeated appeals for friendship and help were heard. An unconfirmed report states that the Soviet leaders asked the Roumanian Government to send forces against Hungary and that it refused on the ground that it could not count on the obedience of its Army. Student demonstrations took place in some Roumanian cities, both in Transylvania and in the Old Kingdom, and it seems that there was some unrest among workers in Bucharest. The Yugoslav Government expressed sympathy for Nagy in the first days, then justified the second Soviet intervention. In Czechoslovakia there was no sign of activity. At least these countries did not join in the repression.

In 1849 Kossuth sent representatives to West European capitals to beg for help, but the West did nothing. Here at least in 1956 the parallel is exact. The difference is in the relationship of the Western governments to Russia. In 1849 the Tsarist and Habsburg régimes were distasteful to Western statesmen, but they were certainly legitimate governments, conventionally correct in their international behaviour, and they did not threaten Western security. In 1956 the Soviet Government is the declared enemy of the West, seeking permanently, by every means available, and in every part of the world, to destroy Western and democratic interests and ultimately liberal democracy itself. Moreover, Western spokesmen have often declared their sympathy for the peoples of Eastern Europe; yet in the crisis they did nothing for them. This is not, of course, to say that Western propaganda had incited the Hungarian people to rise in arms. This it never did. The myth of 'Western incitement' is designed to secure a scapegoat. This is needed both by the Communists themselves and by various Right-wing groups in Western Europe who hope to make their own terms with the Soviet Union at the expense of others. The truth is that the Hungarian Revolution was a result of Hungarian conditions, and that it was abandoned not by Western radio broadcasting stations but by Western governments.

A special feature of the 1956 Revolution is the part played by the working class. The workers were slower to move than the intellectuals, but once they were fully engaged they showed themselves very stubborn. It was the workers who provided the main fighting forces in Budapest, stiffened, of course, by Army units. The last centres of organised fighting were the great industrial centres – Csepel island and Dunapentele. It is ironical that the latter, a new steel plant founded with Soviet equipment, had been named Sztálinváros as a symbol of Hungary's enslavement to Soviet Russia. After military resistance had ended, the workers in factories and mines continued strikes and passive resistance. Throughout the winter 1956–7 resistance still continued.

If the disparity between the strength of the combatants is taken into account, one may say that the effort of the Hungarian workers is the greatest single effort of resistance ever made by an industrial working class against an oppressor. It surpasses the Paris Commune, the St Petersburg Soviet of 1905, or the Viennese fighting of 1934. It is equally true that the Soviet Government has shown itself more systematically, ferociously, and consciously 'anti-working-class' than any capitalist Government in history. The Budapest Workers' Councils are historical heirs to the Russian Soviets, but the Soviet Government is a monstrously distorted and inflated offspring of Nicholas II.

The Soviet story that there was 'counter-revolution' in Hungary is a myth. The suggestion that great landowners and capitalists were plotting to recover their properties is ridiculous. Landowners and capitalists are strong only as long as they possess wealth: once this is gone they lose all power and influence and can do nothing. In Hungary in 1956 they did nothing. Fascism might have been a more serious danger, for Fascism has its roots in the masses; in a country with Hungary's past one might have expected an outbreak of Fascism and anti-Semitism. But the remarkable fact is that no such outbreak occurred. Some members of the security police were lynched. The correspondent of the Polish Communist *Nowa Kultura* estimated the victims in Budapest at eighty. Though these men had

The Hungarian Tragedy

for years subjected thousands of their compatriots to unspeakable tortures and humiliations, one must still deplore lynchings. To compare them with the White Terror of 1919, is, however, absurd. The correct parallel is the mob violence to which some dozens of Tsarist Okhrana men fell victims in the February Revolution of 1917. It is also worth stressing that Cardinal Mindszenty, released by the freedom-fighters, showed himself no 'reactionary' seeking vengeance, no 'chauvinist' denouncing neighbour nations, but a Christian patriot pleading for the unity of the nation and peace with neighbours great and small.

The well-known political names which reappeared in October were the Smallholders' leader Béla Kovács (who had been allowed to return from Russia some months before the Revolution) and the Social Democrat Anna Kéthly. Both enjoyed great popularity in Hungary. Some of the intellectuals of the National Peasant Party also reappeared under a new name as the Petöfi Party. But essentially the Revolution was the work of the younger generation, of new forces which would have crystallized into new political shapes if the Soviet imperialists had allowed them to develop freely.

Though the Revolution was crushed in blood, and the vanquished nation is inundated with lies and calumny, it has shown two immensely encouraging facts. One is that indoctrination of youth with lies does not work. Orwell's *1984* is only a nightmare. The Hungarian students, children of workers and peasants, saw the truth for themselves. It was they who led the Revolution. The second is that a totalitarian régime can be overthrown by its own subjects. Totalitarianism, with its one party, its omnipresent propaganda, its scientifically planned torture, its elevation of moral relativism into absolute dogma, is a more formidable enemy than a nineteenth-century dictatorship. Yet it, too, is no stronger than the will and loyalty of those who execute its orders. Within a few days nothing was left of the totalitarian régime of Rákosi and Gerö. Only foreign intervention crushed the Revolution. Totalitarianism has been overthrown once, and it will be overthrown again.

The most important effects will be felt in Russia itself.[1] The three social groups which made the Hungarian Revolution were the

[1] I did not expect, when writing these words in 1957, that immediate sensational results would be seen in Russia, but rather that the events in Hungary would have a profound effect on the minds of thinking Russians, especially of young people. There is some evidence that this was the case. Whether the seeds sown by the Hungarians will bear a harvest, it is still far too early, in 1964, to predict.

intellectual youth, the workers, and the Army. It is these three groups that form the weakest points in Soviet society. Since October 1956 there have been stormy political meetings in Moscow University, political discontent in Moscow factories, and mutinous incidents and desertions in the Soviet occupation forces in Hungary. Soviet soldiers are workers or peasants, brought up in school on Marxist historical mythology, with its tales of heroic workers fighting their oppressors on the barricades. In Hungary this has been not legend but reality, with the Soviet worker-soldiers shooting at working-class women in food queues, arresting leaders of Workers' Councils, and suppressing strikes. The Soviet soldiers know very well what they have been doing, and the story is already spreading in Russia. Since Beria fell, the Soviet police has lost the power it had over the Army, the power to segregate and intern and indoctrinate troops returning from the West. The truth is beginning to spread in Russia, and Russian students and workers and soldiers are beginning to express their thoughts. This was inconceivable while Stalin lived. A new process has begun.

The Hungarian Revolution may prove to have been Bolshevism's 1905.

The East European Communist Parties
1944-58

In the period of seizure of power (1944-8) and in the period of the purges and the intense drive for heavy industry (1949-52) the East European scene impressed the free observer with its uniformity. Admittedly the East European nations had different origins and traditions, but they were all being subjected to the same process of Stalinization; and this was being done by the same instruments, the Communist parties. Since the death of Stalin, however, it is not the uniformity of the pattern but its diversity which impresses the free observer. The 'New Course' policy of 1953 was differently applied in each country; the effects of the 20th Congress of February 1956 were different; and the climax came in October 1956 in Poland and Hungary where the revolutions were of different kinds – elsewhere there were no revolutions. In the light of the diversity of recent years, it seems worth while to look back into the past and see whether the different Communist parties were really such similar instruments as one was earlier inclined to assume.

Between 1918 and 1944 the East European parties differed greatly from each other. The Czechoslovakian party essentially resembled the German Communist party. It was made up of workers who were drawn from the left wing of the social democratic movement which had existed under Austria-Hungary. In the Czech lands the working class was divided into two approximately equal halves, and in Slovakia and Ruthenia a certain number of poor peasants and intellectuals also were attracted to Communism. The Hungarian party was originally similar, but it soon grew into artificial size and power in the disturbed conditions of the winter of 1918-19. After the defeat of the Communist government of 1919, the Communist Party was reduced by police persecution and popular disillusionment to a tiny sect; it was never again of importance in

This article was first published in the *Annals of the American Academy of Political and Social Science*, May 1958.

Hungarian political life until the Soviet invasion of 1944. In Poland, too, the Communist Party could trace its descent from the old labour movement; it was a combination of the doctrinaire Marxist Social Democracy of Poland and Lithuania with the left wing of the old Polish Socialist party. In the winter of 1918–19 the Polish Communists had some support among a minority of the working class which was itself a minority of the nation. But the defeat of the Soviet invasion of Poland in 1920 was a deadly blow to the party. Though there were times in the following twenty years when it increased its following, it was never much more than a small sect.

If the Czechoslovakian, Hungarian, and Polish parties were workers' parties – the first strong, the other two weak – the Communist parties of Yugoslavia, Bulgaria, and Roumania were essentially parties of revolutionary intellectuals, supplemented by a rather unstable following among workers and peasants; at times this was great and at times negligible, rapidly rising and falling according to changes in economic conditions and the intensity of police pressure. These three parties had the structure of the old pre-1917 Bolshevik Party in Russia, rather than that of a Western radical labour group such as the German Communist Party. Of the three, the most impressive was the Bulgarian party; in the years 1919–23 it polled in free elections about 25 per cent. of the popular vote and was supported by almost all the small working class. From the mid-1920's it was savagely persecuted, but it always managed to keep a hard core of underground conspiratorial cadres. It went into action with some success in World War II and emerged in 1944 as a genuine internal force to be reckoned with. The Yugoslav party had a much more erratic record. It had large but unreliable mass support between 1919 and 1921; afterwards it completely disintegrated under the double effect of persecution and public indifference. In the 1930's it re-emerged as the most active if the smallest of the groups fighting for a Popular Front and for resistance to native and foreign Fascism. In these years it won over a large part of the most politically minded section of the student youth. In World War II these new cadres, mostly derived from the intelligentsia, were able to mobilize vast masses of peasants in their national and civil 'war of liberation'; this ranks beside the Russian and Chinese revolutions and civil wars as one of the three epic victories in the history of Communism. In contrast to these two, the Roumanian party was a negligible sect. Such as it was, its structure was of the second, or

'Balkan', rather than the first, or 'Mid-European', type. But in fact its membership amounted only to a few hundred, and it had not the slightest effect on Roumanian political life between the wars or during World War II.

In 1945 it was clear that the two strongest Communist parties in Eastern Europe, in the sense that they had enthusiastic support from at least a large minority of the population and possessed an apparatus of power of their own making, were the two 'Balkan' parties, the Yugoslav and the Bulgarian. The two weakest and most miserable sects of Soviet agents imported from Russia or blackmailed into service on the spot were the Polish and the Roumanian parties. Czechoslovakia had numerically the most impressive Communist Party. In the free election of 1946 it won 40 per cent. of the votes in the Czech lands. In the trade unions the Communists seized the key positions. They were helped not only by the presence of the Red Army in the first months of 'liberation' but also by the fact that the German occupation of six years had destroyed the old Social Democratic organizations. Most Czech workers voted Communist, and so did many intellectuals and many opportunists in the administrative machine. The Czechoslovakian Communist Party was a rather bourgeois organization in its spirit, based on vested interests and ambitions rather than on the fanatical revolutionary zeal which marked the two Balkan Slav parties. The Hungarian party was numerically far less impressive. At the free election of 1945 it won 17 per cent. of the popular vote. It did, however, build up a certain following among the workers, especially among the unskilled and in the newer industries. The older trade unions were still in Social Democratic hands.

Between 1945 and 1948 the Communist parties, strongly supported at decisive moments by the Soviet military power, established their one-party dictatorships. By terror, threats, bribery, or intrigue they divided or destroyed first the peasant parties and then the Social Democratic parties. By 1948 the Socialists, their ranks thinned by well-planned purges, were 'fused' into the Communist parties. Then came the breach between Moscow and Belgrade, the witch-hunting campaign against 'nationalist deviations,' and the later anti-Semitic purges which reached their height just before Stalin's death. This was also the period of greatest economic pressure on the masses. The aim was maximum creation of heavy industry and general militarization. The timing of this pressure

(1951–2) left no doubt that it was connected with the international tension caused by Communist aggression in Korea.

But though this general pattern was the same, its application was not uniform. The purges were not equally severe in all countries. Some impression can be obtained by a comparison of the proportion of members of the Central Committees of the parties who disappeared from public life during these years. The highest turnover was in Czechoslovakia and Hungary. In Czechoslovakia, of 97 persons elected members in 1949, 53 were not re-elected in 1954, and of 84 persons elected in 1954, 39 were new names. Thus, 55 per cent. of the 1949 Central Committee disappeared and 45 per cent. of the 1954 Central Committee were new people. In Hungary, of 92 persons elected to the Central Committee in 1948 or 1951, 46 were not re-elected in 1954. Of these, 21 disappeared between 1948 and 1951 and 25 between 1951 and 1954, making a total turnover of just 50 per cent. In Bulgaria and Poland, on the other hand, the turnover was low. Of 48 persons elected to the Central Committee of the Bulgarian party in 1948, only 14 had disappeared by 1954. Of 72 persons elected to the Polish Central Committee in 1948, 16 had disappeared in 1954. In the Roumanian party the turnover was similar – 12 disappeared by 1954 from a Central Committee of 46 elected in 1948. These figures are liable to minor error and to some uncertainties about individual cases, but the picture which emerges of the differences in turnover between the different party leaderships is clear. Detailed information is not available to the author on the turnover in the lower levels of the party apparatus, but the general impression, based on such scraps of evidence as have come his way, is that at this level, too, the purge was severest in the Czechoslovakian and Hungarian parties and lightest in the Bulgarian and Polish parties.

Another difference between the parties concerns the intensity of the 'personality cult'. Three Communist leaders of this region were quite outstanding as regards propaganda build-up – Georgi Dimitrov of Bulgaria, Klement Gottwald of Czechoslovakia, and Mátyás Rákosi of Hungary. Dimitrov died in the Soviet Union in 1949, supposedly as a result of illness for which he was undergoing treatment. But his death occurred at a very convenient moment, when world-wide Communist propaganda was concentrating on the 'unmasking' of the Yugoslav leaders with whom Dimitrov had had rather friendly relations; it was also not long after Dimitrov had incurred official Soviet wrath for speaking in favour of East European federation. His successor, Vulko Chervenkov, received a certain amount of build-up, but not on a scale comparable to that which Dimitrov had enjoyed. Gottwald died in 1953, supposedly as a result of a cold contracted in Moscow on the occasion of Stalin's funeral; but this also coincided with a moment of major change in international Communist policy. His successor to the presidency, Antonin Zápotocký, received no special build-up, and since that time the Czechoslovakian leadership has remained remarkably colourless and anonymous. It is a régime without personal glamour and is more genuinely a 'collective leadership' than any in the Communist world, the Soviet Union included. Mátyás Rákosi, however, lasted longer and retained far more power. Indeed, the much-purged Hungarian party became more truly a one-man show than any other Communist party with the exception of the Soviet prototype. The Central Committee consisted of Rákosi's creatures, and the party was ruled by an absolute autocracy. Even the 'New Course' period of 1953-5 did not change this. Imre Nagy became Prime Minister and introduced substantially different policies. But Rákosi remained First Secretary, controlled the party machine, and was able, when the fall of Malenkov in Moscow gave him his opportunity, to overthrow Nagy. In Poland and Roumania there was never any build-up comparable to these three cases. Boleslaw Bierut was the most publicized figure in Poland and Gheorghe Gheorghiu-Dej in Roumania, but neither was elevated to the stature of a pocket-Stalin like Rákosi, Gottwald, or Dimitrov in their great days. Bierut died in Moscow, also supposedly of natural causes, at the time of the 20th Congress of the Communist party of the Soviet Union – yet another landmark in international Communist policy.

During the 'New Course' period the parties acted differently from each other. The much-purged Czechoslovakian and Hungarian parties were glad of the opportunity of milder policies. It was in Hungary that the relaxation of pressure went furthest. It appears clearly from Imre Nagy's memorandum in 1955, recently published in the United States, that the Soviet leaders directly intervened in favour of concessions. Nagy not only made great efforts to conciliate the peasants and reduce the tempo of industrialization, but he also treated the churches more mildly, demanded greater freedom for the intelligentsia, and released a considerable number of persons from prison or labour camp; these included those Communists and socialists who had been arrested in connexion with the purges of 1949–52, especially those regarded rightly or wrongly as followers of the executed László Rajk. In Czechoslovakia there was little relaxation of political terror, but considerable economic concessions were made. During these three years the Czechoslovak leaders were able to build up a more sound economy and to create the conditions for Czechoslovakia's present status as the most prosperous of all the satellites. In Poland change came somewhat later and was not so much in the economic field as in the intellectual. Already in 1955 the 'thaw' in cultural life was very visible. Here one of the most important factors was the reduction in the powers of the police; this was brought about by the fall of Lavrentii Beria in Moscow, the defection of the Polish security police official, Jósef Swiatlo, and the massive propagation of his revelations to Poland by broadcasts and balloon-borne leaflets of Radio Free Europe. The Polish Communist leaders had less popular support than most East European Communists. On the one hand, this basic situation made them dependent on Soviet support; on the other, the almost universal anti-Soviet sentiment among the Polish masses spread upwards into the party hierarchy. The Polish leaders were not isolated from this sentiment by a protective cushion. The solid layer of middle-level, devoted, indoctrinated cadres was weaker than in most parties, and the feeling of the party members and the masses penetrated to the leaders. In 1956 the effect was that the leaders ended by identifying themselves with the masses rather than with their Soviet patrons. The death of Bierut and the 20th Congress accelerated the trend. The Roumanian leadership was in a similar situation: if anything, it had even less support and an even thinner protective cushion than the Polish party. But in both the intellectual and the economic fields the Roumanian leaders were more sparing with their concessions; and they talked less about what few concessions they did make. In Bulgaria there was no 'New Course' at all. The Bulgarian party, stronger in the past and less purged since seizure of power than any other, maintained its own policies. It was more radical and more brutal; this was not because Moscow forced it to be so but because its leaders wished it to be. Paradoxically it may be argued that this, the most 'Stalinist' of all the East European parties, was and is the most independent of Moscow. It is true that Traicho Kostov was executed and that there were some dismissals and disgraces, but by and large the leaders of the party from the underground period have remained in power and have been loyal to each other. Among other reasons why they did not yield to Khrushchev's recommendations in 1955 and 1956 for a milder policy was probably a reluctance to accept policies which seemed to be inspired by Yugoslav advice. Added to the old dislike of Bulgarians for Serbs and the rivalry for control of Macedonia – in the sphere of Communist Party affairs as well as in the interstate sphere this rivalry goes back to the 1920's – may be added the belief of the Bulgarian leaders that their party has as good and as long a revolutionary record as the Yugoslav. They therefore proceeded with their 'tough' course, especially by increasing the collectivization of agriculture; and they never accepted the 'soft' policy introduced in the rest of Eastern Europe.

In the crisis of October–November 1956 these differences between the Communist parties appeared more clearly. The two countries in which revolutions occurred were the two in which there was a definite cleavage of opinion at the highest level of the party and in which there was one surviving Communist leader of great prestige who symbolized all the desire for reform and freedom which had accumulated inside the party for years past. The hopes placed in Gomulka and in Nagy were essentially the same. In the other parties, however, no such clear cleavages existed, and no outstanding figures were available around which opposition could crystallize. In Czechoslovakia and Bulgaria collective leadership was a reality – in the first case of a 'soft' and in the second of a 'tough' type. In Roumania the leadership was unsure of itself, but the whole party was so weak and so lacking in persons of intellectual or political distinction that no action was likely.

In other respects, however, the situations in the Polish and the Hungarian parties were very different. In the Hungarian party everything depended on the autocracy of Rákosi. Once Khrushchev had decided, in the summer of 1955, to come to terms with Tito, it was clear that the Yugoslav leader would press for the removal of the Hungarian boss; for it was he, of all the East European satraps, who had gone furthest to insult him and his régime. But Rákosi fought back, and it must have been extremely hard for Moscow to find a successor. Rákosi even survived the 20th Congress and himself had the effrontery to make public speeches denouncing the cult of personality. At last, in July 1956, he was removed, but his successor was Ernö Gerö who had been his closest collaborator for ten years past. Gerö was a man of undoubted ability but hardly any feeling for political tactics. He was no less a fanatic and a dogmatist than Rákosi, but unlike Rákosi he commanded no respect. Gerö was accepted by Tito and visited him in Belgrade in October 1956. Believing that his prestige had been increased by this visit, he returned to Budapest determined to preserve his authority; here he was faced with the popular October demonstration. Inflexible and frightened, he refused to yield, and the party leadership, composed of Rákosi's creatures, could think of nothing to do but throw themselves on the protection of Soviet arms. In Poland, the dead Bierut was replaced by the moderate Stalinist, Edward Ochab, a man very different from Gerö. He and his colleagues decided that they must yield to popular pressure. The Poznań rising of June 1956 confirmed them in this intention. Pressure from within the party and within the Warsaw working class for the return of Gomulka grew during the summer. Ochab and a majority of the Central Committee voted for making Gomulka First Secretary. That there was a minority in the Committee is shown by the fact that twenty-three out of seventy-six members voted for the re-election of Marshal Konstantin Rokossovsky to the Politburo. But even this minority voted for Gomulka's appointment. The demand for the return of Nagy was no less strong within the party and the working class in Hungary. But where Ochab yielded, Gerö resisted. Moreover, whereas the Polish security police had lost power in the previous year – the armed security forces were commanded by a man loyal to Gomulka, General Waclaw Komar – in Hungary the security police and armed security forces had retained their previous powers and outlook, and in the emergency they loyally obeyed Gerö and fought beside the Soviet army against their compatriots.

It is not any difference in ability or moral character between Gomulka and Nagy—which may or may not exist – but the difference between the Polish patriotism of Ochab and the doctrinaire treason of Gerö that explains the different course of events in Poland and in Hungary. Generalizations about sensible, realistic Poles and silly, romantic Hungarians have even less validity. Nor is the argument convincing that the Poles refrained from extreme action because they believed in the Polish–Soviet alliance against Germany, while the Hungarians cast aside discretion because their neighbour was only peaceful Austria. This difference in the geographical situations of Poland and Hungary, and their different foreign policy problems, is of course a fact. But I know of no evidence that this was a decisive factor in the events of October 1956. If, when Khrushchev and his colleagues appeared in Warsaw, they had found a divided leadership, if Ochab and the old team had asked for Soviet help, and orders had been given to the Soviet Army to attack, then there would have been a far greater blood bath in Warsaw and in Poland than there was in Budapest and Hungary. Not all the high qualities of Gomulka, the realism of the Polish people, or the concern for the Oder–Neisse line could have stopped it.

The other basic factors of discontent without which revolutions do not occur were the same not only in Poland and Hungary but throughout Eastern Europe. Everywhere the peasants wanted freely to use their land, the workers to be paid better real wages and work shorter hours, the intellectuals to talk and write freely, the whole nations to be independent of Moscow. But the special superficial factors which decide whether there shall or shall not be a revolution were present only in Poland and Hungary. The two most important of these factors were the existence of prominent Communist leaders around whom opposition within the party could crystallize and the existence – especially in Hungary – of a number of Marxist intellectuals of an older generation; this group was disillusioned with the régime and even with Marxism itself and was able to give leadership and direction to the rather inarticulate discontent of the intellectual youth. We have already seen that the first condition was absent in both Czechoslovakia, Roumania, and Bulgaria; the second was also absent. In both Czechoslovakia and Roumania, the student youth in 1956 expressed its discontent, but it found no support from its elders.

A year after the Hungarian Revolution, the parties of Czechoslovakia, Roumania, and Bulgaria remain much as they were before it. The Czech and Slovak leaders can congratulate themselves that they escaped disaster and that they have ensured tolerable living conditions to their subjects. The Bulgarian leaders remain united in their savage fanaticism, proud of its results and little troubled by criticism from within or without. The Roumanian leaders remain as cautious as ever. All have, of course, been impressed by the Soviet victory of 1956, the inability of the West to do anything for Hungary, the double standard of morality accepted by the United Nations, the successful mobilization by Soviet policy of racial hatred throughout the world, and the sputniks. Yet the parties are internally unstable; the relationship of their countries to the Soviet Union is insecure, and they know it. Western observers would do well to follow the small differences in personalities, policies, and tactics which differentiate the parties from each other, for at a not distant date, in changed international circumstances, they may prove politically important.

Five Years after the Hungarian Revolution

Five years have passed since the counter-revolutionary assault by Soviet troops which suppressed the Hungarian uprising of 1956. The year 1961 seems likely to see a new crisis in Eastern Europe over the future of Berlin and East Germany. It may therefore be appropriate to look back at the recent past of this region and compare it with such present trends as can be discerned.

The history of Eastern Europe since the Second World War can be divided into four periods. The first (1945–8) was one of mixed hopes and fears. The destruction by Hitler of the old régimes, followed in turn by the destruction of Hitler's empire in Eastern Europe by the Soviet Army, brought widespread hopes of a social and political new deal, of the establishment of democracy and social justice. The first post-war governments were coalitions of democrats and Communists. But soon the behaviour of the Soviet occupying forces and the subservience to them of the local Communists made it clear that the Communist parties were not just the most radical of the democratic political groups (as many sincere East European democrats, especially young people, had believed), but were totalitarian machines designed to set up a type of régime no less oppressive, in its own different way, than that of the Nazis.

This became evident in Roumania and Bulgaria already before the fighting in Germany stopped. In Hungary the illusion lasted a little longer, and in Czechoslovakia hopes of peaceful co-operation between democrats and Communists were not killed until February 1948. Looking back, it may seem absurd that anyone should have had such illusions about the Communists; yet it is a fact that the illusions were strongly held. The sincerity of the East European democrats' determination to co-operate with the Communists and to carry out very radical social reforms makes their betrayal by their Communist partners the more monstrous. And when one observes the prevalence of similar illusions in Asia, Africa, and Latin America today, the tragic history of Eastern Europe in those three years is shown to be of much more than academic interest, and the failure

---

This article was first published in *Problems of Communism*, September 1961.

of non-Communists to learn its lessons becomes the more disheartening.

The second period (1948–52) saw the consolidation of the Communist totalitarian régimes, which were closely modelled after that of the Soviet Union. The local Communist parties were purged, first of 'nationalists' like Kostov and Rajk, and then of 'cosmopolitan' Jews like Slansky and Pauker. The purges were especially severe in the Czechoslovak and Hungarian parties, where 50 per cent. or more of the Central Committee members disappeared from public life, but comparatively milder in the Bulgarian and Polish parties, where the proportion of purges was around a quarter. Economic and social policies were based on those of the Soviet Union in the 1930's, with some inevitable adjustment to the differing local economic structures. Living standards were kept low, and in 1951 the increased priority given to war industries as a consequence of the Korean conflict forced them still lower. Workers were at the mercy of the state-boss, and the first phase of the collectivization of agriculture began. The East European economies were subjected to colonial exploitation by the new imperial power, the U.S.S.R.

The third period (1953–6) was one of renewed hope and increased liberty. Although the death of Stalin did not bring any immediate improvements, the rising in Plzeň, Czechoslovakia, in June 1953 and the much bigger revolt in Eastern Germany two weeks later, both of which were led by industrial workers, brought about a series of gradual concessions. These were both economic and political in Hungary, and only economic in Czechoslovakia, but they were far-reaching in both countries. In Roumania and Poland there was less change, and in Bulgaria, ruled by fanatical Stalinists, there was virtually none. However, the Soviet *rapprochement* with Yugoslavia in 1955 and the denunciation of the 'cult of personality' at the 20th C.P.S.U. Congress in February 1956 had repercussions throughout the whole of Eastern Europe. There followed the Poznan rising in Poland, the dismissal of Rákosi in Hungary, the election of Gomulka to be First Secretary of the Polish party, the October crisis in Warsaw, and finally the Hungarian Revolution. Hopes were at their highest at the end of October 1956. But they were quickly dashed by the ruthless action of the Soviet Union and the inaction of the Western powers.

The fourth period (1957–61) has been one of declining hopes. It is true that there have been some gains over the earlier years.

Poland had preserved elements of independence, and the standard of living has generally improved throughout the region, most strikingly in Czechoslovakia and East Germany, and least in Bulgaria. But against this must be set the obvious evidences of Soviet strength, of Khrushchev's implacable determination to maintain Communist rule wherever it has been established, and of Western hesitancy. The last five years have been regarded by the peoples of Eastern Europe, no less than by those of the 'uncommitted' countries outside Europe, as a period of rapid Western decline.

A brief comparison of the situation in 1961 with that of 1956, from the particular standpoint of the factors which made for revolution in 1956, may be instructive. Four factors in particular should be noted.

The first was the prevalence in 1956 of discontent among the East European masses. The years of Stalinist rule had weighed heavily on them, and they were certain to welcome a change of régime if such became possible. This was especially true of the working class. Its discontent was dramatically expressed in Plzeň and Berlin in 1953, in Poznań and Budapest in 1956. The peasants, too, had plenty of reason to be discontented. But agrarian populations, dispersed in villages over large areas, have less contact with one another and less effective means of protest than workers concentrated in a few big cities. This is, of course, a basic fact of political power not confined to Eastern Europe or to the twentieth century. This fact and the brief duration of the uprising account for the small part played by the peasants in the Hungarian Revolution of 1956. There are absolutely no grounds for believing that the Hungarian peasants were less interested in liberty than the workers.

Comparing the situation of the masses of East Europe in 1961 with their situation in 1956, we can admit that there have been some improvements. To conclude from this, however, that the masses are content with the existing régimes, or that Hungarian workers have forgotten or forgiven the brutal repression of 1956 – which was as clearly an act of 'class vengeance' against the workers as any repression in the long history of labour movements everywhere in the world – would be quite unjustified. Moreover, the material improvements have generally been less appreciable for the peasants than for the workers in the East European countries, with the important exception of Poland where the exact reverse has been the case. Collectivization has been speeded up in Czechoslovakia,

Roumania, and Hungary, and has already entered the new phase of amalgamation of collectives in Bulgaria. All this has meant increased pressure on the peasants, the denial of their remaining rights, and interference with their personal liberties and family privacy. Greater severity against the churches, which has been true also in Poland, has been an added cause of discontent, especially among the peasantry. Thus, we can conclude that the situation of the masses in 1961 is only slightly better than in 1956.

The second stimulus to revolution in 1956 was the hostility of the educated *élite*, or intelligentsia – especially of the younger generation – towards the Communist régimes. The latter had placed great hopes in the new 'toiling intelligentsia', which they had created by making all stages of education accessible to children of workers and peasants on a scale unknown before 1945. But it was precisely this new generation of educated working-class youth which led the revolt against them. The acquisition of knowledge and the opportunity to think for themselves had the same effect on 'toiling youth' under Communism as it had had on 'bourgeois youth' under the pre-war semi-Fascist régimes of Eastern Europe: they saw through the lying slogans, understood the cruelty and oppression, and felt a growing desire to help their peoples to freedom. These trends were clearly visible all over Eastern Europe in 1956, although they expressed themselves most clearly in Poland and Hungary.

Since the Hungarian Revolution the régimes have shown great distrust of the intelligentsia and have subjected them to increased controls of various kinds, while allowing some improvement in their material condition. Thus, the basic causes of discontent among the intellectuals remain; yet, because they tend to be more susceptible to purely political arguments than the workers and peasants, it is possible that they may have been influenced to some extent in the direction desired by the régimes. It has often been asserted in the West that the suppression of the Hungarian Revolution lost the Communists the support of the intellectuals. This was doubtless true of Left-wing intellectuals in Britain and France, but in Eastern Europe the revulsion aroused among the intelligentsia by Soviet ruthlessness – which they already knew well – was offset to a considerable extent by their disillusionment at the failure of the Western powers to come to their defence. The massacre of Budapest certainly did not make the East European intellectuals love Moscow and its

Danubian satraps any more than they had before, but the spectacle of Turtle Bay could not but dampen their hopes for the future.

Power and success in some ways appeal more strongly to intellectuals than to workers or peasants – and not only beyond the Iron Curtain. This reaction takes different forms in different countries. In East Germany the appeal derives force from a long German tradition of worship for power and success, a tradition from which Bismarck, Hitler, and Ulbricht have all profited. Visitors to East German universities in recent years have found unmistakable traces of its survival. In Poland there has long existed, side by side with hatred of Russia and attachment to Western culture, a tradition of respect for Russian strength and of resentment against the West for its failure to help Poland (in 1815, 1831, 1863, 1939, 1945, and 1956). The argument that there is a place for the Poles as the ablest subjects of the Soviet Empire has its attractions. The disillusioned Polish writer who said that he expected to see the West again from the driver's seat of a Russian tank spoke for this tradition. In Czechoslovakia the equivalent attitude is a specifically Czech form of self-complacency – a belief that the whole world is forever in debt to the Czechs because of Munich, that they need never fight for their own freedom, and that meanwhile they are doing very well for themselves by supplying arms to Cuba and Syria, industrial goods to Asia, and security experts to Guinea.

Another element in the outlook of the intelligentsia throughout Eastern Europe is a certain kind of moral puritanism. They feel that they are suffering while 'the capitalist world' is obsessed with consuming, and that this places them on a higher spiritual level than the Western peoples. This feeling may be found even in East Germany, where the régime probably has the least support of all. The East Berlin worker is perhaps impressed by the shop-windows of the Kurfürstendamm; but the East German intellectual speaks with contempt of the West German *Wirtschaftswunderland,* and in his bitterness and frustration he can even reconcile himself to the idea that the ultimate reunification of Germany must come through the imposition of the odious régime of Ulbricht or his successors on the whole German people, if only because then, at least, those comfort-loving Rhineland bourgeois will know what it is to suffer as he has suffered. In short, the intellectuals' hatred of the Communist régimes remains, but it would be a mistake not to recognize that the events of the past few years have robbed it of its intensity, thus making the intelligentsia a somewhat less dangerous adversary in the eyes of the Communist rulers.

The third factor which made for revolution in 1956 was the lack of self-confidence displayed by Stalin's successors – their vacillations towards semi-liberalism and their denunciation of the 'cult of personality'. If even Khrushchev himself spoke bitterly of the system of terror, torture, and forced labour imposed on East European Communist régimes by Stalin, if the security police were no longer to be allowed a free hand, if the big and medium bosses were already busy ingratiating themselves with their former victims, it was not surprising that rebellious spirits both within and outside the Communist parties spoke and acted boldly. But by 1961, the Soviet vacillations have ceased, and the régimes, having weathered the storms of 1956–7, have become more firmly entrenched. In the West, on the other hand, there are still signs of indecision and vacillation; the anti-white racialism of the Afro-Asians is powerfully echoed by the inverted racialism of the American and European *bien pensants* of the Left; and a generous share of the energies of the press is devoted to polemics against one's own allies.

The fourth revolutionary factor in 1956 – perhaps the least significant from a general point of view, yet decisive in the circumstances – was the division within the Communist leaderships of Eastern Europe. This division existed in all the satellite countries, but it was effective in only two, Poland and Hungary. The reason was very simple. These were the only two countries in which there was still a public figure well known to both party members and non-Communists as standing for a more liberal and more national policy. The Polish leader was Wladyslaw Gomulka; the Hungarian was Imre Nagy. Though previously disgraced and deprived of power they had survived, whereas similar or potentially similar figures in the other East European countries had been killed in the purges. If Gomulka and Nagy had not been there, so that discontent could crystallize around them, the events of October 1956 might well not have occurred. (The fact that events developed differently in the two countries was due to the different character and behaviour, not of these two men, but of their predecessors – in Poland, Ochab, who willingly gave power to Gomulka; in Hungary, Gerö, who refused to give real power to Nagy and invoked the intervention of the Soviet Army, which inevitably transformed a revolt within the party into a popular revolution.)

Five Years after the Hungarian Revolution 179

In 1961, differences no doubt exist within the East European Communist parties, but the situation is not comparable to that of 1956, if only because the party leaders and their Soviet patrons have learned their lesson. In Poland the Stalinist rump has recovered only a little ground, but Gomulka himself has adopted a 'tough' line which is on the whole acceptable to Moscow. In Czechoslovakia there is probably some ill feeling between the survivors of the Gottwald team and the group of *apparatchiki* headed by Novotny. The recent removal of Bárák from the Ministry of the Interior may have been due to a factional struggle in the party, or it could be explained by economic or administrative problems; but in any case there do not seem to be sufficient grounds for believing that a dangerous degree of disunity exists within the party leadership. In Roumania Gheorghiu-Dej appears unassailable, as does Ulbricht in East Germany. Perhaps it is precisely because these are the two weakest and most-hated Communist parties in the whole of Eastern Europe that their second-rate but obedient bosses are indispensable to the Soviet leaders.

In Hungary Kádár likewise has a strong position, chiefly because he is the least objectionable of the party leaders. He appears to enjoy the personal confidence, perhaps even the affection of Khrushchev, and he has thus far been able to balance his team of former Rákosi men, ex-Social Democrat traitors and once imprisoned Communists (such as himself and Gyula Kállai). In Bulgaria there is talk of rivalry between Anton Yugov, former resistance leader and now Prime Minister, and Todor Zhivkov, whose background is in the party *apparat*; and there is also some uncertainty about the role of Vulko Chervenkov, who succeeded Georgi Dimitrov as the centre of the 'personality cult' but was, at least apparently, demoted in 1956. But the Bulgarian party, which has always been nearer to the model of a steel-hard Bolshevik party than any other in the region, does not look as if it were facing very serious internal trouble. It is true that two formerly prominent party leaders, Dobri Tarpeshev and Yonko Panov, already expelled from the Central Committee in 1957, were denounced in the party organ *Partiina zhizn* in March 1961 for dissident activities, and that there have recently been purges in the middle levels of the party hierarchy. These purges are probably designed to provide scapegoats for economic troubles caused by the very unrealistic planning of the last two years, and may also be connected with polemics against

Yugoslavia. Nevertheless, it seems premature to speak of a crisis in the Bulgarian leadership.[1] Thus, to sum up, even though Communist parties are by their very nature addicted to factional struggles and purges, there appears in the summer of 1961 to be no reason to anticipate internal disunity in the East European parties on the scale of 1956.

The strongest régimes at present appear to be the Czechoslovak and Bulgarian. Both have the advantage that their peoples are traditionally friendly to Russia. For the Czechs, the argument that the Soviet Union alone provides them security against future German revenge and firmly guarantees their frontiers has considerable force. As for Bulgaria, the fact that two of its traditional enemies, Greece and Turkey, are allied to the West, and that the third, Yugoslavia, is at least an object of suspicion in Moscow, reinforces the case for its association with the Soviet Union.

Internally, however, the Czechoslovak and Bulgarian régimes are dissimilar. The strength of the former is largely due to its economic successes. It has been able to give its subjects a decent and rising standard of living, something which no other régime in the bloc except the East German has accomplished. The Czechs can also take pride in the success of their products in world markets, as well as in such minor but pleasing triumphs as the prize won at the Brussels Fair. It may indeed be argued that Czechoslovakia is better known in the world today than ever before, enjoying a degree of international prestige which raises it above the level of a 'small state'. Guinea is largely ruled by Czech experts, Cuba is a happy hunting ground for still more, and Prague has become a centre for the training of Africans in such varied fields as the natural sciences, Marxist-Leninist ideology, security police techniques, and the arts of guerrilla warfare. Some Czechs may reflect that their new achievements express little of the spirit of their president-liberator, Thomas Masaryk, but there are perhaps not many left who are distressed by such considerations.

The Bulgarian régime owes its internal strength to the simpler expedient of terror and brutality. Pre-war Bulgaria once boasted the

[1] In December 1962 the Congress of the Bulgarian Communist Party was informed of the dismissal of Yugov from the Premiership and the expulsion of Chervenkov from the party. This purge marked the definite triumph of Zhivkov, and undoubtedly was brought about by the direct intervention of Khrushchev, who on several occasions, especially during his visit to Bulgaria in the summer of 1962, showed that Zhivkov enjoyed his full confidence.

most brutal of the Balkan semi-Fascist régimes, and since 1945 it has had the most brutal of the Communist satellite régimes. The Bulgarian leaders, however, have had a disappointment. They pushed ahead more rapidly than all the other satellite régimes in imitating the Soviet model of the 1930's. In particular, they not only completed the forcible collectivization of agriculture long before the others, but already in 1958 began the amalgamation of collectives, which had started in the Soviet Union only in 1951. They therefore expected to be credited with having completed the 'building of socialism' in Bulgaria – and indeed, by the criteria which had enabled Stalin to declare the Soviet Union a 'socialist state' in 1936, they had a strong case. However, something went wrong. It was Czechoslovakia which was the first satellite to be given the honour of calling itself a 'socialist republic', a title formally incorporated in the new Czechoslovak Constitution of 1960. By that time Czechoslovak agriculture had been collectivized, but the amalgamation of collectives had only begun. Industrially, of course, Czechoslovakia was far more advanced than Bulgaria – indeed, more advanced than the Soviet Union of 1936 in terms of *per capita*, but not total, industrial output.

Of Roumania, Hungary, and East Germany little need be said. All three régimes remain extremely weak and unpopular. In Roumania, at the beginning of 1961, collectivization embraced about half the peasant population, and most of the remainder were members of agricultural co-operatives already in the process of being transformed into collectives. In Hungary the peasants were at first left to themselves by the Kádár régime. There had been two periods of mass exodus from the collective farms, the first in 1953 under Nagy's Premiership and the second during the revolution of 1956. The Kádár régime at last began a serious effort to remedy the situation in the first months of 1959, when very heavy pressure was applied to force the peasants into collectives. A second drive, less brutal but no less resolute, was carried out in the early months of 1960, and by mid-1961 Hungarian agriculture has been predominantly collectivized. General living conditions in Hungary at present are probably better than in Roumania, and intellectual life also appears to be somewhat freer, at least in the sense that writers and artists, if they steer clear of politics, are allowed a little more freedom of expression. Ever since 1945 Roumania, in addition to all the normal pressures of Communist totalitarianism, has suffered from a policy of Russification. This has been particularly resented by educated Roumanians, who take pride in their non-Slav culture and their connexions with the Latin nations. In East Germany material conditions have substantially improved, but the bitterness of being separated from the majority of the German people and subject to a foreign imperial power remains.

Of Poland, too, little need be said, since its special situation is already well known in the West. Although the broad freedom of public expression won in October 1956 soon disappeared, there is still 'freedom of conversation' in private. The Catholic Church, too, has lost most of the freedom gained five years ago, and religious instruction in the schools has virtually ceased to exist, but the popular influence of the Church remains undiminished. The peasants have retained the largest share of the gains of 1956. Though there is talk of the ultimate necessity of a 'socialist agriculture', there are no signs of pressure for collectivization. In foreign policy, Poland remains completely tied to the Soviet Union, and the Government makes frantic and unceasing efforts to whip up hatred against West Germany. Whether the Polish people, now generally disillusioned with the Gomulka régime, will eventually become tired and bored with the barrage of anti-German propaganda it is too early to say, but at present, the national fear of Germany remains the one political asset the régime still possesses. On balance, the Polish régime is still far more tolerable for its citizens than any other in Eastern Europe.

During the last few years, the Council for Mutual Economic Aid (Comecon) has become a significant factor in bloc economic relations. Since its ninth session at Bucharest in June 1958, Comecon has made an effort to co-ordinate the East European economies, and the Soviet policy of the Stalin era – characterized by the subjection of each individual East European economy to that of the Soviet Union, the minimization of links between the satellite economies, and maximum autarky for each economy at the cost of developing industries for which there was no natural aptitude – appears to have been abandoned. The cruder forms of 'colonial exploitation' by the Soviet Union have been given up; individual countries have to some extent been encouraged to concentrate on those types of industry for which they have an aptitude; and multilateral trade and economic co-operation have somewhat increased. When the Soviet pipelines to East Germany and Hungary are completed, the cost of fuel transport will be greatly reduced. Czechoslovak co-operation with Hungary in the creation of two large power plants utilizing the water power of the Danube, Czechoslovak aid to the Polish and Bulgarian mining industries, and joint assistance by Poland, East Germany, and Czechoslovakia for the construction of a proposed Roumanian cellulose plant are examples of co-ordinated economic activity within the East European bloc.

The East European states have also played their part in the overall strategy of the bloc for penetrating the underdeveloped countries. The most important contributor has been Czechoslovakia, whose economic credits to such countries during the years 1957–61 may be estimated at about $260 million (out of an estimated total of more than $400 million for all the East European satellite states in that period). The most important Czechoslovak credits in 1960 were to Cuba ($40 million), Indonesia ($30 million), and the United Arab Republic ($27·5 million). Polish credits to underdeveloped countries in the 1957–61 period are estimated at $70 million, and East German at $53 million. In 1960 there were probably about 1,000 East European technicians working in non-bloc countries, and about 2,000 students from non-bloc countries undergoing training in the satellite countries. The largest number of technicians were in the U.A.R., which also provided the largest contingent of trainees.

There has also been an increase in trade between the East European states and some of the new countries. By far the largest increase up to 1960 was with the U.A.R., while there was a smaller but still considerable increase in trade with Indonesia and Guinea. No doubt East European trade with Cuba has been growing rapidly in 1961, although accurate figures are not available at the time of writing. The total effort of the East European satellites – and indeed of the whole Sino-Soviet bloc – in trade, aid, and training is still small in 1961 compared to the effort of the West, but it has been growing at a rapid pace and will doubtless continue to do so.

The divergence between Soviet and Chinese policies, which became clearly visible with the establishment of the 'people's communes' in 1958 and reached a climax on the eve of the Moscow Communist conference of November–December 1960, had as its main repercussion in Eastern Europe the defection of Albania, the most backward and isolated satellite, from the Soviet to the Chinese camp. Slight indications of Chinese influence have at times also been reported from East Germany and Bulgaria. On this obscure problem it may be worth while to suggest one general point.

One possible line of division within the Sino-Soviet bloc is between those states which are satisfied in terms of territory and those which are not – 'haves' and 'have-nots' in the terminology of the 1930's. From this point of view the Soviet Union and Czechoslovakia are clearly 'haves'. Poland and Roumania, relatively speaking, are also 'haves' inasmuch as their only remaining unredeemed lands would have to be claimed from the Soviet Union (eastern Poland, northern Bukovina, and Bessarabia), a thought too impious to be considered by any good Communist. Hungary is potentially a 'have-not', her potential claims being at the expense of two bloc countries (Czechoslovakia and Roumania) and one non-bloc country (Yugoslavia). Unquestionably 'have-nots' are East Germany, whose leaders aim not only at the annexation of West Berlin but also at extending their régime to the whole of Germany; Bulgaria, whose unredeemed lands lie in Greece and Yugoslavia; and Albania, whose leaders and people share the desire to incorporate in the Albanian state the one-third of the Albanian nation living in Yugoslavia, as well as the small Albanian minority within the boundaries of Greece. All three Communist states of Asia are 'have-nots': China demands Formosa, and the Communist régimes of North Vietnam and North Korea wish to extend their rule to the whole of their respective countries.

Even though no sane Communist leader, not even Mao Tse-tung, can positively desire a thermo-nuclear war, it is reasonable to suppose that the 'have-not' governments would be more inclined, and the 'haves' less inclined, towards tactics of 'brinkmanship'. It is therefore interesting to note that two of the three clearly 'have-not' European satellites (East Germany and Bulgaria) have given some indications of sympathy for China, while the third (Albania) has definitely espoused the Chinese point of view. Here it may be argued that Albania's physical isolation from the rest of the bloc, which one would normally consider a dangerous weakness, has proved in fact a source of strength. Whereas neither the Bulgarian nor the East German Government can openly take the Chinese side so long as the Soviet Government peremptorily demands their support, Albania can and does. If the hostility of Yugoslavia, Greece, Italy, and the West has not intimidated Enver Hoxha, there is no obvious reason why he should bow before the wrath of distant Moscow. Albania is a poor country, its economy primitive, its people accustomed to little, its Army and police ruthless; it can survive at a low level of welfare and happiness. Any help that it can get from China will be a windfall of marginal value.

Thus, in general, the picture presented by Eastern Europe in 1961 is bleak. It is bleak for the people, who see no prospect of liberty in the near future. It is bleak for their friends in the West, who see no immediate prospect of helping them. It is bleak for the Communist leaders, who see little prospect of winning the allegiance of the East European peoples.

The problem of Berlin is vitally important to the East Europeans. There can be little doubt that any substantial Western concessions on Berlin would depress most of the East European peoples, and that the surrender of West Berlin to the tender mercies of Ulbricht would depress them exceedingly. Whatever Ulbricht's own scheme of priorities may be, Khrushchev's aims are probably not so much to enslave the Berliners as to drive a wedge between the whole German people and the West, and to prove to the East Europeans generally that Western sympathy is worthless. Yet, in any political trial of strength with the West, Khrushchev's position is far from invulnerable. Not the least of his weaknesses is the fact that the peoples of Eastern Germany and of Eastern Europe as a whole continue to dislike their Communist régimes and wish, above all, to be rid of the yoke of the new Soviet imperialism.

Four: International Problems

Soviet Foreign Policy on the Eve of the Summit

Any general survey of the nature of Soviet foreign policy must, I think, begin with the well-known fact that the Soviet Union is both a great territorial empire and the homeland of a worldwide revolutionary totalitarian movement. Let us not forget that it is an empire. The 1959 census showed 114,588,000 Russians in a total population of 208,826,650. To these we should add about 96 million people under indirect Soviet rule in Eastern and Central Europe. We have 115 million Russians out of 300 million subjects of the Soviet Empire. This empire has of course the usual strategic and economic interests that any great empire must have. Many of them are similar to those of the old Russian Empire of the Tsars. I need only mention Poland, the Black Sea Straits, Persia, Korea, and Manchuria to make this point clear. But of course all that the recurrence of these names, so familiar to Lord Palmerston or Lord Salisbury, proves is that the facts of geography remain facts, that Russia is the same piece of the earth's surface as ever.

Before the Second World War, when the Soviet Union was rather weak, the Communist aspect of its policy received relatively more attention (though not necessarily well informed or intelligent attention) than today, when its status as one of the world's two giant Powers tends to obsess us to the exclusion of all else. This is, I think, unfortunate.

Communism is not just a political opinion like any other. Communists believe that Marxism-Leninism, as interpreted by the currently authorized ideological spokesmen of the Central Committee of the Communist Party of the Soviet Union, is a full scientific explanation of human history and social development. The ineluctable laws of human society ensure that all the branches of the human race will move through socialism to Communism, most but not all of them passing through the stage of capitalism. But the fact that this progress is certain does not mean that Communists should sit

---

This paper was delivered at Chatham House, 5 April 1960, and subsequently published in *International Affairs*, July 1960.

back and let history do their job for them. On the contrary, passivity is one of the worst of sins. The more convinced a Communist is of the inevitable victory of his cause, the more urgent is his duty to expedite it by all means in his power.

In the first years of the Soviet régime, pursuit of world socialist revolution was the manifest and unquestioned duty of those responsible for Soviet foreign policy. In the years of Stalin's rise to power in the mid-1920's, the revolutionary aim to some extent receded into the background, partly because the general world situation was unfavourable, and partly because Stalin was preoccupied first with the elimination of his rivals in the party leadership and then with the epic tasks of collectivization of agriculture and industrialization. But the aim was never abandoned. Indeed, Stalin always maintained that 'the *complete* victory of socialism' in the Soviet Union was possible only when 'capitalist encirclement' had been ended by socialist revolution in the most powerful industrial countries.

A new stage began about the end of the 1930's, when a great measure of success had been achieved in economic construction. At this point Stalin decided that what had been built in the Soviet Union *was* socialism. This is in fact stated in the Constitution which he introduced in 1936. If 'socialism' meant the Soviet system, then 'socialist revolution' could only mean the adoption of a régime designed from the Soviet blueprint. In 1936 this was an academic point, but between 1944 and 1948 the principle was put into practice in the most realistic manner in eight European countries, six of which had been occupied by the Soviet Army.

But Stalin has now been dead seven years. Has the doctrine not been scrapped, together with adulation of Stalin?

The most authoritative recent pronouncement is the declaration of 16 November 1957, signed in Moscow by the representatives of the twelve ruling Communist parties of Europe and Asia. One passage reads:

> The processes of the socialist revolution and the building of socialism are governed by a number of basic laws applicable in all countries embarking on a socialist course. These laws manifest themselves everywhere, alongside a great variety of historical national peculiarities and traditions which must by all means be taken into account.

The first of these laws is:

> guidance of the working masses by the working class, the core of which is the Marxist-Leninist party, in effecting a proletarian revolution in

one form or another and establishing one form or another of the dictatorship of the proletariat.

During the Soviet-Yugoslav reconciliation of 1955-6 there was much talk on both sides of 'different roads to socialism'. But the limits were shown when the government of Imre Nagy in Hungary, an overwhelmingly socialist Government supported by the working class, was suppressed by Soviet arms-not by Stalin but by Khrushchev. In the spring of 1958 there was a most illuminating controversy in connexion with the Draft Programme of the League of Communists of Yugoslavia. The Yugoslavs had argued that it was possible to achieve socialism without a revolution, and that the struggle for socialism need not necessarily be led by a Marxist-Leninist party. They were probably thinking not so much of social democratic parties in Europe as of more or less socialist parties in Asia and Africa, for example the followers of U Nu in Burma. But the Soviet publicists were inflexible. The struggle for socialism must be led by Marxist-Leninist parties, and there must be a revolution. However, they distinguished between 'violent' revolutions and 'peaceful' revolutions. In the first case the enemies of the Communists must be overthrown by force, and state power must then be used to suppress them. In the second case, if the enemies would yield without a fight, it would be possible to seize power peacefully, and force would be needed only to crush those who had surrendered. Mikoyan had made this clear already at the 20th Congress of the C.P.S.U. in February 1956, when he gave, as examples of a 'parliamentary road to socialism', the cases of Czechoslovakia and Eastern Germany.

To sum up, socialist revolutions are revolutions made by Marxist-Leninist parties, operating according to principles and tactics approved in Moscow. Socialist revolutions may be 'violent' – in which case violence is used before and after seizure of power – or 'peaceful' – in which case it is used only after.

All this was made clear by Soviet ideologists writing in 1958, when Khrushchev was undisputed master of the Soviet Union. Has he changed his view? Mr Khrushchev rose to supreme power by his control over the apparatus of the Communist Party. His victory was the victory of the party machine, of its *apparatchiks* and its lay priesthood of ideologists. In Stalin's later years the party was one of a number of instruments of power wielded by the autocrat: the most important other instruments were the police, the armed forces, and the industrial bureaucracy. Today there is no doubt that the party is, as it was in Lenin's time, the supreme instrument of power. Party officials and propagandists have more prestige and power in the Soviet Union than they have had since the 1920's. Foreign policy is therefore likely to be more, not less, influenced by ideology than under Stalin.

And why should Khrushchev wish to abandon his Communist convictions? As he sees it, and as the leading people in the party and State see it, Communist ideology has been a remarkably useful guide to action. Under its inspiration, the leaders of the Soviet Union have made their country immensely powerful. The same Moscow declaration of November 1957 gives the following description of the world political scene. It describes the 'forces of peace' in the world in six categories. They are:

> the invincible camp of socialist countries headed by the Soviet Union; the peace-loving countries of Asia and Africa taking an anti-imperialist stand and forming, together with the socialist countries, a broad peace zone; the international working class and above all its vanguard – the Communist parties; the liberation movement of the peoples of the colonies and semi-colonies; the mass peace movement of the peoples; the peoples of Latin America and the masses in the imperialist countries who are putting up increasing resistance to the plans for a new war.

These forces the Soviet Government is confident that it can mobilize for the world-wide victory of 'socialism' – that is, of the Soviet régime. Mr Khrushchev has never given any indication that he disagrees with the diagnosis or the exhortations put out by the most eminent spokesmen of the régime of which he is the double head – First Secretary of the party and Prime Minister. We would I think, do well to pay him the compliment of taking his convictions, and the resultant policy, more seriously.

The pursuit of these aims – the imposition, whether by force or by capitulation of their opponents, of the Soviet type of régime on all nations not already subject or allied to them – places the Soviet rulers in a relationship to the non-Communist world which can only be described as permanent warfare. It differs in kind from the traditional relationship between states. England and France were enemies for centuries, because they were rivals for the control of Aquitaine, or the Low Countries, or North America, not because Englishmen wanted to destroy France as such, or the reverse. But the Soviet leaders are not primarily concerned with strategic problems such as the Black Sea Straits (though these may play their part at times), but with their duty as Communists to expedite

Soviet Foreign Policy on the Eve of the Summit 193

the ineluctable process of history by destroying what they call 'capitalism'. It is not what we do, or what we want, but what we are, that marks us out as their victims.

I have used the word 'warfare', but this must be understood in a very broad sense. The Soviet aim is to destroy their chosen enemies, and their effort is systematic and permanent. But all sorts of methods may be used, of which 'war' in the traditional sense is only one. The methods include diplomacy, propaganda, the granting or witholding of trade and of economic aid, subversion, guerrilla warfare, open warfare by satellite armies or 'volunteers', open warfare by Soviet forces with conventional weapons, and thermo-nuclear war. The selection and admixture of the methods of struggle are a matter of expediency, depending on the concrete circumstances of each case. Questions such as, 'Should we rely on military or economic means?', so often asked in the West, must appear meaningless to a Soviet observer. In the conduct of Soviet policy, the availability of all the necessary political, economic, and military weapons all the time is assumed.

The Soviets' attitude to 'shooting war' is empirical. They have no trace of the romantic love of war proclaimed by Mussolini and practised by Hitler. They have also no trace of pacifism. Their military doctrine assumes that they must be capable of fighting any sort of war – with conventional weapons, with small-range atomic weapons, or with the full thermo-nuclear panoply. Hitherto the military force of the Atlantic Alliance has deterred them from military action. In the economic and political fields, however, they have, since 1945, shown themselves far more successful than the West. Should the Western Powers now decide, not only to devote greater resources to the economic and political struggle – especially in Asia, Africa, and Latin America – but also to pay for this new effort by economizing on defence expenditure, then the opportunity for military action might appear favourable to the Soviet leaders. The West cannot in fact choose to meet the Soviet challenge in one field only – military or economic or political. It has to meet it in all fields, and pay the cost, or be driven from defeat to defeat and to ultimate destruction.

The picture I have presented is, I fully realize, unpleasant. It does not correspond to the general picture that emerges from the popular press and the statesmen's speeches in this country or America today. Surely, you will be thinking, there have been great changes in the Soviet Union in the last years?

Certainly there have been changes. Let me briefly mention what seem to me to be the five most important points. First, the security police has less power, and exercises the power it has much more moderately, than in Stalin's time. Soviet citizens are far less afraid, and even speak freely to foreigners. However, the whole machinery of the security police is still there, to be used if and when the leaders need it. Secondly, both workers and peasants are earning more, and far more consumers' goods are available. However, the priority on heavy industry and war industry is still there. The Soviet economy is richer, the productivity of labour is higher, and as the cake grows everyone's slice is bigger. But economic policy is planned not by the consumer but by the party leaders. Thirdly, there are fewer troops under arms. But the armed forces, and especially the land army, are still far larger than ours, and the proportion of combat troops to total forces is higher. Fourthly, the managerial or technocratic element in Soviet society is extremely important. There are people in important posts in the administration for whom the principal criterion is not ideological orthodoxy but professional efficiency. This conflict between ideology and practical outlook is found even inside the party machine. The pressure for normality in everyday life, and against the ideological crusades whether at home or abroad, are undoubtedly growing. One might even say that the other-directed young executive, the 'organization man', of American society is beginning to appear in the Soviet Union. Finally, there is evidence that among the educated youth there is even a spirit of critical inquiry, which spares no political or economic dogmas, and which was strongly stimulated by the events in Hungary, Poland, and Yugoslavia.

All these trends undoubtedly exist, and they promise much for the future. But do not let us confuse the future with the present. The Soviet Union is not ruled by consumers demanding cars with fins or durable household goods, or by organization men, or by angry young students, but by the Central Committee of the party led by Mr Khrushchev.

Unfortunately Western public opinion about foreign policy is still suffering from a hang-over from McCarthyism. There is no need for me to waste words on the late Senator for Wisconsin, and this is no place to consider the roots of McCarthyism in American society. But the effects of McCarthyism on Western attitudes to the Soviet Union are too important to be passed over. During the height of the anti-Communist hysteria in the United States (which McCarthy exploited without caring a cent about the issues involved), it was frequently asserted that the Russians were crude savages, incapable of civilized achievements, and that they were monsters of wickedness. But in the last few years tens of thousands of Americans have been to Russia, and have seen for themselves that Russians are charming people, that they lead virtuous (perhaps boringly virtuous) lives, and that their country is well ordered. At the same time the achievements of Soviet science have impressed the whole world. Indeed the enthusiasm with which, in the months after the first sputnik, Americans denounced their own system of education and extolled that of the Soviet Union could not fail to strike anyone who was living in the United States at that time.

But if all that had been said in the McCarthy era about the barbarism and the wickedness of the Russians was shown to be untrue, then, it was quickly assumed, everything that had been said about the implacable hostility of the Soviet Government to the rest of the world must also be untrue. It is one of the most widespread of democratic fallacies that a nation of enemies must consist of wicked men, and that a nation of decent and kindly men and women cannot be a nation of enemies. Unfortunately this is a fallacy. Russians have been intelligent and charming for centuries, but the Soviet leaders were implacably hostile to all non-Communist states long before Senator McCarthy was heard of, and remain so now that he is dead. But not the least of the damage that his lies did to the free nations was the uncritical revulsion which their discrediting produced. In fact there is today in the West, perhaps especially in Britain, an arrogant orthodoxy of anti-anti-Communism which inhibits clarity of thought no less than the preceding anti-Communist hysteria. One may even speak of a new McCarthyism of the Left, with its own special smear words. It is hardly an exaggeration to say that anyone who today argues that the exercise of power plays an important part in the Soviet system of government, and still more anyone who tries to analyse the methods by which Communists have achieved power or the instruments by which they pursue their international policies, is bound to incur the reproach of being 'a professional anti-Communist', and to have his arguments dismissed, without rational examination, as 'just cold war propaganda'. This mentality is of course exploited by Communists in the West, but it was certainly not created by them.

Senator McCarthy in two years did more for the Soviet Communist cause, at least in the Anglo-Saxon countries, than their Communist parties had achieved in forty.

What are the main dangers to the West at present from Soviet policy? It seems to me that there are four.

The first is a technological break-through by Soviet science such as to convince the Soviet Government that it could destroy the retaliatory power of the Atlantic Alliance. As to the likelihood of this, I have no ability to form an opinion. If it should occur we should be placed before the choice, of which so much is made in various contemporary publicity campaigns, but which mercifully does not confront us today – the choice between annihilation or submission to Soviet rule. The only action against this danger is, of course, a sustained effort of scientific research and nuclear armament on the part of the West – certainly of the United States, perhaps of the other Western Powers, perhaps not. The only solution in the long term is, of course, a mutually accepted plan of nuclear disarmament, of whose efficacy both sides are confident.

The second danger is the superiority of the Soviet Union in conventional forces. This enables the Soviet Union or its satellites to intervene if war breaks out anywhere along the borders of the Soviet orbit, and place on the West the onus of resorting to nuclear war. Here I shall make only one point. The Soviet superiority is not a fact of nature, but a result of political decisions by Western governments and electors. The Soviet Union has 210 million people, the N.A.T.O. countries about 400 million. The peoples of the East European countries (with another 100 million) are a dubious military asset to the Soviet bloc. The West has the power, if it has the will, to match the Soviet capability in conventional weapons.

But it is of the third and fourth dangers that I should like to speak at rather greater length. These I will describe as 'encirclement' and 'demoralization'. The first of these consists of the unremitting efforts of Soviet policy to exploit the conflicts between the West and the Afro-Asian nations, to mobilize the Afro-Asians under their leadership, and so to transform the balance of political and economic power in the world that the West will in the end have no choice but to capitulate. The second consists of the no less persistent effort to exploit for the Soviet advantage those trends of Western public opinion about foreign policy which are favourable to Soviet interests (though in most cases in no way created by Soviet policy) in order to produce the same result – capitulation of the West before Soviet power, the equivalent in the international field of the 'peaceful revolution' of which I was speaking earlier in the field of internal politics, and which would be its direct and inevitable consequence.

I should like to develop these points by taking three problems which illustrate them, and which are, or ought to be, much in our minds at the present time – African nationalism, Persia, and Germany.

The great question of the next years in Africa is not, it seems to me, whether the African nations will make themselves independent of their Western colonial rulers, or obtain equality with, or power over, their white fellow citizens. To me it seems beyond doubt that they will. I say this although I am fully aware of the terrible complexities and tragedies of South Africa and of the Rhodesias. I say it also without any pleasure, for I have the gravest doubts as to whether the triumph of the nationalist intelligentsias of the African nations will be a triumph for human liberty or human civilization. But it is what is happening. The great questions for Africa, to which we do not know the answer, are different. The first is, will independence be obtained in circumstances which make possible normal, mutually advantageous, and even, if you like, friendly relations between the independent states and their former rulers, or will it take place in a climate of hatred, of desire for revenge, of a passionate obsession to humiliate the white man and to help his enemies? And the second question is, will the independent states preserve their independence or will they be enticed, deceived, or compelled into the Soviet or Chinese empire? I cannot answer these questions, but I must stress that Soviet policy towards Africa is designed to ensure that the answers to both are favourable to its aims. And I must also insist that the Soviet rulers are putting into the study of Africa and the penetration of Africa a wealth of human ability, economic resources, and plain hard work which puts the nations of the West to shame, and which is still largely ignored by the African experts in Western countries.

Secondly, Persia. This is, I think, in relation to its international importance, the most underrated problem in world politics today – at any rate the question on which Western public opinion is least informed. Thanks to the CENTO alliance, the Soviet Union has no direct access by land to the Arab countries. This seriously restricts the scale of Soviet influence in Iraq and in Egypt. If, from the Soviet point of view, Egypt is the key to Africa, Persia is the key to Egypt. Persia is by far the weakest of the three Muslim members of CENTO. It suffers from almost all the weaknesses from which Nuri Pasha's régime in Iraq suffered, especially from the two most dangerous of them – the terrible contrasts of wealth and poverty in city and countryside, and the alienation of the educated class, the intelligentsia. The Shah is said to have a programme of social reforms. How sincere and how enegertic a reformer he is, I do not know. But even if he were a genius, a hero, and a saint, he could not cure Persia's ills in a few years. Meanwhile the country must be governed, and this depends, to put it in the crudest terms, on whether his security service is more reliable than was Nuri's. If a revolution took place in Persia, even one in which Soviet agents had had no hand at all, the Soviet Government could hardly refrain from exploiting it. In so large and mountainous a country as Persia, revolution in the capital might well lead to civil war in the provinces. The strategic importance of Persia, both for the Western defence of the Middle East and the Soviet penetration of Africa, is such that all sorts of frightening possibilities occur to one. In such a situation, the inferiority of the West in conventional forces, and the absence of an adequate, airborne strategic reserve might well force the N.A.T.O. Powers into the choice between nuclear war and a capitulation that would be likely to bring Africa, within a few years, under Soviet domination. This is a very dangerous situation. One might even argue that it is a common interest of the West and the Soviet Union to prevent the Persian situation getting out of hand. One might even hope that at the Summit Conference they would actually talk on these lines. But of course common action means a compromise. And the Soviet Union has no reason to compromise if it believes that it can get all it wants for nothing. And I can hardly believe that its study of Western public opinion on Persia has convinced the Soviet Government that it is likely to meet with much opposition, provided it avoids the crudest forms of direct aggression. The Western press shows a fairly complete indifference to Persia. The main exception to this statement are the political declamations in Left-wing weeklies against Persian landlordism which, though largely justifiable in terms of the social facts, do not help to clarify the problem. The question is not whether Persian landlordism, which has existed for centuries, is a bad thing – it is – but whether Persia will become a means of Soviet expansion.

Denunciations of the Shah in the British press merely make the Soviet leaders more inclined to take risks.

Thirdly, Germany. The aim of Soviet policy is perfectly clear. It is the unification of Germany under the Ulbricht régime. In East Germany an efficient system of political and economic power has been built up under a Communist Party which is much hated by its subjects but is fully backed by the Soviet Union. Unification is to be brought about by some form of confederation on the basis of parity between the two German Governments. A government imposed by force on a quarter of the German people is to have as many posts in the confederal government as a government freely elected by three-quarters of the German people. Holding positions of power at the centre while denying to the democratic forces any influence in its own territory, the Communist Party could infiltrate and terrorize the whole of Germany in much the same way as the Communist Party of Czechoslovakia infiltrated and terrorized that country between 1945 and 1948, and with the same result.

Such is the aim, but it is still far from realization. The immediate aims are more modest. They are to make the Ulbricht régime internationally respectable, to undermine freedom in Berlin, and to destroy the confidence of the German people in the Western alliance. This is no time to enter into the details of the Berlin question. But Soviet policy has, I think, three aims – to detach West Berlin economically from Western Germany, to create some machinery for interfering in freedom of speech in West Berlin, and to convince the Berliners that the West is abandoning them. The aim in fact is the demoralization of Berlin, and as its consequence the demoralization of the whole German people. At the Summit Conference various concrete proposals will no doubt be put forward by both sides. It seems to me that they should be judged by the extent to which they promote or hinder the realization of these Soviet aims.

The Soviet aim of demoralization of public opinion on foreign policy is not confined to Berlin or to Germany. And looking no farther than our own country, one cannot surely deny that the opportunities are excellent. The climate of capitulation is being built up more successfully and more consciously than in 1938. And it is certainly not the work of the Communist Party or of Soviet agents. When one finds articles in the same tone, and sometimes from the same pen, denouncing Dr Adenauer as the main obstacle to peace, appearing in the *Evening Standard* and the *New Statesman*, it is difficult to know what to think. In the months before Munich, at least there was a division in public opinion. Today the impression is created by a large part of the British press that Western Germany is ruled by the adolescents who scribble swastikas on synagogues, and that Eastern Germany is a democratic state ruled by progressive humanitarians. One wonders what our press would have said if a prominent German bishop had signed a letter to be handed to our Ambassador in Bonn protesting against the Notting Hill outrages. When refugees from beyond the Oder declare that the Oder–Neisse line cannot be accepted, this is treated by our press as a statement of the West German Government's intention to invade Poland. Personally I believe that the Oder–Neisse frontier has come to stay, and I would even say that on balance, taking everything into account, it is a just frontier. But I do not consider that I have the right to moral denunciation of an East Prussian who feels it is an outrage that he was driven from his home, and will feel so all his life. Nor do I equate such a man's words with the foreign policy of Bonn.

One last point on Germany. It was a commonplace of liberal writing on Germany for the last fifty years – a commonplace on which I was brought up, and which still seems to me true – that the sickness of Europe for the last century or more has been the sickness of its heart – Germany. Or, to use a different but equally familiar formula, that the great historical treason of Germany was that she betrayed her mission to unite Europe, preferring vainly to seek to dominate it. And another commonplace of the same kind was that the future peace of Europe depended on the healing of the ancient conflict between Germany and France. Well, now we have a German Government that bases its whole policy on European unity, and in particular on Franco-German friendship, and actually does something about it. And we splutter with indignation, shout that we are being victimized, and talk about a Paris–Bonn Axis. The spectacle of the relations between the Western Powers at the present time must give great comfort to the Soviet leaders.

Finally, a few words about the Summit Conference.

Summit conferences are usually considered to be occasions for diplomatic negotiation. An enormous amount of nonsense has been talked about negotiating with the Soviet Union. In the McCarthy era it was widely held that it was in some way surrendering to the powers of darkness to have any dealings with Soviet diplomats at all.

It was also widely believed that Soviet diplomats were so clever that they would always out-manœuvre Western diplomats. These views were silly six years ago, and they are still silly today. But the opposite view, that negotiation is a sort of magic talisman which will cure all our troubles, is also silly. Obviously it has always been, and still is, desirable to negotiate with the Soviet leaders whenever there is something to negotiate about. Successful negotiations between Powers which are in conflict with each other end in compromises, with each side giving something and getting something. The trouble about the present situation is that though it is very easy to think of lots of things which we would like the Soviet Government to give us, it is rather hard to see what we can offer in return that is of the slightest value to the Soviet Government.

But summit conferences, if we may judge from the past, are not necessarily only, or even primarily, occasions for negotiation. They can also be propaganda tournaments. Propaganda-by-conference is indeed one of the forms of propaganda for which the Soviet leaders have shown the greatest aptitude. The object is, of course, to choose the right moment to end the serious negotiation, and to place the maximum odium on the Western governments, in the eyes of Western electors and of Afro-Asian intelligentsias. Personally I do not see why the Soviet Government should always have the better of these propaganda battles. I do not believe that the West has a weaker moral or political case than the Soviet Union. But, of course, one does not get one's case accepted if one does not even put it. And that is what has happened at past summit conferences. One must hope that the Western leaders will go to this summit conference prepared both to negotiate and to make propaganda, ready for whatever turn events may take.

Certainly the Soviet First Secretary and Prime Minister will be in a strong position. His Government has an almost unbroken record of successes in foreign policy since 1945. The surrender of Persian Azerbaidjan in 1946 and the survival of Yugoslavia after 1948 are the only notable failures. Mr Khrushchev is in no hurry. Nobody demands quick results from him. He does not have to face a presidential or parliamentary election. He doesn't have to worry about his allies. We comfort ourselves by saying that the unanimity of the Soviet public is the result of police terror, and that free societies are morally healthier. But one should not make too much of this. Certainly the police terror is there, even if in the background.

Certainly the forcible indoctrination of the masses with Marxist-Leninist cant is there. Personally I am convinced that the picture of the world that emerges from this cant is false, that their ideology misleads the Soviet statesmen more than it helps them. But the Soviet régime has other sources of strength – the serious-mindedness and self-righteousness of the Soviet urban citizens, their acceptance of discipline and hierarchy, their conviction that their country is getting more and more powerful, their sense of a world mission, their belief that they are on the side of progress. The successes of the Soviet Union in fact are due not so much to 'scientific' Marxism-Leninism as to the social processes which they have been through in the last thirty years and which the people of England and Scotland went through from a hundred and fifty to fifty years ago. Visitors to the Soviet Union understandably mock at the comic and pompous features of Victorianism in the arts. But the Soviet people have the Victorian virtues, and these are formidable. Victorian England was a force to be reckoned with, and so is neo-Victorian Soviet Russia. The affluent society, with its fin-tailed cars, waist-high culture, angry young men and all, faces a vast industrial and military power led by men who combine something of the outlook and the virtues of Lenin, Tsar Nicholas I, and Samuel Smiles. It is a rather formidable prospect.

The 'National Bourgeoisie' in Soviet Strategy

THEORY AND POLICY

Ever since the Bolsheviks, in Lenin's lifetime, began to pay serious attention to the world beyond Europe, their polices have had to face the conflict between nationalism and Communism, between the struggle for independence and the class struggle. This unresolved contradiction led to the failure of the first attempts to influence events in Turkey and Persia in the nineteen-twenties. Still more important was the disastrous defeat of the Communists by the Kuomintang in China in 1927, the debate on which in international Communist circles was linked with the last stages of the conflict between Stalin and Trotsky. But it was in China, twenty years later, that the contradiction was first successfully transcended when the Communists were able to mobilize for their own purposes the Chinese patriotism which, in the first stage, had been used against them by Chiang Kai-shek. China was thus the scene of the greatest defeat and the greatest victory of Communism in the task of combining the national and class struggle in a single 'national liberation movement' under its leadership.

Since the Second World War, nationalism has spread through southern Asia and the Arab world, and has become a mighty force even in Africa beyond the Sahara. In Latin America, too, where nationalism of a sort has existed for more than a hundred years, it has taken on a more virulent revolutionary form. The policies of the two Communist Great Powers, the Soviet Union and China, have had to adapt themselves to this new situation, and the professional ideologists and academics have had to carry out the necessary adjustments of Marxist-Leninist theory. Afro-Asian nationalism has to be treated on two distinct levels – Government action and Marxist theory. Both are considered important by the Soviet and

---

This article was published in *Unity and Contradiction*, edited by Kurt London, Praeger, New York, 1962, under the title 'The Communist Powers and Afro-Asian Nationalism'.

Chinese leaders. Theory influences political action. Political action is, however, also influenced by the facts of international politics. When a new policy is adopted for empirical reasons, a new theoretical justification has to be found for it. The new theory, in turn, has its effect on policy. It is therefore important for observers of Communist policy to study the interplay of action and theory.

The grant of independence to India and Burma in 1947 was treated by Soviet spokesmen as a fraud. Nehru and Nu were regarded as agents of British imperialism, maintaining the stranglehold of British monopoly capital over their countries while covering it with an outward appearance of respectability. The Soviet attitude to Sukarno and to the first governments of independent Indonesia was similar. The outbreak of war between the Vietminh and the French in December 1946 was probably due mainly to local conditions, and was subsequently approved by the Soviet leaders rather than brought about by initiative from Moscow. However, the 1948 outbreak of armed rebellion in Burma, Malaya, the Philippines, Indonesia, and the Telengana district in India can hardly be attributed to local factors and coincidence. It seems more plausible to attribute these events to a definite 'left' strategy in Moscow, possibly associated with the predominant influence of A. A. Zhdanov. The death of Zhdanov in July 1948, and the execution of a number of his associates in the 'Leningrad Affair' of 1949, did not cause the 'left' strategy to be abandoned. This strategy was associated, in theoretical discussions by Soviet experts on Asia, with an emphasis on the leading role of the working class, the treacherous role of the bourgeoisie, and the close link between the class struggle and the struggle against imperialism.

Chinese Communists had played little part in Communist policy toward Asia in the nineteen-forties, either in theory or in practice, since they were fully occupied with their civil war. But in November 1949, only a few months after their victory, a far-reaching Chinese claim was made in the statement by Liu Shao-ch'i to the conference of the World Federation of Trade Unions in Peking that whereas the Russian October Revolution is the great example for carrying out a socialist revolution in an industrial European country, 'the path taken by the Chinese people in defeating imperialism and in founding the People's Republic of China is the path that must be taken by the peoples of the various colonial and semicolonial countries in their fight for national independence and people's democracy'.

The historical justification of this claim is doubtful. The Russia of 1917 can hardly be regarded as a representative example of an advanced industrial society. It is true that in the events of February–October 1917, the working class played an important part, which has no parallel in the history of the Chinese Communists' rise to power. It is also true that the peasants contributed a larger share of the manpower used by the Communists, for a longer period of time, in China than in Russia – though it would be wrong to underrate the peasant soldiers used by the Bolsheviks both in the subversion of the Provisional Government and in the Civil War of 1918–20. In essence, however, by comparison with the industrial West of the twentieth century, both Lenin's Russia and Mao's China were 'underdeveloped societies', and in both revolutions the leadership came from no social class, but from the classless cadres of professional revolutionaries that have been the ideal for Communist parties ever since Lenin wrote *What Is to Be Done?*

Here, however, we are concerned only with the fact that the claim to provide a specially relevant model for Asia was made by Liu in 1949 on behalf of the Chinese Communists. This claim was neither accepted nor directly rejected by Soviet spokesmen. Soviet theoretical discussions, however, such as that which took place under the auspices of the Academy of Sciences in 1951, showed clearly that Soviet views on these problems were different.[1]

Differences in practical policy towards Asia appeared during the Korean War. It soon became clear that independent Asian states were taking a different attitude to the war than their former European masters or the American allies of the latter. This the Chinese recognized earlier than the Russians. The Indian Ambassador in Peking, Sardar Panikkar, was treated with courtesy, and the Chinese leaders ceased to denounce Nehru, Nu, or Sukarno as imperialist agents. Soviet policy, however, lagged behind Chinese even in the first years after Stalin's death, when the Moscow Government was more concerned with Europe than with Asia. It was during this period that the strategy developed that has been analyzed in John Kautsky's interesting book.[2] The name given to it by Kautsky – Neo-Maoism – does not seem to me entirely satisfactory. But the essence of the strategy was, as he shows, the inclusion of the bourgeoisie in the front to be led by the Communist parties. It was a new

[1] *Izvestia Akademii Navk* ('Seriya istorii i filosofii'), IX, Part I (Moscow, 1952).
[2] *Moscow and the Communist Party of India* (New York; John Wiley and Sons, 1956).

version of the old strategy of 'united front from below' extended to cover the bourgeoisie. Communists were now to claim to represent the interests not only of workers and peasants but also of capitalists. The decisive criterion was to be neither class nor ideology but solely willingness to join 'anti-imperialist' – that is, anti-American and anti-European – movements. There was less talk of the workers' class struggle, but the need for Communist leadership of the anti-imperialist front was not forgotten. This, of course, raised difficult problems when the question arose of co-operation with nationalist organizations that were not controlled by Communists and were strong enough to have a will of their own. Should the united front from below with the bourgeoisie (Kautsky's Neo-Maoism) be developed into a united front from above with the bourgeoisie? This question appears at present to be the occasion for disagreement between Soviet and Chinese policy in the Arab world.

However, in the period following the conclusion of the Korean War, whose first most striking events were the Bandung Conference of April 1955, and the Khrushchev–Bulganin visit to India in November 1955, the theorists' main task was to elaborate a doctrine about the role of social classes in the 'anti-imperialist' movements in the 'lands of the East' – including Africa and Latin America in addition to Asia – that would give doctrinal sanction to Soviet support for nationalist movements, and would also assist infiltration of Communists into such movements. Soviet theoretical discussions of this sort increasingly centred around the role of what was now called 'the national bourgeoisie'.

WHAT IS THE NATIONAL BOURGEOISIE?

In all Communist literature, from Karl Marx onward, the use of the word *bourgeoisie* has been ambiguous. At times, it has been used to denote only the business class, the capitalists. At others, it has been extended to include the whole upper stratum of urban society, the various social groups known in European history as the 'middle classes'. These, in the Europe of which Marx was a citizen, included not only capitalists but also Government servants (both civil and military) and members of the independent professions (in Russia, increasingly described by the then newly invented Russian word *intelligentsia*). Marx himself maintained, and his followers have adhered to this view, that the capitalists were the most important of these middle classes, and that in the period of capitalist economy, both the state machine and the intellectuals were essentially hangers on of the capitalists. Nevertheless, there is a difference between bourgeoisie meaning capitalists alone and bourgeoisie meaning all the middle classes. In present-day Communist literature, this difference is usually blurred. Even if one accepts Marx's views on the subordination of the other middle classes to the capitalists, the confusion between the wider and narrower uses of bourgeoisie is bound to inhibit clear thinking. In my own opinion, Marx's view in this matter was only partially true of the country and period that served as the main model for his analysis – mid-Victorian England. It was less true of nineteenth-century Germany, not at all of Imperial Russia, and even further from the truth in most of twentieth-century Asia and Africa.

The confusion of thought, and distortion of social reality, that arise from Marx's writings extend also to contemporary Communist discussion of the 'national bourgeoisie'. At times the 'national intelligentsia' is mentioned as a separate category, at times it is clearly included under the heading of 'national bourgeoisie'. The Government officials of independent Asian and African states are seldom separately discussed in the Communist literature that I have studied, but many observations about the 'national bourgeoisie' clearly apply to them as well.

For the most part, however, contemporary Communist use of the phrase 'national bourgeoisie' in the Asian and African context refers to the business class, and the main problem in Communist definitions of 'national bourgeoisie' is to decide which sections of the business class of a given country belong to it. The author of the main paper produced in a discussion on the 'national bourgeoisie' by Soviet academic experts in 1956, A. I. Levkovski, defined it as that section of the local bourgeoisie for whom 'national capitalist production is the foundation of its existence'.[1] He distinguished it from the 'usurer merchant bourgeoisie' on the one hand and from the 'comprador bourgeoisie' on the other. The national bourgeoisie even included sections of the 'monopolist bourgeoisie' in both India and the Philippines. In the discussion, G. I. Levinson argued that even such Filipino big capitalists as the steel magnate Marcello and the chemical-trust owner Garcia should be reckoned as members of the national bourgeoisie because their interests were in competition with those of American monopolists. In India, according to I. M.

[1] *Sovetskoe Vostokovedenie*, January 1957.

Reisner, the Indian-owned monopoly interests have a dual character: 'On the one hand, they represent forms of capitalism that exhibit decay and parasitism, and hinder capitalist development; at the same time they show themselves to be bearers of an extremely important national entrepreneurship.' It was pointed out by A. A. Guber that Soviet specialists were inclined to misuse the word 'comprador' and thereby indiscriminately damn all capitalists who had business links with foreign imperialist interests. This point was given much attention in another discussion of the 'national bourgeoisie', which was held in Eastern Germany in 1959 and attended by Communist intellectuals from many countries (but not from China).[1] Messouak, of Morocco, pointed out that the national bourgeoisie in many countries is obliged to trade with imperialist countries, because there is no other source from which to import the raw materials needed for industrialization. 'If we designate as compradors all who import foreign goods, and sign agreements with foreign firms, and if we regard them as agents of foreign monopolies, we not only risk the retarding of the advance of the national economy, but risk jeopardising our relations with the national bourgeoisie.' On the other hand, Eskandari, of Iran, suggested that the national bourgeoisie be defined as 'that part of the bourgeoisie which struggles against the imperialists, for a national industry and a national domestic market'. In his view, traders who handle imports of such goods as motor-cars or refrigerators, though they have an interest in the development of the home market, cannot be reckoned a part of the national bourgeoisie because 'it is they who help the foreign monopolies to gain access to our home market'. Walid Samman, of Syria, went so far as to say that Nasser was the representative of the comprador bourgeoisie of Egypt, especially of the Misr and Cairo Banks, which were taking over the economy of Syria. Idris Cox, of Great Britain, made the same point, insisting that the Syrian national bourgeoisie were resisting Egyptian business interests, and that the latter wished to extend their domination also over Iraq.

In the Soviet academic discussion, an attempt was made to divide the national bourgeoisie into three subdivisions – 'big, medium, and small'. M. A. Kocheryan even suggested that in the case of India, precise limits could be given. Small national bourgeois were

[1] The discussion is fully summarized in *World Marxist Review*, August 1959, and September 1959.

those with incomes up to 10,000 rupees (about $500); medium national bourgeois, with incomes of 10,000 to 100,000 rupees (about $500 to $5,000).[1] This arbitrary categorization, which recalls the attempts made in Soviet Russia in the twenties to define *kulaks*, *serednyaks*, and *bednyaks* in the Russian peasantry, was not supported by other speakers. In his concluding reply to the discussion, Levkovski distinguished the 'small national bourgeoisie' from the 'petty bourgeoisie': the former employs labour and appropriates surplus value, whereas the latter consists of self-employed producers. He also excluded even the richest peasants (*krestyanskaya verkhushka*) from the national bourgeoisie, on the ground that in Asia, the peasantry is much less differentiated than it was in Russia in 1917. The kulak can only be included in the national bourgeoisie when his main function is that of a capitalist entrepreneur.

The main impression that emerges from these published discussions, and from articles in the Soviet specialized press, is that no satisfactory social or economic criteria can be found to define the national bourgeoisie. The problem, in fact, is not social or economic, but political. The national bourgeoisie, in fact, consists of those Asian or African businessmen who can be manipulated for the aims of Soviet foreign policy. Nevertheless, Marxist-Leninist orthodoxy requires that quasi-economic terminology be used to state political aims. However, Idris Cox put the problem fairly frankly: 'Their role varies not because they are big or small, or whether they are a trading or industrial bourgeoisie, but whether or not they have economic and political ties with imperialism.'[2]

It is all fairly obvious. As long as the Soviet Government hopes to influence Indian policy, big capitalists in India, even if they are 'monopolists', can be given the respectable label of 'national bourgeois'. But as soon as Nasser pursues a policy disliked by Moscow, he becomes an agent of the comprador bourgeoisie and the Misr Bank. As the Communist Party is stronger in Syria than in Egypt, Syrian resistance to Egypt is generally encouraged, and the Syrian capitalists count as 'national bourgeois'.

THE POLITICAL ROLE OF THE NATIONAL BOURGEOISIE

From the Communist point of view, the non-Communist states of Asia and Africa fall into three categories. First are the independent states that pursue a neutralist policy. These are regarded as being

[1] *Sovetskoe Vostokovedenie*, loc. cit.   [2] *World Marxist Review*, loc. cit.

genuinely independent. Second are the sovereign states that belong to alliances with the West (the CENTO and S.E.A.T.O members). These are not admitted to be independent: at most, they are semi-colonies, victims of indirect imperialism. Third are the remaining colonies directly ruled by European powers.

In the first category of countries, the national bourgeoisie must be brought to support as strongly anti-Western a foreign policy as possible. In the second group, they must be brought into the movement for the repudiation of alliances with the West. In the third group, they must be brought into the struggle for independence.

The national bourgeoisie, however, has an inescapably dual character. On the one hand, it is, or is capable of becoming, anti-imperialist. On the other hand, it is an exploiting class, the enemy of the working class. In a joint discussion by Soviet and Chinese academic experts on 'The Disintegration of the Imperialist Colonial System in the Postwar World', held in 1959, A. A. Guber put the problem as follows:

> The working class ... has regarded the gaining of national independence merely as a stage, a necessary requisite for social change and the subsequent growing over of the national colonial revolution into a socialist revolution. The national bourgeoisie saw in national independence the attainment of its ultimate aim, namely, the establishment of its undivided rule in a sovereign state.[1]

Another eminent Soviet political expert on Asian affairs, V. V. Balabushevich, in an article published about the same time, observed that after independence has been won,

> ... a certain community of interests is preserved between the national bourgeoisie and the toiling masses in the cause of the defense of peace, the struggle against colonialism, and the strengthening of political and economic independence, but at the same time, the objective conditions arise for a further sharpening of the class struggle. In the fight for the strengthening of national independence, and for the most consistent solution of the tasks of the bourgeois-democratic revolution, the working class under the leadership of the Communist and workers' parties has the possibility of attracting to its side the broad popular masses, and in the first instance the peasantry.[2]

Shorn of its quasi-socio-economic terminology, this means simply that Communist parties must grasp political leadership from the other groups that have participated in the earlier phases of the independence movement. In all Communist literature on this

[1] This discussion is fully reported in *Mezhdunarodnaya Zhizn*, March 1959.
[2] *Problemy Vostokovedenia*, No. 2, 1959.

subject, for 'the working class' one should understand 'the Communist Party', and for 'the hegemony of the working class' one should understand 'the political dictatorship of the Communist Party'. Idris Cox makes the point clearly in comparing events in India and in China: In India, independence was won 'under the leadership of the national bourgeoisie as a whole, including the big bourgeoisie . . . as distinct from China where the leadership of the workers in close alliance with the peasants merged the national revolution into a socialist revolution.'[1]

A recurrent theme is the 'uneven development' of the process of emancipation of 'the peoples of the East' from 'colonialist oppression'. In the words of a leading Soviet orientalist, E. M. Zhukov, the majority of the new states 'have secured differing degrees of political independence but economically still remain – some more, some less – dependent on foreign capital'.[2] The main aim for these states must be economic independence, by which is meant the expropriation of Western capital and the rupture of economic relations with the West. V. Y. Avarin, in the same discussion, argued that Western writers deliberately misinterpret the facts of economic development in order to 'prove' that the new states need Western economic 'aid' for economic progress. The claim of Western writers that these states should accept Western private capital 'in a climate that will secure adequate return to the investors and creditors', is interpreted by Avarin as a demand by the West that the new states should 'submit to unlimited exploitation by foreign capital and to unequal exchange', and that they should 'agree to restore the situation that prevailed . . . before colonial oppression was overthrown'.

If all foreign private capital is depicted as an unmitigated evil, qualified approval is expressed for state capitalist enterprise in the new states. India and the United Arab Republic are mentioned by Zhukov as states where the existing economic leadership can be helped by Soviet experience of planning. In Zhukov's words:

> Given a comparatively low level of general economic and technological development in the East – not for nothing is the term 'under-developed' frequently applied to these countries – and given the economic diversity of these countries, the progressive tendency towards the transformation of the state (more correctly, the state-capitalist) sector of the economies of the nonsocialist countries of the East into an important factor strengthening their economies and sovereignty should not be underrated.[3]

[1] *World Marxist Review*, loc. cit.　　[2] *Mezhdunarodnuya Zhizn*, loc. cit.
[3] Ibid.

However, it must not be thought that the policies of state enterprise pursued in India or the United Arab Republic add up to 'socialism'. In the words of A. A. Guber, 'We should not be misled by the adoption of programs for "building a society of a socialist type," for the "building of socialism," by the socialist names taken by bourgeois parties, etc.'[1] Balabushevich, in the article already quoted, stresses the same point. The national bourgeoisie, he argues, is intensifying its efforts at influencing the ideas of the workers and of the broad masses. It hopes to counteract the spread among them of Marxist ideas by representing itself as the exponent of the general national interest. It 'makes great efforts to discredit the Communist Parties in the workers' eyes ... using the slogans of socialism that have become so popular as a result of the enormous successes of the Soviet Union and the socialist countries. ... The achievement in several countries of state-capitalist measures, and the presence of elements of economic planning, are advanced as proof of development along a "socialist path," but one which takes account of "national peculiarities." '[2] It is characteristic of those who argue thus that they show sympathy for the revisionist idea of 'national Communism' and for Yugoslavia. Soviet theorists, as was indeed to be expected, stick to the dogmatic view – expressed in the Moscow Declaration of November 1957 – that there is only one way to socialism, through the dictatorship of the proletariat, inspired by the example and obeying the directives of the Soviet Communist Party. Asians who call themselves socialists without accepting this hierarchical relationship to Moscow, are no more socialists than are the British Labour Party or the German Social Democrats. Nehru, Nu, and Sukarno are basically no better than Gaitskell.

Even more important than the development of state enterprise, as a factor favouring the development of the new states in the direction desired, is the increasing strength of the 'socialist world system' as a factor in the world economy. The new states can do without foreign private capital, loans, or 'aid' from the 'imperialists', because there is available to them the 'unselfish disinterested aid of the socialist countries'. The Soviet Union and the other socialist countries not only have valuable experience of the problems of economic growth and economic planning, but are willing to grant aid on generous terms, without any strings attached. All aid from the 'imperialist', on the contrary, is inspired by selfish motives, and

[1] *Mezhdunarodnuya Zhizn*, loc. cit.   [2] *Problemy Vostokovedenia*, loc. cit.

is offered on onerous terms. It is only the reactionary forces in the new states that seek agreements with imperialism. 'Such agreements', wrote Zhukov in March 1959, 'must in fact always be of an unequal character and lead in the ultimate analysis to the renunciation of independence, subjection to the rule of the foreign monopolies, and surrender to imperialism,' and be directed 'not only against workers, peasants, and intellectuals, but also against the vital interests of the national bourgeoisie. . . . The interests of imperialism and those of the national bourgeoisie are directly opposed.'[1] Very different is the relationship within the world socialist system, as described by V. A. Fomina:

> The successful construction of socialism is possible precisely within the framework of the world socialist camp, on a basis of close mutual relations and co-operation, on the principle of full equality and respect for the integrity, state independence, and sovereignty of the countries of socialism, and also of noninterference of one country or several countries in the affairs of others.[2]

Moreover, all writers on this subject stress that the socialist camp is steadily overtaking the capitalist countries in its industrial output, and that before long, its total economic power will exceed that of the capitalists.

To sum up, the national bourgeoisies of the new states are encouraged to expropriate Western private capital, to refuse economic co-operation with or economic aid from the 'imperialists' and to rely on disinterested Soviet aid, and their efforts in the field of state capitalism are mildly praised, though it is made clear that these are not 'socialism'. At the same time, the inevitability of class conflict is not concealed. The 'working class' – that is, the Communist parties – will impose its will on the national bourgeoisies in due course. As for the fate that will be in store for them at this stage, the relish with which Soviet writers describe the 'three anti' and 'five anti' campaigns in China in 1952, and the general policy of re-education of the bourgeoisie by the Chinese Communists, leave little ground for optimism to any 'national bourgeois' who is willing to learn the lessons of the recent past and to look ahead.[3]

[1] *Mezhdunarodnaya Zhizn*, loc. cit.
[2] *Vestnik Moskovskovo Univerziteta*, No. 4, 1958.
[3] See, for example, F. S. Pavlov, 'The Alliance and Struggle of the Chinese Working Class with the National Bourgeoisie in the Period of Transition to Socialism', *Voprosy Istorri KPSS*, No. 2, 1959.

SOME INDIVIDUAL PROBLEMS

The new emphasis on the appeal to the national bourgeoisie called for a reappraisal not only of India's role as an independent State, but also of the historical significance of the Congress and in particular of Mahatma Gandhi. This was strongly emphasized in the Soviet academic discussion of 1956. I. M. Reisner called for a re-examination of Stalin's assertions on India in the nineteen-twenties, and of 'certain other dogmas, especially the untrue definition of Gandhi as an agent and accomplice of imperialism'. However, not much light was thrown on the subject during the discussion.

The following statement by Levkovski shows the intellectual limitations that restrict any Soviet attempt to understand or to interpret a view of the world basically different from the Marxist-Leninist:

> The most general ideology of the national bourgeoisie in India was Gandhism, and the most important party that reflected its fundamental interests was the Indian National Congress, the main mass of whose members belonged to the petty bourgeoisie, the peasantry, and in part, the workers. The specific essence of Gandhism, and the peculiarities of the National Congress, were the reflection, and the concrete expression in the field of ideology and politics, of the distinct character of the Indian national bourgeoisie.[1]

Exactly what these words mean it is impossible for the reader to detect, and one suspects that the author, too, was a little less than clear in his own mind.

Another Indian problem that arose in this discussion was that of linguistic nationalism. L. I. Reisner suggested that more attention should be paid to the distinction between the bourgeoisie which competed mainly on the all-Indian market and that which confined itself to local, but very large, markets such as Bengal and Maharashtra. He suggested that there were thus two subdivisions of the Indian national bourgeoisie – the all-Indian and the 'local bourgeoisie that is developing within the national regions'. The political implications of this distinction, and their relevance to Communist tactics in India, need no comment.

In Soviet writing on tropical Africa, special attention is devoted to the emergence of nations. Here the main expert is I. I. Potekhin, Director of the African Institute in Moscow and a regular contributor to several Soviet journals, both the purely political and the

[1] *Sovetskoe Vostokovedenie*, loc. cit.

more scientific. Potekhin has been developing a theory of the development of tribes (*plemeni*) into peoples (*narody*), and of peoples into nations (*natsii*). It is only in the last phase that a national bourgeoisie becomes an important factor. Potekhin, of course, discusses the familiar Marxist themes of the transformation of patriarchal into feudal, and of feudal into capitalist relationships. But he also pays great attention to language. He maintains that Western experts in African affairs have exaggerated the number of languages spoken by the Africans, as part of the imperialist policy of 'divide and rule'. Not only are there a few languages that are widely spoken, but others can quickly develop by the elimination of dialects and the establishment of standardized literary languages. It is obvious that the development of languages is considered by Potekhin to be at least as important a means of creating national consciousness as the development of capitalism. The Soviet Communists have a rich experience in the manipulation of linguistic nationalism, and have certainly shown themselves no less adept at the practice of 'divide and rule' than the 'imperialists' of the West: the story of the small peoples of the Volga Basin, and of Central Asia, bears witness to their skill. Potekhin gives the example of the Ewe, a single language group divided between Togoland and Ghana. The Bakongo, divided between French Equatorial Africa, the Congo, and Portuguese Angola, are another case. Yet another are the Somalis. The encouragement and exploitation of the aspiration to unity of African peoples so divided by arbitrary colonial frontiers offers enormous opportunities to Soviet policy. Potekhin also has interesting things to say about the Nilotic peoples, divided between Sudan, the Congo, Uganda, and Kenya. These do not, he admits, form a single people, but the Nilotic languages form 'a single fundamental supply of words', and three of the languages have an identical grammatical structure. 'It is by no means out of the question that in favorable conditions, the Nilotics may be able to form themselves into a single people.'[1] It should be stressed that Potekhin's articles show a striking combination of intelligent and well-informed analysis with obvious political aims. It is no empty boast that Soviet experience of nationality problems can throw light on African problems. The conflicts between linguistic, religious, and national groups, which played so important a part in the history of both the Russian and the Austro-Hungarian empires in the

[1] *Sovetskoe Etnografia*, No. 4, 1957.

nineteenth century, and which were carefully studied by both Lenin and Stalin, are genuinely illuminating for all who wish to understand contemporary Asia or Africa. Potekhin's statement that the new states of Africa – Ghana, Nigeria, Sudan, and the Congo, as well as the states that have still more recently emerged from French West and Equatorial Africa – are 'multinational states' is perfectly true. If national consciousness is not yet far advanced, the conditions for linguistic nationalism are clearly present. British and French colonial administrators or academic experts on Africa, who lack the advantage of Central or East European experience, have been slow to grasp the nature of these problems. The makers of Soviet policy in Africa have plenty of explosive material to hand. As in Eastern Europe after 1945, they can come forward alternately as champions of state unity, of irredentism, or of separatism, depending on political expediency. Their record in the Congo in 1960 showed that they were determined to play a hand in this game; the fact that in the first rounds they have not done very well should not cause either African nationalists of Western observers to be complacent.

In Central Asia, the Soviet Communists have encouraged the development of separate Turkic- or Iranian-speaking nations, but have steadily opposed the notion of a single Turkestani or Turko-Tatar nation. Similarly in Africa, while favouring the formation of large language groups, and the development from tribes through peoples to 'bourgeois nations' (*burzhuaznie natsii*),[1] with a recognizable national bourgeoisie, Soviet writers have shown little sympathy for Pan-Africanism. In so far as this movement is anti-Western, it has their qualified approval, though they strongly object to the emphasis placed at Pan-African conferences on non-violent methods of struggle. But Pan-Africanism as an aim does not appeal to them. It is regarded as a bourgeois ideology, which must in time be superseded by 'proletarian internationalism', whose bearer is the 'working class' – that is, the Communist parties, each of which is individually and hierarchically subordinated to directives from Moscow. In South Africa, there is a direct conflict between the Pan-Africanists and the Communists, who have a considerable influence in the old African National Congress.

The expression 'Afro-Asian' is also not much used in Soviet political literature, though the Afro-Asian Solidarity Committee

[1] This phrase is used by Potekhin in an article in *Problemy Vostokovedenia*, No. 1, 1960.

enjoys Soviet support and is subject to some Communist infiltration. It is interesting to note that the word most frequently used to describe the whole so-called underdeveloped world is 'East', or 'Orient' (in Russian, *Vostok*). The 'peoples of the East' include not only Africans, both of the Arab Maghreb and south of the Sahara, but also the peoples of Latin America.

Pan-Arabism is also viewed with suspicion by Soviet writers, especially since the Iraqi revolution of 1958 and the consequent estrangement from President Nasser. In the Communist intellectuals' 1959 discussion in East Germany, R. Schulz declared: 'It should be said outright, we Marxists must undoubtedly recognise that certain aspects of bourgeois nationalism – such as the "Pan-Arab" ideology in the forms it has assumed in the U.A.R. – hinder the Arab people's struggle for liberation from the imperialist yoke.'[1] The Chinese went further. In an article by Yu Chao-li in *Red Flag*, 1 April 1959, the following passages occurred:

> President Nasser, who once won the people's respect, has recently made vicious attacks on Iraq, the Communist Parties, and the Soviet Union.... At present, Iraq and the U.A.R. are two independent and sovereign countries.... If one ... insists on annexing the other, this will only ... harm the very interests of Arab unity. Those doing so, no matter how much they talk about Arab national interests, are in fact making it easy for the imperialists to carry out their scheme of getting Arabs to fight Arabs.... [The U.A.R. press slogan] 'neither East nor West' is only a deliberate attempt to confuse friends with enemies. It is tantamount to saying 'neither enemies nor friends.' But those who want no friends will naturally not be feared by any enemy. Indeed, this will become a step toward going over to the enemy. The Chinese people are very familiar with such anti-Soviet, anti-Communist tunes. In his vilification of the Soviet Union and the Chinese Communist Party, Chiang Kai-shek long ago wore to shreds such phrases as 'Red imperialism' and 'foreign agents.'... [In 1927,] Chiang Kai-shek plunged completely into the embrace of imperialism and literally became an agent of imperialism in China.

The reference to 1927 is revealing. In that year, a policy that may not unreasonably be described as 'united front from above with the national bourgeoisie' brought the Chinese Communists to disaster. In Peking in 1959, it looked as if Moscow, which after all had been responsible for the Chinese catastrophe of 1927 (even if Chinese spokesmen do not usually publicly attribute it to Stalin, its true author), was repeating a similar policy with Nasser, who was

[1] *World Marxist Review*, loc. cit.

persecuting the Egyptian and Syrian Communists. The Chinese favour an alliance with the national bourgeoisie, but only in the form of a 'united front from below'. That is to say, although the national bourgeoisie must be welcomed into the movement, and flattered and reassured as much as possible, political leadership and power must be securely in Communist hands. It is tempting to interpret differences between Soviet and Chinese policy in Baghdad in terms of a difference between united fronts 'from above' and 'from below', between acceptance of Kassem as an equal and insistence on the 'hegemony' of the Communist Party. Evidence is, however, too scanty to permit a conclusion. Moreover, in Algeria, the Chinese Communists seem willing to give support to a movement that is certainly not controlled by Communists.

No clear conclusions can be drawn, in this connexion, from the statement issued in Moscow as a result of the long-drawn-out deliberations of the Communist parties' leaders in November – December 1960. The statement essentially upholds the Soviet tactic of supporting the national bourgeoisies (i.e. it approves of the united front from above with the national bourgeoisie). It may be assumed that Soviet aid will continue to be offered to régimes ruled by non-Communist nationalists, on which, indeed, a new respectability is conferred by the invention of the new term 'national democracies'. This must be a disappointment to the Chinese. On the other hand, the somewhat more violent language of the statement, as compared with that of November 1957, and the fact that the Soviet Government at last gave a measure of recognition to the Algerian 'Provisional Government', perhaps represent concessions to the Chinese.

FUTURE PROSPECTS

In very general terms, it is clear that a policy of supporting anti-Western nationalism in Asia, Africa, and Latin America is sound from the point of view of world Communist strategy. In this sense, the emphasis on the appeal to the 'national bourgeoisie' makes good sense.

However, one cannot help doubting whether the Soviet analysis is not to some extent out of focus. The particular emphasis on the capitalist element appears misplaced. In fact, it may be argued that it is the other two main middle classes of society in underdeveloped countries – the intelligentsia and the bureaucracy – rather than the business class that are most strongly nationalist and most likely to be attracted by Soviet appeals.

During the last hundreds years, in almost all national independence movements in underdeveloped countries (from the Bulgaria movement against the Ottoman Empire to the movements in Kenya or Senegal in our time), leadership has come from the intelligentsia. It is the intelligentsia that has both the greatest pride in the real or imagined glories of the nation's own traditions, and at the same time, the greatest interest in the new ideas of democracy and social justice that since the nineteenth century have spread out from Western Europe and North America over the rest of the world. It is the intelligentsia's indignation and sense of national humiliation at the spectacle of poverty and backwardness of its peasant compatriots, rather than the active discontent of the peasants themselves, that made land reform a major political issue, for example, in the Egypt of King Farouk or the Iraq of Nuri es-Said. The definition of the intelligentsia, which is a distinct social group with a distinct political role of its own, clearly separable from the business class on the one hand or the bureaucracy on the other, is a question of the greatest importance for the study of underdeveloped societies, but one which exceeds the scope of the present survey. Here it may suffice to note two trends that are visible in varying admixtures in the intelligentsias of Asia, Africa, and Latin America at the present time. One is populism – the desire to serve the people, to lift it up out of its poverty and squalor, which are a source both of suffering to the people and of shame to the nation. The second is careerism – the desire to obtain both material rewards and social status commensurate with the intellectuals' sense of their own merits, and indeed to create a society in which the intelligentsia will be the ruling group, a society based on scientific and rational principles rather than on antiquated hierarchies and obsolete traditions.

The appeal of Communism to the intelligentsia is understandably powerful. It appeals both to their desire to serve the people and to their desire to dominate it. The Russian Communists consider themselves the heirs to the Populists of the eighteen-seventies – the revolutionaries in whom the desire to serve the people and to sacrifice themselves to the people's liberation burned with a purer flame than ever before or since. At the same time, the Soviet Union can be represented as a state managed on scientific principles, based on the 'science' of Marxist-Leninism, a society in which the scientist and the intellectual have their true reward, enjoy the unlimited admiration of a grateful people, and have enormous authority over the people. This double appeal of Communism to idealism and ambition can affect the intelligentsia in all three of the main types of situation mentioned earlier. It can appeal to the intelligentsia that is leading, or still struggling to create, a movement for independence in colonial conditions. It can appeal to the intelligentsia of a country that possesses sovereignty but is still allied to the West, a country whose continuing social injustices and political abuses can be conveniently ascribed to the indirect influences of 'imperialism'. Finally, in countries of whose sovereignty and independence there can be no doubt – such as India or Indonesia – it can appeal especially to the younger generation of the intelligentsia, to those who inevitably react against the generation of the 'fathers' of independence, who protest against the many injustices that are still there – perhaps even in more acute form – although independence is more than a decade old. As an object lesson of the danger that the disillusionment of the educated youth can represent to a newly independent state, the Indians and Indonesians would do well to look at the history of such Balkan countries as Bulgaria, Roumania, and Yugoslavia in the first half of the twentieth century.

As for the bureaucracy, a distinction must clearly be made between colonial and independent countries, and between traditionalist and democratic régimes. Clearly, Communism has no appeal to the remaining colonial administrations of European imperial powers. In the case of independent states, it can also hardly be expected to appeal to the bureaucracies of such countries as Persia, ruled by an autocratic shah, or of Thailand, under military rule, or of such Latin American countries as Peru or Ecuador, in which, though formal democracy exists, the mass of Indian peasants remains a race of helots whose aspirations the rulers fear. But in independent Asian, African, or Latin American states that possess a more or less genuinely democratic system of government, or in which a genuinely popular dictatorship based on mass organization exists (such as Ghana or Guinea), the appeal of Communism may be powerful. It combines the two elements of appeal to idealism and to ambition mentioned above, but with perhaps an even more pronounced emphasis on the second. The approval given by Soviet spokesmen to the state-capitalist trend in India and the United Arab Republic is likely to make an especially good impression on the bureaucracy, for it is they, rather than the private capitalists, whose interests are bound up with such enterprise. The other side to the

Soviet doctrine – its insistence that such enterprise cannot be called 'socialist', and that those Afro-Asian politicians who use 'socialist slogans' in this context are deliberately deceiving the people – is less publicized, and is therefore unlikely to counteract the appeal in Afro-Asian bureaucratic minds. The offer of Soviet loans and the establishment of steel mills or other factories by Soviet technicians (or by Czechs or East Germans) are also likely to appeal more immediately to bureaucrats than to private capitalists.

Thus, in so far as Soviet theorists include in the category of 'national bourgeoisie' both bureaucrats and intelligentsia, in addition to capitalists, it would seem that they are showing a realistic appreciation of the relative value to them of the social classes of underdeveloped societies. In so far as they confine the phrase to the capitalists it would seem that their appeal is to some extent misdirected. However, Westerners should derive little comfort from this observation. In the first place, the Soviet leaders – none more than Khrushchev – are capable of ignoring doctrine when they see practical opportunities: the study of theory is at best only an incomplete and approximate guide to Soviet policy, as also to Chinese policy and to the relations between the two. Secondly, even the capitalists are undoubtedly influenceable by Soviet appeals, especially in the field of trade. If the Soviet Union emerges within a few years as one of the great trading Powers of the world, and manipulates its prices according to political priorities rather than economic factors, it can have an enormous impact on the whole business communities of the new states. This is one of the great unknown factors of the future. It will certainly prove extremely important for the success or failure of Communist movements within the Asian, African, and Latin American countries, for the world-wide political struggle between the Soviet block and the non-Communist countries, and for the relations between the Soviet Union and China.

The Great Schism

No problem of world politics today is likely to have greater effects on the fate of the human race in the rest of this century than the relationship between Russia and China. Plenty of mystery still surrounds this subject, and it is hardly surprising that the leaders of the two countries are unwilling to speak plainly about it to citizens of hostile states. But this does not mean that nothing is known of it. On the contrary, not only are many of the Chinese materials available in English, but there is already a large secondary literature of the subject in Western languages which includes some works of high quality. This literature certainly makes it possible for persons who are not Old China Hands, know no Chinese, but are politically literate and possess critical powers, to get a reasonable idea of the issues involved.

It is convenient to distinguish three periods: the background before the Communist victory in China, the first eight years of the Communist régime, and the period of acute Sino-Soviet conflict since 1958. In the first two periods an attempt will be made to separate the relations between the Governments from the relation between the Communist parties, but in the more recent period these have to be taken together. The survey of the course of the conflict will lead to some observations about future prospects.

First among the historical factors is Chinese pride, the survival of the belief that China is 'the Middle Kingdom' and that the rest of the earth consists of outer barbarians, placed around the periphery of the civilized world, and destined to pay tribute to it. China, we are repeatedly assured by the Sinologues, is not a nation or an empire, but a civilization. The non-Sinologue gets the impression, from reading or conversing with Sinologues, that there is some unique quality in Chinese arrogance, and something with which very often Westerners who have lived in China consciously identify themselves. This special essence, if it exists, is something which those of us who do not know China cannot grasp. But at least it is not difficult to understand that the educated class of a country which for

---

This article was first published in *Encounter*, May 1963.

millenniums was either the greatest or one of the greatest Powers, and whose civilization, if not the oldest, was perhaps the most uninterruptedly maintained for the longest consecutive period in human history, should have passionately resented the humiliations of the last two hundred years at the hands of Europeans. Among the Europeans, perhaps even outstanding among them, were the Russians.

Second only in importance are the territorial problems that have caused conflict between China and Russia since the mid-nineteenth century. The Russian Government exploited China's involvement in war with Britain and France to seize the land between the Amur, the Ussuri, and the Pacific, and to found there a naval base with the arrogant name of 'Ruler of the East' (Vladivostok). Russia did its best to seize Korea, a tributary state of China, and its plans were defeated, not by China, but by Japan. In Manchuria the Russians were more successful, and even after their defeat by the Japanese in 1905 they kept their Chinese Eastern Railway, a fortress of political and military as well as economic value. When the Bolsheviks took the place of the Tsar, they first talked of handing the railway back to China, but they did not repeat the promise when they were in a position to implement it. (They kept the railway until 1935, and then sold it to the Japanese.) In Mongolia the Russians in 1911 appeared as protectors of the Mongols against the Chinese, and though Mongolia was nominally autonomous under Chinese suzerainty it became a vassal of Russia. In 1919 the Bolsheviks repudiated the privileges held by the Imperial Government in Mongolia, but in 1921 they invaded it, and since then the Mongolian People's Republic has been a vassal of the Soviet Union. Chinese Turkestan (Sinkiang) was also an object of contention between Imperial Russia and China. Here, too, in the 1930's, Soviet influence was strong, at the expense of the Chinese Government.

The story of relations between the Communist parties of the Soviet Union and China is not one of happy comradeship. Soviet advice to the Chinese Communists in the 1920's was close alliance with the Kuomintang. This continued long after Chiang Kai-shek had shown himself an enemy. Insistence by the Comintern (which meant Stalin) that the Chinese Communists should take no action against Chiang led to the massacre of Communist workers in Shanghai in April 1927, and to further humiliations and repression by the Kuomintang later in the year. These disasters have never been forgotten by Mao Tse-tung, who saved a remnant of Communist forces in the wilderness, and built up his nucleus of power in the following ten years, despite Stalin's preference for his rivals within the party. Factional disputes were connected with the question whether greater reliance should be placed on urban workers or peasants. But essentially this was a dispute, not about social analysis, but about power. Mao used peasants because they were the only people available, to be used by any Chinese revolutionary movement, whether Marxist or not. Mao showed later that he was no romantic, 'peasant-loving Populist'. But his struggle against the Moscow leadership did not teach him to love Stalin.

The Chinese Communists are often called 'Stalinists'. This is only true in the very vague sense that they are men who use 'hard' rather than 'soft' methods. It would be better to drop the adjective 'Stalinist'. The striking thing about them, when they emerged into the public view at the end of the Second World War, was how little they conformed to the universal Communist practice of fawning on Stalin. In his speech to the 7th Congress of his party, on 14 May 1945 (published in 1951 under the title *On the Party*), Liu Shao-chi at one point referred to Mao as 'a disciple of Marx, Engels, Lenin, and Stalin'. But this homage is dwarfed by the endless references to 'the Thought of Mao Tse-tung', repeatedly described as that which 'unites the theories of Marxism–Leninism with the actual practice of the Chinese revolution . . .'. Mao is described as 'boldly creative' as a theorist, and is credited with 'discarding certain specific Marxist principles and conclusions that were incompatible with the concrete conditions in China, and replacing them with new principles and new conclusions that are compatible with China's new historical conditions'. In fact, it is not only in the age of Khrushchev that Mao was proclaimed one of the prophets of Marxism.

After the Communists had conquered China in 1949, it seemed at first that their relations with the Soviet Union were friendly. But behind the façade things were not so good. Stalin had given little help to the Communists in the civil war. He admitted to the Yugoslavs in 1948 that he had 'underestimated their chances'. In 1945 he had secured the interests of the Soviet Union by a treaty with their enemy Chiang Kai-shek which had given him control of the Manchurian railways, Port Arthur, and Dairen. These were not given back to the Communists until well after their victory – the railways in 1952 and Port Arthur in 1955. The Soviet Government continued to insist on the independence of Mongolia, which Communists and Kuomintang alike regarded as part of China. Perhaps most important, the Soviet Government showed itself far from generous with economic aid. In 1945 the industrial equipment of the factories built in Manchuria by the Japanese since 1931 was removed to Russia. It was not until the mid-1950's that it was replaced (admittedly by equipment of higher quality than that which had been removed). It is true that in the post-war years the Soviet Union, painfully recovering from war-time devastation, was not in a position to give much help to anyone. But it remained a fact that the total aid given by the Russians to the Chinese was negligible in relation to China's needs for economic development.

In November 1949, at a Peking conference of Asian and Australasian trade unions belonging to the W.F.T.U. Liu Shao-chi, after paying tribute to the example given to the Communist parties of industrial countries by the Bolshevik Revolution, made the claim that

> the path taken by the Chinese people in defeating imperialism and in founding the People's Republic of China is the path that must be taken by the peoples of the various colonial and semi-colonial countries in their fight for national independence and people's democracy.

There was no official Soviet comment on this claim, but discussion of problems of Asian revolution in the Soviet press, both political and academic, showed clearly that the claim was not accepted.

The relations between the Soviet Union and China during the Korean War (and the effect of Chinese military intervention on the relative strength of Soviet and Chinese influence within the Korean Communist Party) are still obscure. But one important consequence of the war is clear. The Chinese learned that the newly independent states of Asia, and especially India, were not – as Soviet propaganda since 1947 had said they were – puppet creations of the Western imperialists who continued to rule them by other means. The Chinese learned that India was an independent State, and that it was both desirable and possible to have friendly relations with her. The Chinese led the way in adopting a new Communist policy towards 'Asian neutralists', which received its most striking expression at the Bandung conference of 1955. In the Soviet Union the death of Stalin did not bring a change, perhaps because the new Soviet leaders were exclusively concerned with Lenin's old problem of 'Who-whom?' They lagged behind China, and it was not until the Khrushchev–Bulganin visit to India in November 1955, that courtship of neutralists began to be a priority of Soviet foreign policy.

The 20th Congress of the C.P.S.U. seems to have been received with mixed feelings in Peking. As we have seen, Mao had little love for Stalin, but Khrushchev's impetuous launching of 'de-Stalinization' was hardly to his taste. In the summer of 1956 the Chinese began to take a hand in the affairs of Eastern Europe. In September 1956, a Polish delegation to the 9th Congress of the Chinese Communist Party, led by Edward Ochab, found much encouragement for the Polish party's independent attitude (including its opposition to the Soviet view of the Poznań rising of July). For months after this, the 'liberal' elements in the Polish party were convinced that China was on their side. In reality, the Chinese were interested not in 'liberalism' but in equality between parties, that is, in reducing the predominance of the Soviet party. This became clear when they came out strongly in defence of the Soviet action in Hungary. In an emergency all Communists must stand together. However, this did not mean perpetual deferment to the Soviet commands, nor did the Chinese patronage of the Poles improve Sino-Soviet relations.

During 1957 the Chinese made their curious experiment with the 'Hundred Flowers' campaign. Strongly urged by Mao himself to express their opinions freely, the intellectuals fiercely attacked the régime. The party replied with brutal repression, and a general change of course, in economic and political affairs, from a 'right' to a 'left' policy. The other event of 1957 which most impressed the Chinese was the launching of the first sputnik. This seems to have convinced Mao that the balance of world power had decisively changed, and that a much bolder foreign policy was possible for 'the socialist camp'. At the conference of Communist parties in Moscow in November 1957, Mao declared:

> I think the characteristic of the situation to-day is the East wind prevailing over the West wind. That is to say, the socialist forces are overwhelmingly superior to the imperialist forces.

At the end of the year, with the definite restoration of Soviet superiority in Eastern Europe, with Khrushchev's victory over the 'anti-Party group' of Molotov and the failure of the Army's challenge represented by Marshal Zhukov, and with the publication of the militant manifesto of the twelve ruling Communist parties,

Sino-Soviet relations seemed once more to be on a sound basis.

However, the year 1958 brought the worst conflict yet seen between the two régimes. The adoption of a 'left' course in China led to a rush forward into extreme policies and fantastic ideological claims. A Resolution of 29 August 1958, announced the introduction of 'People's Communes'. This decision must no doubt mainly be explained by economic factors. China's economic backwardness was being made more intolerable every year by steadily mounting population pressure. The only line of advance seemed to be the ruthless exploitation of the country's main resource, manpower. The Communes were designed to mobilize manpower still more ruthlessly and systematically than had been the case in Russia at the beginning of the First Five-Year Plan. Public hardships could have been reduced only if substantial aid were forthcoming from an advanced industrial country. The only possible source was the Soviet Union, and it seems reasonable to assume that an important reason for the decision to embark on People's Communes was the knowledge that the Soviet Union would not give large-scale aid. But if economic necessity was the motive, the opportunity was taken to claim ideological virtue. The Chinese asserted that through their Communes they had discovered a short-cut to *Communism*. They clearly implied that they might reach Communism ahead of the Soviet Union, whose Revolution had preceded theirs by thirty years. This monstrous affront was greeted in Russia with public silence (though there was plenty of indirect evidence that it was repudiated). What arguments or recriminations were conducted in secret, is not known. But in December the Chinese publicly retreated. A resolution of the Central Committee of 10 December admitted that even the completion of *socialism* in China would still require 'ten, fifteen, twenty, or more years. . . .' There was no more talk of achieving Communism in the near future. But it would take more than a party resolution to remove the ideological rage caused on both sides by the earlier claim.

In July 1958, the revolution in Iraq and the civil war in Lebanon caused an international crisis. Khrushchev suggested a summit meeting. At first he agreed that this should take place at the Security Council of the United Nations – of which the Government of China was not a member but the Formosan Government was. A few days later he rejected this idea, but still favoured a summit meeting at which India was to be present, but not China. Thus, he was placing the 'non-socialist' India above his 'socialist' ally China, and also according India a higher status as a Great Power than the 600-million Power China. It is hardly surprising that when Khrushchev arrived in Peking on 31 July 1958, he received a cold reception.

There was a further reason for this. Acting on the assumption that, with the launching of sputnik and of a Soviet I.C.B.M., 'the East wind prevailed over the West wind', Mao Tse-tung decided that the time had come to 'liberate' Formosa. He expected his Soviet ally to go to the brink of war to support him. But Khrushchev would do nothing more than promise that if the United States attacked mainland China with nuclear weapons he would retaliate on the United States. This of course was not enough. The Chinese alone could not take Formosa, or even the off-shore island of Quemoy. Nor would the Soviet Union give them nuclear weapons to use on their own behalf. The shelling of the off-shore islands from mid-August to the end of September 1958, ended in a Chinese retreat.

The importance of the Formosa issue in Sino-Soviet hostility cannot be overrated. It is interesting in this connexion to note a parallel between the Chinese position and that of some of the East European satellite states. Some of these are territorially 'satisfied', while others have 'irredentas' of their own, to acquire which is a matter of urgency for their public opinion and for the status of their régime. The most obvious European case is Albania, a country of less than two million inhabitants, along whose border, under Yugoslav rule, live nearly a million Albanians. Two others are Bulgaria (which has claims on Yugoslav and Greek Macedonia) and East Germany (whose rulers cannot be content or secure until they have extended their régime to the whole of Germany). On the other hand the most 'satisfied' state is Czechoslovakia, while of the three other satellites only one has claims on lands outside the 'socialist camp', (Hungary or Yugoslavia), though all three secretly cherish the idea of recovering lands from 'socialist' neighbours (Poland and Roumania from the Soviet Union, Hungary from Czechoslovakia and Roumania). It is interesting – and can hardly be a coincidence – that in the Sino-Soviet dispute Albania has strongly taken the Chinese side, the satisfied states the Soviet side, while both Bulgaria and East Germany at times during the autumn of 1958 showed sympathy for the Chinese.

At the beginning of 1959 there was a lull in Sino-Soviet relations.

The doctrine expounded by Khrushchev at the 21st Congress of the C.P.S.U. in February, that all socialist states would enter Communism 'at about the same time', was intended to smooth over the difficulties. But Chinese resentment at Soviet failure to support China in Formosa, and at its attitude to India and to the new states generally, remained bitter. The bitterness was greatly increased by two factors which continued to operate for the next three years. One was the growing economic chaos in China, largely resulting from the People's Communes policy and the fantastic projects for small-scale heavy industry associated with it. The other was the growing economic aid offered by the Soviet Union to 'non-socialist' countries of Asia, Africa, and Latin America. Every year the plight of the Chinese people became more desperate, and every year the discrepancy between massive Soviet aid outside the bloc (or to European countries of the bloc) and Soviet indifference to China's needs became more shocking.

In April 1959, an article by Yu Chao-li (almost certainly the *nom de plume* of a member, or a group of members, of the Chinese Politburo) in *Red Flag* bitterly attacked the Nasser régime in Egypt. It denounced his neutralism: the slogan

'neither East nor West' is only a deliberate attempt to confuse friends with enemies. It is tantamount to saying 'neither enemies nor friends.' But those who want no friends will naturally not be feared by an enemy. Indeed, this will become a step toward going over to the enemy.

The article then compared Nasser with Chiang Kai-shek in 1927. The fact that both Nasser and Chiang imprisoned Communists was noted. The memory of the bitter events of 1927, and of Moscow's fatal advice to the Chinese Communists, was certainly fresh in the author's mind (thought it was not mentioned). Moreover, nearly all that was said in the article against Nasser could equally be said against Nehru. The article was essentially an attack on the whole Soviet policy of support to neutralist states. The whole Soviet doctrine of the progressive role of the 'National bourgeoisie' and of the 'state sector' and 'state capitalist forces' in the new states was clearly unacceptable to the Chinese. Historical memories, genuine ideological disagreement, jealousy of India, and economic needs combined to produce hostility to Soviet policy. Things were made worse by the development of the Tibetan rebellion in March 1959, and the flight of the Dalai Lama to India. The influx of Tibetan refugees drew the attention of the Indian public to the frontier with

China, and led to the discovery of the large extent of the territory occupied by Chinese troops. This led to public pressure on Nehru at least to speak boldly against China. But when the Indian–Chinese quarrel thus became public knowledge, all that Khrushchev would do was to speak of Soviet friendship for both China and India and to express the pious wish that they would settle their dispute in 'a friendly spirit'. He then paid his visit to the United States, and went to Peking on 30 September. His reception was even colder than in the previous year. Contrary to normal Communist protocol, no joint communiqué was issued on his departure. In a personal statement he asserted: 'We Communists of the Soviet Union consider it our sacred duty, our primary task, to utilise all possibilities in order to liquidate the cold war. . . .'

During 1959 it is clear that there was a bitter struggle within the Chinese party. The extremist policy was attacked by a 'right wing' which blamed it for the country's economic misery. The conflict reached a climax in the meeting of the Central Committee at Lushan in August 1959. An interesting article in *The China Quarterly* by David Charles, based on reports from refugees who left China in this period, shows that the chief spokesman of the 'Right' was the Minister of Defence, Marshal Peng Teh-huai. It appears that during a visit to the Soviet Union and Eastern Europe from April to June he had written a memorandum criticizing the Chinese leadership and passed it to the Soviet Government. If there was in fact a combined attack by the Soviet leaders and the Chinese Right on the dominant group in the Chinese party, it was defeated. The Lushan meeting ended in a resolution which upheld the existing course; a campaign was launched against the Right; and at the end of September – just as Khrushchev reached Peking – Peng was removed from his Ministry.

The next major event in the Sino-Soviet controversy was the publication on 22 April 1960, the ninetieth anniversary of Lenin's birth, of an article in *Red Flag* entitled 'Long Live Leninism!' This boldly stated the Chinese doctrine in what was to become the main ideological issue in the Sino-Soviet conflict, the issue of 'the inevitability of war'. It insisted on the incurably bellicose and predatory nature of the imperialists, and dismissed the argument that nuclear war was an unacceptable disaster for the human race. Should the imperialists resort to nuclear war, the sacrifices endured by the human race would be worth paying.

On the débris of a dead imperialism, the victorious people would create very swiftly a civilisation thousands of times higher than the capitalist system and a truly beautiful future for themselves.

During the summer the conflict sharpened. At the congress of the Roumanian Communist Party in Bucarest in June, it seems that Khrushchev and the Chinese delegate Peng Chen quarrelled bitterly. According to David Charles, Khrushchev reproached the Chinese with persecuting Marshal Peng Teh-huai for having communicated his views to the Soviet party, and also asserted that Kao Kang, the former Communist boss of Manchuria, who had committed suicide in April 1955, had suffered only because he had opposed the incorrect policy of his party towards the Soviet Union.

In November–December 1960, a conference of the Communist parties of the world wrestled for more than a month with the Sino-Soviet conflict. It ended with the publication of the manifesto of the eighty-one parties, which solved nothing. The document indicated a victory for the Soviet point of view, though there were some phrases which appeared designed to placate the Chinese. But in fact the Chinese abandoned none of their positions. They were strongly supported by the Albanians. The basic reason for Albania's sympathy for China – territorial irredentism – I have already mentioned. To this two points should be added. First, ever since Khrushchev's reconciliation with Yugoslavia in 1955, Albania's relations with the Soviet Union had been uneasy. When Yugoslav-Soviet relations were good, the Albanians sulked. When they deteriorated, as in 1958-9, the Albanians expected Soviet action against Yugoslavia, and were disappointed. The second point is that Albania is the only East European Communist state which has no common frontier with either the Soviet Union or another satellite. It is thus less vulnerable to Soviet pressure. Distance from the Soviet Union was a disadvantage in earlier years, when it was difficult to get supplies, but an advantage when relations with the Soviet Union became really bad. Apart from Albania, the Chinese had some support from the Indonesian and Vietnamese parties, and possibly enjoyed more sympathy in some Asian and Latin American parties than their official leaders would admit. But overwhelmingly the Communists of the world supported Moscow against Peking.

The manifesto contained one new idea, the invention of the new category of 'State of National Democracy'. This was intended to be something intermediate between a 'national bourgeois' state such as India and a 'people's democracy'. In the first type of state the Communists are in opposition, and in the second they not only possess, but are seen to possess, all the power. If one studies the conditions enumerated for the 'State of National Democracy' in the manifesto, and in subsequent official Soviet commentaries, it appears that there are in practice two significant differences between the 'national democratic' model and the neutralist 'national bourgeois' states. The first is that their foreign policy must be aligned with the Soviet bloc, the second that the Communist Party – even if not formally represented in the Government – must possess a considerable portion of real power. In subsequent months it was made clear that Cuba was the model 'national democracy' – and that Indonesia, Guinea, Ghana, and Mali were moving fairly satisfactorily in that direction. The concept proved, however, of small value. Cuba soon 'developed' so well that it became in fact indistinguishable from a 'people's democracy'. On the other hand, Guinea quarrelled with the Soviet Union, and Mali ceased to evolve in the desired direction. Moreover, the Chinese showed absolutely no interest in the notion. They continued their opposition to Soviet policy towards India, Egypt, and Iraq. For their own part, however, they had no objection to supporting, in Morocco, a 'national bourgeois' régime certainly more reactionary than that of Nasser, and, in the Yemen, a slave-owning 'feudal' monarchy.

During the first half of 1961 there was at least less open hostility between Moscow and Peking, but there was no reconciliation. In China economic failure reached the point of famine, and Soviet help was negligible.

At the 22nd Congress of the C.P.S.U. the Sino-Soviet conflict once more became public, with Chou En-lai's ostentatious homage at Stalin's mausoleum, the Congress decision to remove Stalin's body from it, and the denunciations of Albania. Thereafter the conflict took the form of polemics between Moscow and Tirana, with the Chinese press giving greater publicity to the Albanian than to the Soviet point of view. 'The anti-Marxist liar N. Khrushchev', was an Albanian phrase. Chinese attacks on Soviet policies usually referred to 'the modern revisionists'. In 1962 there was something of a lull in the summer, but a new outbreak in the autumn. At the time of the Cuban crisis it looked for a time as if there would be a *rapprochement*. Already in September, 1962, the Chinese Ambassador, who was thought to have left for another post, had returned to Moscow

The Great Schism

and had been given an exceptionally warm welcome, attended by all the most prominent figures in the Soviet Union.

The Cuban crisis and the Chinese attack on India coincided, and during the Cuban crisis the Soviet Government appeared for a few days to be backing the Chinese. But when the crisis was over, it became clear that Khrushchev was not going to commit himself. The Chinese, speaking through the Albanians, denounced the Soviet Government for failing in Cuba and for refusing to condemn India. For example, at the November Revolution celebrations in Tirana, Hysni Kapo spoke of

> the renegades from Marxism-Leninism – the modern revisionists like N. Khrushchev and Tito's treacherous band . . . the revisionist leadership of the Italian Communist Party.

The same speech had the sentence:

> The armed attacks of Indian reactionary circles with Nehru at their head against the territorial integrity of the Chinese republic as the facts of recent days had clearly shown, were also inspired by the imperialists – American, British, and others – who were now sending vast quantities of arms to India destined for an aggressive war against people's China.

Who, in the Albanian view, were the 'other' imperialists?

At the congresses of the Hungarian, Bulgarian, Czechoslovak, and Italian Communist parties, held in the last weeks of 1962, there were unpleasant clashes between the Chinese delegate and the others. The Peking *People's Daily*, without specifically mentioning the Soviet Government, made clear its view that in Cuba Khrushchev had been guilty both of 'adventurism' in introducing the missile bases and of 'capitulationism' in removing them. A *Red Flag* article at the beginning of January suggested that the modern revisionists had fallen into Trotskyist errors. To them, it argued,

> the differences between proletariat and bourgeoisie, imperialism and oppressed nations, capitalism and socialism, just wars and unjust wars, revolution and counter-revolution . . . have lost significance. In short, they have thrown to the winds all the teachings of Marxism, all the teachings of Leninism.

In his speech at the congress of the Socialist Unity Party of the Soviet zone of Germany, on 16 January 1963, Khrushchev referred to the suggestion by 'some comrades' that there should be a new conference of Communist parties. He said that he was in principle willing to have a conference, but felt that at the present time 'there would clearly be few hopes of successfully settling the existing divergencies', and that a conference would only exacerbate them. It would be better to wait, and to stop polemics for the time being. However, the Chinese delegate, Wu Hsiu-chuan, responded by violent attacks on Yugoslavia. *Pravda's* comment was that Wu had spoken 'in absolutely inadmissible terms'.

A series of articles in *People's Daily* at the beginning of March carried on the ideological polemic against the modern revisionists. It denounced those who 'claim to possess the totality of Marxist-Leninist truth', but are 'cowardly as mice'. The Chinese proudly declared that they had published the articles hostile to themselves, together with their replies, but that the press of their opponents would not do likewise.

> You fear the truth. The spectre of 'dogmatism', the spectre of genuine Marxism-Leninism, is haunting the world, and it threatens you.

Hardly less alarming for the Soviet leaders than this echo of the *Communist Manifesto* was another argument, raised in *People's Daily* on 7 March. Some time earlier, reacting to Chinese criticism of his retreat in Cuba, Khrushchev had taunted the Chinese with their failure to liquidate the imperialist outposts of Hong Kong and Macao. *People's Daily*, replying ostensibly to a similar taunt from the American Communist Party, pointed out that there were nine unequal treaties formerly signed by China with imperialist Powers which had annexed Chinese territory in north, south, east, and west, and held leased territories on the seaboard and in the hinterland of China. These nine clearly included those by which Imperial Russia had acquired the Maritime Province with Vladivostok, and some territories in Central Asia over which China had once had sovereignty. *People's Daily* now asked

> By raising questions of this category, do you aim at reopening all the unequal treaty questions in order to have a general settlement? Has it ever entered your head what the consequences would be?

On 10 March it was announced in Peking that there had been an exchange of letters between the Soviet and Chinese Communist parties which had 'affirmed the necessity of holding talks between the two parties on important questions affecting the international communist movement at present'. The Chinese stated that they would be glad to see Khrushchev or some other leading Soviet comrade in Peking.

Whether this was a genuinely friendly move, or merely another manœuvre in the political warfare, was not clear. It seemed, however, highly improbable that a conference could now remove the most important sources of conflict between the Soviet Union and China. These are: (1) Soviet refusal of brinkmanship on behalf of Formosa; (2) Soviet refusal of economic aid to China on a scale remotely approaching China's needs; (3) jealousy of India and resentment of Soviet aid to India: (4) the ideological claims of Mao as a prophet of Marxism; and (5) latent territorial disputes, of which the most important is probably Mongolia, but which may include even the status of the Far Eastern Province of the Soviet Union. It is impossible to assign an order of priority to these, but together they constitute a formidable body of disagreement.

What are the possible consequences of the Sino-Soviet conflict? I can offer no more than a few working hypotheses which may be worth keeping in mind.

The most important of the unknown factors is the development of the economy. The pressure of population on resources relentlessly increases. It is sometimes argued that because Stalin was able to achieve economic progress in the 1930's by ruthless mobilization of manpower, the Chinese will be able to do the same, even if at greater cost in human suffering. But it is arguable that the problems facing China are different in kind from those which faced Russia in the 1930's. Far too little comparative study has been made of the two economies, and perhaps even in Peking too little is known. Superficial comparisons are not enlightening. China's economic problems may be substantially increased if it becomes necessary to fight a long war with India. In March 1963, it seems possible that the Indian-Chinese conflict may be allowed to smoulder quietly for a time, but this is by no means certain. China was able to achieve successes on the north-east frontier in October and November 1962, because her immediately available striking force was larger and better armed that the Indian; but in a long war India, with substantial help from the West, could put up a resistance which before long would place a severe additional strain on China. Moreover, China has other military opponents of which at least some account must be taken: the Tibetan guerrillas and the Formosa Army. Thus a second unknown factor, the strength of India's will to resist, will be of great importance.

In March 1963, it appears that economic conditions in China have somewhat improved in recent months. However, in the longer term it is difficult to see how China can stand up to its economic and military tasks unless its whole economic policy is reversed and unless it receives substantial Soviet aid. But it is most unlikely that the Soviet Government will do anything to help the present Chinese leadership. It is even arguable that Moscow would rather see Indian victories, the loss of Tibet, economic chaos, and occupation of part of the mainland by Chiang Kai-shek, than see the Mao Tse-tung–Liu Shao-chi leadership strengthened. However this may be, it seems a reasonable hypothesis that a restoration of Sino-Soviet friendship, and a large increase of Soviet aid to China, will require a drastic purge of the Peking leadership. Whether this is likely to occur, I am quite unqualified to predict. Yet even if there were a purge in China, we may doubt whether the Soviet Government would show much enthusiasm for helping China. It may well feel that *any* government in China is likely to frustrate the aims of Soviet policy in regard to Japan, India, and South-East Asia, and to interfere with Soviet–American relations in unpredictable and dangerous ways. It will almost certainly feel that the economic demands of *any* Chinese Government will far exceed the resources which *any* Soviet Government can spare, at a time when the demands of the Soviet people for a higher standard of living can no longer be ignored.

Meanwhile, Chinese action against India has affected Soviet policy both in the *tiers monde* and in Eastern Europe.

Soviet strategy towards the underdeveloped countries has been based for some years on wooing the 'national bourgeoisie'. Countries allied with the West (in CENTO or S.E.A.T.O.) have not been regarded as independent states. But non-aligned countries are considered politically, but not yet economically, independent. The goal held out to them by Soviet propaganda has been 'economic independence', and the bogy which they have been urged to avoid has been 'neo-colonialism'. As long as any foreign private business firms control any important branches of the economy of a new state, neo-colonialism is said to be present. Economic independence can be achieved only when all major foreign business is expropriated, when Western aid is for the most part replaced by the 'unselfish, disinterested aid of the socialist camp', and when trade with the socialist bloc is more important than trade with the West. Meanwhile the 'state sector' of the economy in such countries as India and Egypt is regarded as 'objectively progressive', and is felt to deserve Soviet support, even if it is controlled by the 'national bourgeoisie', and not by 'the working class' (a euphemism for the Communist Party), and though the claims of such men as Nehru,

Nasser, or Nkrumah to be 'socialists' are consequently fraudulent.

This policy brought considerable successes to the Soviet Government in the years 1957–62. The 'neo-colonialist' charge is particularly effective in tropical Africa, in many of whose new states it must be admitted that it is more than a bogy. But the show-piece of Soviet policy was certainly India. The Chinese attack appears to have wrecked Soviet policy in India. Even if the fighting is not revived, it seems improbable that India will for a long time revert to the Nehru–Menon 'double standard' which gave such satisfaction in Moscow. In the perhaps improbable event that the talk about Indian–Pakistan reconciliation were translated into action, the Soviet loss would be still greater. On the other hand it is not certain that India's changed position need damage Soviet interests in Africa. It may be that the Arab states will be worried by India's troubles – but in tropical Africa the Indians are not loved. It is by no means clear that the Indian–Chinese fighting will diminish the attraction of the radical African nationalists towards the Communist world. Nor is there much reason to believe that Latin American revolutionaries will prefer a Chinese to a Soviet orientation. The Soviet Union is in a position to give them far more help than is China. No doubt Castro prefers Mao to Khrushchev, but what can Mao do for him? No doubt those Communists who wish to make greater use of the present guerrillas in Colombia and in north-east Brazil will look to Peking for inspiration, but the existence of 'left-wing sectarianism' within some Latin American Communist parties is not likely to create much alarm in Moscow. In fact, the harm done to Soviet policy in the *tiers monde* by Chinese action may be confined to the Indian sub-continent. Even so, this is a serious loss.

An important effect of the conflict with China has been that Khrushchev has felt an increasing need for the support of other Communist parties, and has had to pay the price of granting them greater freedom from Soviet control.

Two East European Communist parties which have very little genuine support among their peoples – the Hungarian and Roumanian – have used this situation to court greater popularity by giving their subjects better material conditions and somewhat more liberty. This is most striking in the Hungarian case. At the Congress of his party in November 1962, Kádár went so far as to say that discrimination on grounds of class origin should be ended, and spoke of much greater intellectual liberty. In Poland, Gomulka has successfully maintained his autonomy from Moscow as far as internal policy is concerned, though in recent months his policies have been less rather than more 'liberal'. The East German party is probably the most unpopular of them all. But Ulbricht has done nothing to endear himself to his subjects: rather he has profited from his indispensability to Moscow in order to maintain his personal autocracy.

The two strongest parties, the Czechoslovak and the Bulgarian, have been ruled for some years past by advocates of 'tough', or – as it is often though inaccurately called – of 'Stalinist' policies. The Czech boss Novotny was still in control in March 1963. But the intransigence of the Bulgarians seems to have become intolerable to Khrushchev, possibly because he could not afford to permit it in a country which has long frontiers with non-bloc countries, is not far from Albania, and has territorial claims on Yugoslavia. It is reasonable to assume that Soviet intervention had something to do with the purge at the October 1962 Congress of the Bulgarian party, which removed the most prominent 'Stalinists' and placed the reliable *apparatchik* Zhivkov in charge of the party and Government.

In non-bloc Communist parties in Europe the trend has certainly been towards less subservience to Moscow and less doctrinal rigidity – in short, towards a 'right-wing' course. This has been most marked in the Italian party, which has incurred the bitterest insults of the Albanians. It seems also likely that if the French party thinks there are good prospects of a Popular Front in France, it too will adopt a more 'moderate' posture.

In general, Western observers may be pleased that Soviet policy in India has suffered a reverse, and that Hungarians, Roumanians, and perhaps now even Bulgarians are enjoying a more agreeable existence. For both these changes they may thank the Chinese. If there should arise a rival Communist International, Trotskyism with a territorial base, under Chinese leadership, with its agents intriguing within existing Communist parties or creating rival parties, this too would help the West. But extravagant speculations about an alliance 'between the West and Russia against China' would seem to me to have no justification for the predictable future. It is also important not to fall into the error of regarding Khrushchev as 'a liberal' because the Chinese dislike him, or of interpreting the Soviet double-talk 'peaceful coexistence' as equivalent to the Western concept of 'peace'. Before the Cuban crisis, Khrushchev appeared to believe that the incurable decadence of 'the capitalist

The Great Schism

world' and the weak will of its leaders, would give him victory on a world scale without war and – in contrast to the Chinese view – without even having 'to go to the brink'. In Cuba he tried his hand at brinkmanship, thus coming closer to the action recommended by the Chinese (though there are no grounds for believing that he was influenced by Chinese pressure). Having approached the brink, he drew back, incurring Chinese abuse. But this does not mean that his world-wide aims have been abandoned.

A realistic Western policy will bear all this in mind. It will avoid all dogmatism, either a doctrinaire belief in negotiation, or a doctrinaire belief in toughness for toughness' sake. It will recognize that both Khrushchev and Mao are enemies of the West and enemies of each other.

Commonwealth, Common Market, Common Sense

The prospects for international politics in 1963 are more obscure than they have been in any year since the end of the Second World War. Both the Atlantic Alliance and the Soviet Bloc are weakened by schism. The passions of African nationalism are growing fiercer as independence moves southwards. The Caribbean and the Himalayas remain danger zones. Economists talk darkly of approaching slumps. The prospects for Britain within this uncertain world are particularly bleak. Humiliation at Nassau was followed by exclusion from Europe. Both white and black nationalists in Southern Rhodesia utter dire threats if their mutually irreconcilable demands are not met. It seems indeed certain that Britain will incur the contempt of the former and the enmity of the latter. It is some consolation to find that there are nations, notably Italy and Japan, which still think the friendship of Britain worth seeking. But in the world as a whole British influence does not stand high. The probability of a change of government within a year does not make things easier.

This is surely a time for thinking about our position in the world, how we got where we are, and how we can get out of it. Anyone who writes on these subjects from outside the Government machine must be aware that he lacks up-to-date detailed information, and – still more important – that he lacks the experience, possessed by the senior officials who conduct policy, of years spent in taking (or refraining from taking) practical decisions. Yet the outsider's view has its importance, for good or ill. Public opinion influences vote-dependent politicians, and through them the officials who carry out their orders. Public opinion is largely formed by the ideas, prejudices, and illusions of outside writers.

In 1945 Britain was both a world power and a Great Power. Huge forces under arms, on land, at sea, and in the air, held not only the whole British Empire but also large territories of enemy Powers. An

---

This article was first published in *Encounter*, July 1963.

important additional factor in Britain's real strength at that time was the prestige derived from its war record. Britain was the only nation that remained at war from September 1939, to August 1945. British refusal to surrender, between the fall of France and the American landing in North Africa, deprived Hitler of victory. This remains true, although it is equally true that Russian sacrifices were greater than British, and that the Russian Army made a greater contribution to the final allied victory than the British. Without British resistance, Hitler would have crushed Russia, and nobody can say what would have happened in and to America. In this sense Britain was the main victor of the war. This the allies knew in 1945, even though the Russians never admitted it.

Morally and materially Britain in 1945 was a Great Power: in 1963 she is neither. Soon after 1945 British military strength was demobilized. In the nuclear and missile age which has followed, it has become clear that only Powers with gigantic economic resources, can remain in the top class, and there are only two of these in the world today. It is true that Britain and France can have some nuclear weapons today, and it may be that Egypt or Ecuador can have some tomorrow. But to maintain all the expenses of weapons research and development, to explore all the avenues of the missile age and to meet all the new types of threat which arise, is more than any but the two monster Powers can face. It will be a long time before China can enter this class. An integrated Western Europe of 300,000,000 skilled persons could compete, and Britain might have competed if she had kept her Empire. But there is no integrated Western Europe, and the British Empire has disappeared.

Britain gave up her Empire because the British political *élite* had ceased to believe that it could or should be maintained. Indian independence was a proud triumph of the British radical tradition, in which liberals and socialists had played their part. This was what the British Left had fought for, at least since the beginning of the twentieth century. As for the opposite tradition, imperial paternalism, its spokesmen were forced to admit that its time was passing. It could not be denied that British political principles, which the British had brought to India, required that power must be handed to the Indian people when its political feelings had found effective expression, nor that in 1947 popular demand for independence was real. Two great facts obliged the British rulers of India to abdicate, even though they vainly sought a slower pace in order to save their subjects from massacre – the political ferment in India, which was bound in time to affect Britain's most prized creation, the Indian Army; and the massive indifference of the vast majority of the British public, who wanted to settle down to peace and a higher standard of living in Britain and could not care less what happened to an empire created by and for 'them'. Those who cared, the *frères ennemis* who passionately pursued their contradictory aims – to give India her freedom, as the radicals saw it, to protect the people of India from the party demagogues, as it appeared to the paternalists – were a minority. The bitterness of Attlee's victory is that it was made possible by the support of voters who cared little for his ideals.

But the radicals and the paternalists, though numerically a small minority, included most of the political class in Britain. Their emotions mattered, their frayed nerves needed comfort. This was provided by the myth of the Commonwealth.

Commonwealth was the word which came into general use between the world wars to describe the association between Britain and the old Dominions – Canada, Australia, New Zealand, and South Africa.[1] These four countries were independent, yet were associated with Britain by ties closer than those between the most friendly foreign countries. In the case of the Australians, New Zealanders, and the majority of Canadians there was personal kinship, affecting hundreds of thousands separated by the oceans, and a far-reaching similarity of political and cultural outlook. These bonds remained strong in spite of the development of very different societies in very different physical environments. In the case of South Africa, the same considerations applied to a minority of the European population, while the magic of the names of Botha and Smuts for long persuaded many in both countries that the imponderable factors of Commonwealth fraternity extended to some extent even to the vanquished of the Boer War.

The old Commonwealth was a reality, even if there clung to it at times distasteful fumes of after-dinner rhetoric. In 1947 it was decided to extend the concept of Commonwealth to include India and Pakistan, and later still the various other new States that

[1] No better name than 'old Dominions' can be found to describe them. One is inclined to think of them as 'Anglo-Saxon', until one remembers the French Canadians and Afrikaners; or as nations of 'European stock', until one remembers the varied races of South Africa, not to mention the Maoris, Red Indians, and Australian aborigines.

Commonwealth, Common Market, Common Sense 243

emerged from the disappearing Empire. The Commonwealth formula indeed played an important part in the solution of Mountbatten's problems in 1947. Everybody was delighted by the extension of the Commonwealth idea. Indians and Pakistanis found themselves treated as friends. In Britain, the imperial paternalists could feel that much of what was best in the imperial tradition had been saved, indeed that at some rarified spiritual level the old Empire was still in existence; while the radicals, proud of their democratic achievement, could feel that the Empire had been replaced by an association of morally elevated and like-minded nations. As the leading nation in this unique family, Britain remained, it was felt by Right and Left alike, a Great Power of an unique type. As such, they argued, she remained only a short distance behind the two monster Powers. As a nation with world-wide interests, she remained far above any European nation, and so her leaders – not always politely – rebuffed the appeal from Europeans that they should play a leading part in the creation of a new Western Europe. Many British politicians felt that West European politicians had a parochial view of the world as a whole, and failed to notice that they themselves had a parochial view of the continent of Europe. The fact that the leading figures of the new Europe were Catholic conservatives did not endear them to the post-war Labour Party.[1]

As the years passed, the Commonwealth idea became more mythical, but it did not lose its appeal. From the Korean War onwards, Indian foreign policy diverged sharply from British, while the unsolved Kashmir problem ensured continuing hostility between two Commonwealth members. However, relations between British and Indians remained agreeable, and the moralizing rhetoric

---

[1] In May 1950, the French Foreign Minister, Robert Schuman, put forward his Plan for a coal and steel community, and invited the British Government to take part. It refused.

In 1954, when the European Defence Community was running into difficulties in France, it was hoped that Britian might save it by joining, thereby removing the fear held by many Frenchmen that the E.D.C. would be dominated by the Germans. The British Government made no move, and E.D.C. was rejected by the French Chamber.

It is true that the British Government then took the lead in providing a solution for the problem of German rearmament through the West European Union. But when the next step towards European unity was taken, in the economic field, at the Messina Conference in June 1955, the British, once more invited, once more refused. In 1957, after the Six had signed the Treaty of Rome, negotiations began with the British about a Free Trade Area, but these broke down owing to French opposition in November 1958.

of Nehru (the outstanding exponent in the mid-twentieth century of the English Victorian governess tradition) awoke frequent echoes in British hearts. The first African recruit to the Commonwealth, Ghana, also aroused high hopes. But its foreign policy soon diverged no less from British than had Indian. Though a small State, Ghana became an important political factor, as the centre of a Pan-African policy which was increasingly adopted by the new nationalist movements in other parts of the continent, and which saw in the European communities of Kenya, the Rhodesias, and South Africa its chief enemies. In 1961 the Asian and African members of the Commonwealth were able to ensure that conditions were put to South Africa for entry into the Commonwealth in its new status as a Republic, which it was bound to refuse.

The Commonwealth idea played a valuable part in smoothing for the political class in Britain the painful period of the dissolution of Empire. The claim that the manner of the ending of the British Empire has been more elegant than that of other modern empires may or may not be justified. It certainly imposed less immediate suffering on the people of Britain. Half a million people perished when Hindus, Moslems, and Sikhs massacred each other, but there were no British casualties. Most victims of Mau Mau were other Africans, of E.O.K.A. Greeks or Turks, of the Malayan guerrillas Chinese or Malay. If there is a blood-bath in Kenya or Southern Rhodesia, the white victims will be the local settlers. The British have suffered little, but this has not prevented them from showering advice and abuse on those they left behind, especially on those of their own stock. When the legions were withdrawn from the British Isles to Rome, it is not recorded that Roman politicians denounced as reactionaries the remaining Anglo-Romans for not handing over political power to the Welsh or to the Saxon invaders.

In the other empires that have fallen in the twentieth century, the metropolitan nations suffered more. The Ottoman Turks, whose Empire lasted twice as long as the British Raj in India,[1] fought many savage wars against their rebellious Balkan subjects. The Habsburg Monarchy collapsed after defeat in a war waged partly against the kinsmen of some of its disaffected subjects, but in which

[1] The Ottoman Empire in Europe lasted approximately from 1389 to 1913, the British Raj from 1757 to 1947. The rule of the Habsburgs, outside Austria proper and Bohemia, lasted a little longer than the British Raj – approximately from 1699 to 1918.

few of the latter took up arms against it.[1] The hatreds aroused by the conflicting nationalist passions of the Monarchy's last days grew fiercer under the Successor States and exploded in the age of Hitler. Bohemian and Styrian Germans became Nazis, and proved themselves by massacring Czechs and Slovenes, while Hungarians massacred Serbs, and Croats and Serbs and Moslems massacred each other. The dissolution of the French Empire cost thousands of French lives, even if Vietnamese and Moslem Algerians suffered still more.

Such horrors were spared the British, but not their former colonial subjects. And the end is not yet. It would be rash to prophesy that Nigeria will not have suffered the horrors of Balkan nationalist strife before as many years have passed as separated the fall of the Monarchy from the defeat of the Third Reich. On the contrary, the African nations have been quick off the mark when it comes to the creation of dictatorship and the picking of frontier quarrels with neighbours.

But at least, it may be objected, our former subjects hold us in affection because we let them go so graciously? Surely in this at least we have done better than other empires?

It may be so, but it is too soon to be sure. Kindness does not always win love, nor harshness hatred. Austria produced a large proportion of the most bestial Nazis, yet there is little hatred of Austria among the people of Eastern Europe. Neither the continued popularity of Frenchmen as individuals in North Africa and Indo-China nor the unpopularity of Dutchmen in Indonesia seems closely related to the actual record of their governments. Certainly British people enjoy friendship and respect in many parts of Asia and Africa. But excessive desire to please, willingness to admit that Africans (or Asians) are always right, seems, at least in personal relationships to create contempt rather than affection.

It would perhaps be prudent to conclude that, though the British record, both of Empire and of de-colonization, gives ground for pride, it is premature to assume the existence of some esoteric Commonwealth virtue that guarantees a moral superiority of the British over other empires. The end of empire is essentially a similar process wherever it occurs. The predicament of an ex-imperial

---

[1] The total number of Czech, South Slav, and Roumanian volunteers, deserting from the Austrian Army in the First World War, amounted to some tens of thousands.

nation is always painful, and we might endure ours with more dignity if we would show a little more understanding and compassion for our predecessors and our contemporaries in this experience.

The Commonwealth in 1963 is a network of personal and institutional relationships which defies any simple description. Thousands of families are united by ties of affection, some of which go back for several generations. Hundreds of business firms, large and small, are accustomed to work with each other in different parts of the Commonwealth. Then there are the links between universities, and the uniform qualifications in the professions. There is a similar vocabulary in politics, at least at the highest level, and a similarity of bureaucratic structure. As Mr Patrick Gordon-Walker showed in his recent book, in the new states of the Commonwealth there are 'opposite numbers' to most British institutions and officials.

All these things are of value, and they both should and can be maintained. They are of course far more marked in the three remaining old Dominions than in the new states. These three are also bound to Britain by military alliances; their foreign policies are nowhere in serious conflict with that of Britain (even if there are inevitable disagreements from time to time); and they are governed on democratic principles which derive from the same sources as our own. This is not true of the new states. Ghana has a dictatorship of the modern one-party demagogic type which is well on its way towards full-blooded totalitarianism. In Nigeria freedom is clearly in danger.[1] Pakistan has a military dictatorship. Whatever happens in Souther Rhodesia, it is unlikely to be democracy.

In foreign policy, too, there is no unity. Pakistan belongs to the CENTO and S.E.A.T.O. treaty systems, though its devotion has been visibly diminishing since the outbreak of the Indian–Chinese

---

[1] One of the most melancholy aspects of the Commonwealth relationship was revealed by the case of Chief Enahoro. This leading Nigerian was, under existing law, deprived of the right of political asylum to which he would have been entitled if he were a citizen of any foreign country, because he is a citizen of a State member of the Commonwealth. Here the Commonwealth seems to resemble nothing so much as Mr Khrushchev's *sozdruzhestvo*, or commonwealth of 'socialist nations', which of course deny political asylum to persons who have offended against the political principles of a fellow member. The British Government made things still worse by dragging in the irrelevant question of the quality of justice in the Nigeria law-courts – which there was no reason at all to doubt. It thus succeeded in antagonizing all those concerned, depriving Chief Enahoro of his liberty and insulting Nigerian public opinion.

conflict. Malaya has a treaty with Britain. The other new states prefer 'non-alignment', a rather pompous phrase for the obvious and natural policy of the pursuit of their own national interests in their own part of the world. In the case of India, this policy was for many years accompanied by a steady flow of self-righteous moralization from Nehru, and the adoption in words though not usually in deeds, of a double standard which favoured the Communist Powers at the expense of the West. In Africa, 'non-alignment' is in some though not all cases accompanied by an active policy of Pan-African expansion.

The champions of the 'Commonwealth ideology' in Britain have all too often failed to distinguish between polite relationships and political reality. This mistake the French avoided. Though French policy in Indo-China and Algeria took a tragic course, in tropical Africa the French were at least as successful as the British at peaceful decolonization. In West and Central Africa the French enjoy essentially the same type of goodwill and the same complex of personal and business relationships as the British in the new states of the Commonwealth. But the French, while not underestimating the political value of this goodwill and these relationships, have not deluded themselves that they provide the basis for the security of France. This security they have sought in their own immediate neighbourhood, in Europe.

It was perhaps reasonable for British politicians in 1947 to think that Britain, as the centre of the Commonwealth, could remain a world Power, only a little behind the two giants. But as the years went by, with the development of military technology and the revelation of the political disunity and fragility of the Commonwealth, it might have been expected that British governments would have reconsidered the basis of policy, and would have paid more attention to Europe. This did not happen. Labour leaders distrusted European leaders who were not socialists. Conservative governments lacked this particular predjudice, but they showed no more general understanding. Eden clung to the illusion that Britain could still play a leading part in the Middle East, and this led him to the Port Said fiasco of 1956. While the European Economic Community was being formed in the late 1950's the British attitude was indifferent or hostile. For this, and for a long list of earlier grievances, General de Gaulle took his revenge at the beginning of this year.

Britain in 1963 is *not* the centre of a great Empire, or of a great world-wide community of high-minded nations of all colours looking to her for moral leadership. To eyes unclouded by the haze of after-dinner rhetoric, the shape of Britain appears quite clear, in more modest dimensions. Britain is an island inhabited by 50,000,000 highly skilled and potentially efficient people – a powerful compact state but not a monster Power. It also has three further characteristics which distinguish it from other states of similar population and potential strength.

It possesses, scattered across the globe, a number of minor colonial possessions, to whose inhabitants it has obligations, and a smaller number of military bases. The bases are questionable assets, and some may be serious liabilities. One wonders, for example, whether the real military advantages, either to Britain or to the whole Atlantic Alliance, from the retention of Aden outweigh the hostile feelings aroused in all Arab nationalists from Iraq to the Maghreb.

It has its imponderable relations of kinship and friendship with Canada, Australia, and New Zealand. Despite mutual irritation, which was increased during the negotiations with the Common Market, these are a real and valuable asset. It is a great pity that they have been to some extent devalued by rhetoric about the Commonwealth. Increasingly empty talk about the unity of a wider Commonwealth, held together by nothing more than an agreeable sense of membership of the same club, has diverted attention from the unity of the real Commonwealth of four kindred nations. The argument that this unity must not be stressed because it might offend Asians and Africans, is grotesque, and unworthy of a self-respecting people. If the Africans have the right to Pan-African solidarity, have we not the right to solidarity with our kinsmen across the ocean – and with Europe too?

The third special characteristic is one noted by Bismarck nearly a hundred years ago – that the people of the British Isles and the United States speak the same language.

This island state, this medium Power with its imponderable links with the old Dominions, must have a policy towards four parts of the world – the United States, Western Europe, the Soviet bloc, and the underdeveloped societies.[1]

---

[1] This ungainly phrase is still the least unsatisfactory description that can cover the large number of societies concerned. They are to be found in Asia, Africa, and Latin America. Their inhabitants have white, brown, yellow, black, and red skins.

Commonwealth, Common Market, Common Sense 249

Britain is allied to the United States and Western Europe, but its relationship to these two areas has a further dimension which exceeds mere formal alliance. Britain belongs to the community of Anglo-Saxon civilization of which the United States and the three old Dominions are the other members. Britain belongs to Europe, not only in the obvious geographical sense but also because for 2,000 years her history has been part of the history of Europe. The security of the island State is based on its links with Western Europe and North America.

The Soviet bloc is the source of danger. It threatens Europe directly, though at present the threat is not very acute. It threatens also other positions, control of which would increase the pressure on Europe, and would open the way to further expansion and further pressure. Persia and Turkey are the most obvious examples.

Finally, the underdeveloped countries are the area of opportunity for the future. Here it is perhaps worth setting out future possibilities in an inverted order of desirability, while recognizing that the desirable and the possible do not always coincide. From the point of view of British interests, the worst that can happen to an underdeveloped society is that it should be conquered by the Soviet Army or be taken over by Communists completely subservient to the Soviet Union. More tolerable is that it be ruled by some totalitarian régime, Communist or Nationalist, which is independent of the Soviet bloc. More desirable is some humane and modernizing dictatorship. Best of all is a democratic régime. In the economic field, too, a wide range of situations may occur, reaching from chaos and starvation through varying degrees of inequality and corruption to a progressive economy offering a decent minimum living standard to all its citizens. The ability of British or other Westerners to influence the economy or the politics of such societies is limited but real.

Let me briefly consider in turn these three aspects of Britain's tasks in foreign policy – the opportunity in the underdeveloped societies, the menace from the Soviet bloc, and the base of security in North America and Western Europe.

Some have comparatively democratic governments, some almost totalitarian. Some are allied to the West, most are 'non-aligned'. The category should strictly include the Communist countries in Asia, including China. But it will be clear that what is said here is not for the most part applicable to them. On the other hand, it clearly excludes countries, such as Australia, whose *resources* are still less than fully devleoped but whose *societies* are highly advanced and sophisticated.

Britain may possess a larger number of persons who have experience and understanding of underdeveloped societies, and a larger body of useful knowledge on which even the inexperienced can draw, than any other Western country. But the underdeveloped societies are a world problem, and a Western problem, not just a British problem. There is rather widespread British belief that the British do this sort of thing best, a kind of proprietary interest in the underdeveloped, which antagonizes both the receiving nations and the other Western nations. There is also, especially among part of the British Left, a curious survival from the Wilsonian era, a belief that small new nations are more virtuous than other nations simply because they are small and new. This belief easily emerges with the Victorian governess complex, the assumption of British moral superiority. We hear a lot about the duty of Britain 'to give a moral lead to the nations of the world'.

In recent years a mirage has appeared of a happy brotherhood of the virtuous British and the virtuous new nations, free from the guilt of militarism and aggressive alliances, teaching peace to the sinful practitioners of power politics. This mirage appeared to be dissolving after the Chinese attack on its most eminent follower. But it would be unwise to assume that the climatic conditions which led to its formation have ceased to exist.

The truth is that Britain can play a great part in helping the underdeveloped societies, and can thereby benefit both their economies and its own, both their internal stability and world peace. But practical tasks are more important than moralizing dreams, and Britain is not the only Western nation that can contribute. The French effort in this field, both before and since de Gaulle, has been bigger than the British.

Agreement with the Soviet Union is, of course, as desirable as ever, but the prospects do not seem to be improving very fast in any of the three most important, and inter-related, issues – arms control, the underdeveloped societies, and an European settlement. Discussions about disarmament produce only oceans of useless words.[1] Co-operation between the Soviet Union and the West in aid to the underdeveloped, as a common task in the interests of world peace, is unhappily still no more than a dream. Soviet words and actions – from *Pravda* to the specialized academic journals on

[1] Since these words were written the agreement on nuclear tests was signed in Moscow in July 1963.

Asia and Africa, from diplomacy at the United Nations to subversion in Vietnam – point clearly to Soviet determination to 'support national liberation movements' and 'intensify the class struggle' in all these countries, in short, to exploit every crisis in Asia, Africa, or Latin America for their political warfare against the West. It is true that they lay less stress on violence, and are less inclined to brinkmanship, than the Chinese, who accuse them of cowardice and of ideological error in this field. But between implacable hostility pursued by relatively mild means and co-operation there is a vast distance.

Agreement with the Soviet Union in Europe depends, of course, on some agreed solution of 'the German problem'. Here two ideas are at present being publicly discussed in the West. One is the plan attributed to President de Gaulle, that the Soviet Union should allow Germany to be reunited in freedom in return for the removal of all American forces from Europe. The other is the proposal, favoured by a section of the British Labour Party, that the West should recognize the Soviet zonal régime as an independent German State, in return for guarantees for the security of West Berlin, and that this should perhaps be followed by agreements on denuclearized zones in Central Europe. There are arguments for and against these proposals on their merits. Neither seems at all likely to be achieved.

If the Soviet Government would consent to de Gaulle's proposal, this would be a tremendous success for France and Germany, and – it must be admitted – for all Europe. But if one thing has become clear in eighteen years of Soviet policy in Germany, it is that Moscow is not prepared to abandon the Communist régime in Germany, which is the Soviet blueprint for the whole of Germany, and ultimately for the whole of Western Europe, including Britain.[1] Withdrawal of American forces from Europe would not be so valuable a gain as to induce the Soviet leaders to change their mind. A dissolution of N.A.T.O. with a formal repudiation by France and

---

[1] The famous Soviet proposals of 1952 are not an exception. If they are closely examined, it is clear that they never envisaged freedom for the people of East Germany to get rid of the Ulbricht régime. They were designed to bring about a coalition government, similar to that set up in Czechoslovakia in 1945. The intention was that the Communist base in the eastern zone should be preserved, within a confederal German State.

The only moment when it seems *conceivable* that Moscow did think of abandoning Ulbricht, was in the months after Stalin's death when Beria was in the ascendancy. But there is far too little evidence to enable us to assert that such a plan *was* then taken seriously in Moscow. On balance, it still seems improbable.

Germany of the American alliance, might be a sufficient price, for in this case it might be argued that the temporary loss of Communist East Germany would soon be compensated by the conquest and Communization of all Western Europe. But even in his wildest moments President de Gaulle is unlikely to abandon all alliance with the United States, and if he so wished, the Germans would certainly not follow him.

The second proposal is also unlikely to succeed, owing to the almost invincible aversion of all Germans – socialists as well as followers of Adenauer and Erhard – to recognition of the D.D.R. as a German State. This is a matter on which individual British or Americans may legitimately hold various opinions. For my part, I admit to sympathy with the German point of view. This colonial régime, created by Russian military power and ruled by a Russian colonial governor, is not a German State. It has far less right to be regarded as a State than had Tshombe's Katanga. There is no comparison with the other East European states. These do at least include almost all members of their nations, and there is no other Czech State but Czechoslovakia, no other Bulgarian State but Bulgaria, and so on.[1] Apart from this, it is difficult to see what quarantee for the security of West Berlin could be given, in return for recognition of Ulbricht's *pashalik*, that would be more – or less – effective than the present state of affairs. In short, it is unlikely that any West German Government would consent to such an agreement, and unlikely that the United States could act against West German wishes. And without United States consent there is nothing that Britain could do. Britain cannot provide any solution to the West Berlin problem independent of her allies, even if some British Government were prepared to ignore its obligations of honour to the people of Berlin. An unilateral British recognition of the Ulbricht régime would be of no value to the Soviet Government, which would not be willing to pay any price for it.

This brings us, in conclusion, to the home base, to Britain's relations with North America and Western Europe. Here the first and essential fact is that Britain cannot separate herself from either. An Atlantic Community is desirable for the Americans and

[1] There are, of course, still large minorities in Eastern Europe (Hungarians in four neighbouring countries, Roumanians in the Soviet Union, etc.). But none of these *irridentas*, not even Transylvania for the Hungarians, are of the same order of magnitude as, for the Germans, the line which cuts their country in two.

Europeans, but vital for the British. General de Gaulle's remarks about *les anglo-saxons* have a core of truth; yet it need not follow from this that Britain would only enter an European community in order to act as an 'American Trojan Horse'. Certainly the views expressed by some British newspapers, and some of the arguments used by conservative politicians to justify entry into the Common Market, could reasonably be interpreted, even by persons less suspicious than the French President, in this sense. The whole public attitude of Britain since 1945 to efforts for European unity was bound to create resentment beyond the Channel. In fact, it is pleasantly surprising to find that so many Dutchmen, Italians, Germans, and even Frenchmen still do want to have Britain in Europe. Devotion to the Commonwealth myth at the expense of the European and Commonwealth realities, and condescending comparisons of Britain's world-wide obligations with European 'parochialism' inevitably offended many Europeans who in 1945 had been Britain's firm friends. All too often the impression was created that the British were using their 'special relationship' with America to play off America and Europe against each other instead of bringing them together. This may have been an unjust suspicion. Yet the fact remains that in 1963 we are far from the Atlantic Community which is the only guarantee of British security. And it is unwise to put all the blame for this on the Americans or our fellow-Europeans.

Atlantic Community must remain the aim. But Britain is and has always been part of Europe, and cannot live without Europe nor Europe without it. Europe's freedom and Europe's civilization owe as much, in the last two thousand years, to England and Scotland and Ireland as to France. The people of these islands, especially the young people who are growing up without any consciousness of Empire, have still plenty to contribute to Europe. That the British have plenty to learn from Europe is also true.

De Gaulle's refusal decided nothing. The road back from Empire still leads to Europe. There are other forces in Europe besides de Gaulle and Adenauer, and it is at least probable that in the next years their political influence will grow. Britain will have other opportunities to enter Europe, and the Europeans will have new chances to build an Atlantic Community.

But before the new time for decision comes, we must hope that the heads of British politicians will be cleared of the hang-over of Empire and the dreams of Moral Leadership.